FOREWORD BY
TARA STILES

JOY
UNLEASHED

THE ULTIMATE GUIDE TO
LIVING YOUR BEST LIFE

SHARI ALYSE

FEATURING: RENATA ANGELO · MELINDA BOURG · DEANNA COTTEN · JEAN VOICE DART
JEANIE DAVIDSON · JODI DESANTIS-HELMING · ILENE DILLON · ANGEL GOLD
JULIE GOLDBERG · LOLITA GUARIN · REV. DEBRA GUERRERO · R SCOTT HOLMES
SUSAN WALL JOHNSON · MELISSA LEWIS-STONER · MICHAEL G. NEECE · MAGGIE O'HARA
MICHELLE PECAK · FELICIA RANGEL · DR. HEATHER ROBERTSON · TINA MARIE ROMERO
JENNY TASKER · SUSAN THROOP · LULU TREVENA · REBEKAH JOY ZAYIT

JOY
UNLEASHED

THE ULTIMATE GUIDE TO
LIVING YOUR BEST LIFE

SHARI ALYSE

FEATURING: RENATA ANGELO · MELINDA BOURG · DEANNA COTTEN · JEAN VOICE DART
JEANIE DAVIDSON · JODI DESANTIS-HELMING · ILENE DILLON · ANGEL GOLD
JULIE GOLDBERG · LOLITA GUARIN · REV. DEBRA GUERRERO · R SCOTT HOLMES
SUSAN WALL JOHNSON · MELISSA LEWIS-STONER · MICHAEL G. NEECE · MAGGIE O'HARA
MICHELLE PECAK · FELICIA RANGEL · DR. HEATHER ROBERTSON · TINA MARIE ROMERO
JENNY TASKER · SUSAN THROOP · LULU TREVENA · REBEKAH JOY ZAYIT

Stay Connected to Your Joy

Exclusive tips, behind-the-scenes from *Good Morning Joy*, and a boost of joy every week. Plus, receive a free joy guide!

Subscribe at https://sharialyse.com/

DEDICATION

This book is for anyone who's ever thought: *Maybe my joy got lost. Maybe it left a note saying, "BRB" and never came back.*

For every soul who has ever felt like life has dimmed a little, who wakes up wondering if the spark they once had has vanished or if it's hiding somewhere, laughing at them, playing hard to get. It's for anyone who has questioned whether joy is still theirs, whether they're even worthy of it, or who just don't know where to find it. If you're holding this book in your hands right now, take a deep breath. You're in the right place. You're not alone. And I promise, there's so much light ahead, more than you can even imagine.

This book is also lovingly dedicated to my dad, who gave me the gift of joy in ways I never expected. Through his life and even more through his passing, he showed me how to love fiercely, live fully, and choose joy no matter the circumstances. And to my mom, who always encouraged me to chase my dreams and be unapologetically myself, showing me that living authentically is one of the greatest lessons of joy. Their light lives on in every page and in every spark you're about to uncover.

DISCLAIMER

This book is designed to provide competent, reliable, and educational information on mind, body, and spiritual health and wellness, as well as other related subject matter. However, it is sold with the understanding that the authors and publisher specifically disclaim all responsibility for any liability, loss, or risk, personal or otherwise, incurred as a consequence, directly or indirectly, of the use and application of any of the contents of this publication.

In order to maintain the anonymity of others, the names and identifying characteristics of some people, places, and organizations described in this book have been changed.

This publication contains content that may be potentially triggering or disturbing. Individuals who are sensitive to certain themes are advised to exercise caution while reading.

The opinions, ideas, and recommendations contained in this publication do not necessarily represent those of the publisher. The use of any information provided in this book is solely at your own risk.

Our authors represent cultures worldwide, and as such, there may be differences in language and expressions. As a global publisher, we have made the conscious choice not to edit these nuances, so each chapter is authentic and in its author's words.

Know that the experts here have shared their tools, practices, and knowledge with you with a sincere and generous intent to assist you on your personal journey. Please contact them with any questions you may have about the techniques or information they provided. They will be happy to assist you further and be an ongoing resource for your success!

FOREWORD

BY TARA STILES

Joy is easy to feel and appreciate when we are in the middle of experiencing it. Joy supports our well-being and gives us an uplifting boost. When life gets hard and stressful, it can feel impossible and almost unreasonable to find joy, but it's necessary for us to feel connected.

Shari Alyse shows us through the power of unique storytelling that joy is essential for our well-being. *Joy Unleashed, The Ultimate Guide to Living Your Best Life* gathers wisdom from voices who have lived, stretched, struggled, and soared. Each contributing author shares their own spark—a tool, a truth, a practice—to help you reconnect with what matters and create a life rooted in joy.

I've learned one way into joy is through the practice of softening into what's happening right here, right now. When times are joyful, that's easy. When times are hard, it becomes a practice. Joy is always there, waiting to be uncovered, and here to guide us to our most centered and connected selves.

Tara Stiles
Founder of Strala Yoga, bestselling author, well-being expert

Website: https://stralayoga.com/
IG: https://www.instagram.com/TaraStiles
FB: https://www.facebook.com/TaraStilesOfficial
YouTube: https://www.youtube.com/user/TaraStilesYoga
Spotify: https://open.spotify.com/user/stralayoga

TABLE OF CONTENTS

INTRODUCTION

"What do you have to be so happy about?"

That was the question.

And let me tell you, it didn't float across the table like some casual comment. Nope. It hit me like a grenade. *Boom*. Everything I thought I knew about myself, my life, and the way I lived was suddenly blown wide open.

I wasn't faking happy. I wasn't walking around pretending. I worked hard to be positive. I showed up with a smile because I believed that's what strong people do. I didn't want my past pain (or anyone else) to have power over me. So, I pushed through. I made the effort to find the good. I carried optimism like armor.

And it worked. At least on the outside. People saw me and thought, *She's always happy*. And honestly, I thought that too.

But that one question cracked the foundation. It forced me to look deeper. I never really stopped to ask myself that question. I just wore happiness like a mask, convincing even myself. But when I finally looked honestly at who I loved, how I lived, and how I treated my heart and body, the truth was undeniable.

I wasn't happy.

Boom! Emotional shrapnel left everywhere.

I sat in that discomfort for a while, trying to understand what had just blown up inside me. And honestly? I didn't understand it at all. My thoughts were tangled. *I've worked so hard on myself. I smile all the time. I laugh. I'm fun. Isn't that what happy looks like? Shouldn't I know how to feel this?*

Then came the spiral. *What if I've been fooling myself this whole time? What if I've been pretending? Did I miss something? Did I do something wrong? Why can't I just be happy like everyone else seems to be?*

The more I asked, the emptier it felt. And in that moment, all I knew for sure was that I didn't have the answer.

Until Haiti.

I was called intuitively (soul deep) to travel there after the 2010 earthquake. At the time, I planned to go there to help; bring light, compassion, and supplies to people who lost everything. I expected devastation, and I found it on the streets: two little boys scooping dirty water from the ground into plastic baggies, a mother sweeping the steps of a house that no longer stood while her son sat reading on what remained of the porch. Families were shattered. There was rubble everywhere.

As we pulled up to the orphanage gates, I felt my chest tighten. *Get ready*, I told myself. *This is going to break you.*

The gates creaked open, and my eyes swept over what I prepared for—devastation. There were tiny bodies, some missing limbs, lying on wooden, makeshift stretchers. A boy sat in a rusted wheelchair, swallowed by wheels far too big for him. The dormitory stood in ruins. Roofs collapsed, and walls cracked open like wounds.

They have nothing. No parents. No home. Some, not even whole bodies, to carry them through this world.

And then, light.

"Hi!" A little girl with braids and the brightest smile ran toward me. "I'm Ginny!" she announced, proudly holding out a sheet of stickers like they were treasures. Before I could speak, she pressed them onto my cheeks and forehead, giggling the entire time. I laughed, despite the lump in my throat.

"Come," she said, and tugged me gently toward a small boy standing off to the side. "This is Winston," she added, her voice full of teasing, rolling the name like she knew it would make him squirm.

"WIN-ston," he corrected her immediately, his mischievous grin betraying his delight. He didn't rush toward me but lingered back, watching from the corner of his eye, pretending he didn't care. Every time I caught him sneaking a glance, that smile broke wide open—playful, alive, like pure joy couldn't be contained inside him. And then, without warning, he laughed, loud and sudden, for no reason at all. It wasn't a laugh about something. It was life itself spilling out of him, and it pulled a laugh right out of me, too.

I caught myself in awe, taking in the entire scene. *How is this all possible? How can there be such light, such laughter, in the middle of so much loss? How can this be?*

The next day, under the shade of a massive tree, adults and children gathered for a makeshift church service—no walls, no roof, just open sky and open hearts. When the music started, it wasn't just singing; it was magic. Music poured from them like sunlight, voices strong and unrestrained. There was dancing, hugging, and holding each other tight. Something unmistakable was present. It was alive, pulsing through every note and movement.

I stood there, overwhelmed, tears mixing with laughter as I clapped along, feeling their rhythm in my bones. I never felt more alive, more lit up. And it didn't make sense. Surrounded by loss, they found something unshakable, something I couldn't name yet but knew I'd never forget.

I came expecting heartbreak. What I found instead was the purest presence I had ever known. What I found was something alive, radiant, and unexplainable.

And then it clicked!

This was the same spark people always saw in me, but what they mistook for happiness. It was something deeper, something unshakable, that lived and breathed within me even when I wasn't happy on the surface. It's something we all carry, even when we forget it.

JOY.

That trip changed the trajectory of my life and work. It set me on a path to truly understand joy. *What is it, really? Where do we find it? Can we all access it?* I had a million questions and a spark set ablaze.

In my time of self-connection, in conversations with others, and in simply observing life, I discovered something profound. I realized that happiness comes and goes with circumstances, but joy is different. Joy is something we're born with, present before the world teaches us to shrink, hide, or dim our light. Joy is steadfast. Joy survives. Joy is unconditional.

Through this discovery, I realized that joy is rooted in five pillars, all grounded in true connection: connection to self, purpose, creativity, nature, and community. These are the rooms we return to again and again when we want to feel fully alive.

And the definition that changed everything for me, the one that is the surest way to help anyone reconnect to their own joy, is simple:

Joy is the full alignment with your truth and the expression of that truth.

That's it. That's the secret.

Inside these pages, you'll meet 24 extraordinary co-authors, each heart-led, soulful, and creative. Each one shares what I call their "Spark"–a practice, tool, or way of being that helped them reconnect to their joy, light, and truth. And now, they're passing it on to you.

This is more than a book, it's an invitation–not just to read, but to step into your own life differently, to open the doors to the rooms where your joy lives, to meet the authors in these pages not just as storytellers, but as guides lighting the path back to yourself. Their "Sparks" are yours to try, play with, to adapt, to awaken something in you that has always waited.

Take a breath.

Feel the weight of the world release just a little.

Let yourself be curious.

Let yourself be surprised.

Let yourself remember that the joy you thought was out of reach is already inside you, waiting for the spark that brings it fully alive.

This is your journey now, your joy, your light, your truth. All you have to do is open these pages and step in.

With Joy,

Shari

A Heads-Up

Some stories in this book are raw and real. They touch on abuse, addiction, sexuality, mental health, and other heavy stuff.

Read what inspires you, skip what doesn't, and protect your heart. This is your journey to joy, and you get to set the pace.

CHAPTER 1

THE GIFT I ALMOST MISSED

THE SECRET TO JOY IS RIGHT HERE

Shari Alyse, TV Host, 2x TEDx Speaker

MY STORY

I didn't know it would be the last time my dad told me he loved me.

There was no fanfare, no dramatic music playing, and there certainly wasn't an angel whispering in my ear, "Pay attention, this is it!"

It was just another afternoon at Dad's bedside in the living room converted into a hospital room. Dad lay there in his bed, almost invisible under the blankets, his body barely moving. ALS stole nearly everything from him: his strength, voice, even the simplest ability to scratch an itch. All that remained were his eyes and the faintest traces of his smile on my lucky days.

That particular afternoon, my stepsister was there, helping me with our usual bedside dance: talking, joking, trying to make him laugh, keeping him tethered to the life he could no longer fully move in. We became performers, comedians, weather reporters, Broadway directors, pillow whisperers—you name it.

And then, in the middle of the ordinary, it happened.

"Did you see that?!" my stepsister gasped, excitement and awe tumbling out of her in equal measure.

I could barely find my voice. It felt like a laser beam pierced my chest, burning straight into the center of me. My throat tightened, heavy with something holy. "See it?" I whispered. "I felt it."

After months of caregiving, exhaustion, questions, and wondering if I was enough, this moment was my answer. More than that, it was the answer to a lifetime of questions.

I didn't just see it. I unequivocally felt it.

And as that feeling settled, I realized just how much life had shifted. Everything changed in ways I never expected. And yet, just a few months earlier, things felt completely normal–ordinary in the best way.

BEFORE ALS

Dad came out to LA to visit me. We hiked and ate too much, and he flirted with the young waitresses like he hadn't aged a day. He was Dad, slower at 78, sure, but still that same mischievous sparkle, still hungry for life, still impossible to keep up with.

"Dad, do you want to stop and rest for a minute?" I asked, slowing my steps to match his.

He shook his head firmly. "No. Keep going." His voice was steady, matter-of-fact, even though his chest rose and fell faster than usual.

We kept climbing. The trail got steeper, and I could hear his breath grow heavier. I glanced over. "Are you sure? We can stop for just a second."

He didn't even hesitate. "No. I'm fine."

He made it to the top, chest heaving but proud as ever. That was my dad.

But even then, there were tiny hints of what was to come. Opening jars became a struggle. Twisting caps hurt his hands more than they used to. He brushed it off, more annoyed than worried, but the change was there. Independence meant everything to him, and this was something he couldn't simply power through.

He could tell I was worried, though.

"When I get back to Tuscaloosa, I'll get this checked out," he promised. "Maybe it's carpal tunnel or something."

Dad always updated us after a doctor's appointment, proudly reporting his clean bill of health, as if he were collecting gold stars. This time, though, there was silence. No calls. Just a quiet that grew heavier by the day.

"Dad, what happened at the doctors?" We texted him for days. Nothing. Then finally, "I'm not ready to talk about it," he replied.

That's when we knew it was serious. Nothing prepared us for the Zoom call.

ALS (Amyotrophic Lateral Sclerosis). Lou Gehrig's disease.

The words landed slowly, like stones dropping into water, ripples spreading but not quite reaching me. I stared at the screen, Dad's face on one side, the diagnosis on the other, and it felt like I floated somewhere outside myself.

I knew it was serious, but my mind refused to catch up. Images and fragments flashed through me like a movie on fast-forward. Ice bucket challenge from years ago. Viral videos I scrolled past. Headlines screaming devastation. Whispers of the disease, stories I only half-listened to. And now it was real. My dad. Right in front of me.

This can't be happening. Not him! He was just laughing with me on that mountaintop. He's not supposed to be here yet.

It felt unreal. Like the universe mixed up the storyline. He wasn't ready to go. We weren't ready for him to go.

And yet, there it was, ALS, sitting in the middle of our lives, uninvited.

The full weight hadn't dropped yet. And maybe it couldn't. Not all at once.

THE MEETING

For the first few months after the diagnosis, Dad's girlfriend stepped in. She was devoted, a gentle presence who tried to keep him comfortable, laugh with him, and maintain some semblance of normalcy. But Dad was a man of six-foot-plus stature, and she, sweet as she was, stood just five feet tall. Logistically, the care became impossible for her to manage on her own. Emotionally, too, the weight was immense, and we saw it wearing her down.

That's when the family meeting happened. My sister, my uncle, and I hashed out the logistics: who could do this, who had the flexibility, and who could potentially carry the mental and emotional load without falling apart.

It was clear quickly that this wasn't a role for a part-time visitor. This wasn't a help-you-out-on-weekends type of gig. This was full immersion. This was uprooting a life and temporarily displacing it to dedicate yourself entirely to another human being.

And that human being was my dad.

I had the most flexibility with work, the ability to shift schedules, and pivot career demands. I could leap. But let me be honest, it wasn't a romantic notion. I had a life in Los Angeles, a partner, my cats, my job, and my growing TV career.

I hesitated.

Can I handle the responsibility, exhaustion, and emotional weight? What if I'm not enough? What if I fail him?

It felt inconvenient. It was messy. I was scared. I wanted to deny it, to pretend this wasn't really happening. Some days, I secretly wished that everything could return to normal life. I wasn't completely selfless.

And yet, somewhere beneath all the fear and doubt, I knew the choice was clear.

My dad needs me, and I can't and won't turn away.

I went to Tuscaloosa.

I'll be fully present for him every day. Not half-heartedly, not with guilt or resentment, but truly.

I decided that if I was going to step into this role, I would bring as much joy, laughter, and love into his life as possible. So that became my mission.

Dad and I are going to out-joy ALS!

OUT-JOYING ALS

And for a while, we did. Each morning, I flung open the shades in his living room and announced like I was the local weather girl:

"Let's see what's happening out there in T-town! Ohhh, it looks cold and gloomy out there, Dad, but it's warm and sunny here in our hearts with Daddy and daughter!" His face lit up every single time, and my heart right along with it.

I sang for him. Broadway tunes became our daily ritual. I did the Rockettes kick line with his fingers to exercise them. His compression boots didn't just sit on his feet; they danced. "These boots were made for walking!" I sang, dramatically removing them each morning.

Each morning, I waited anxiously to greet him with his favorite little ritual. I started by taking off his BiPAP mask, planting a kiss on him, then looking at him with a wide-eyed, playful shock, as if it were the first time, and asking, "How is it that you get better looking every day?" He blushed every time. Dad loved being complimented, and that question never failed to bring a smile to his face.

Even the most intimate and uncomfortable caregiving moments, helping him with personal care, were broken up with an inappropriate joke.

"Well, looks like we've found ourselves in a crappy situation."

Dad had a warped sense of humor, so I knew it was just enough to make us both laugh and remind us that life was still here and we were still us.

ALS might have been the villain lurking in the background, but if this disease was coming for him, joy was coming louder.

However, ALS is relentless.

As his disease progressed, our smiles faded.

The small, interactive joys that carried us started to slip away as his body declined. Words, once so easily spoken, became garbled. Eventually, they stopped entirely. The alphabet board we resorted to, the laminated one where I pointed to letters and he nodded, became cumbersome. Nods were harder, slower, and more taxing. I learned to read him through grunts, moans, and gestures.

I became attuned to every micro-movement, every breath, and every blink. Hours of watching turned me into an expert on the smallest details. I could tell when he was in pain before he said a word, when he wanted to be left alone, and when he needed me near.

Mostly, I learned his eyes.

The subtle language they spoke became my guide. The way they sparkled when he remembered a joke. The way they narrowed slightly when he disagreed with something I said. The way they softened when he felt safe. They were warm, filled with depth, and held decades of love, wisdom, and humor.

I wasn't the only one who noticed his eyes. One hospice nurse even admitted she couldn't bear to leave him. "His eyes kill me," she said as her own welled with emotion every time she had to leave.

When words and movement failed, those eyes became our language. They became my everything. They were my map, lifeline, and the one thing I held on to, the one thread still tying us together.

And then it happened.

THE MOMENT

I stood at his bedside, cracking jokes with my stepsister. It was what we did, our way of keeping the heaviness from swallowing the room. We were mid-routine, bouncing off each other like always, when I glanced at him.

He was watching us, entertained, the corners of his mouth twitching in quiet amusement. Then his eyes found mine. At first, I thought it was just another look. But then something shifted. His eyes, which were dull and clouded from exhaustion, transformed in front of me. Sharp. Present. Alive. It was like watching a storm clear.

I felt the whole room slow down and get very still.

And then, it poured out of him.

It was unlike anything I had ever known.

LOVE. Pure. Total. Eternal.

Not the kind of love you casually say with a "love you" before hanging up the phone. This was different. It was thick, encompassing, like it was wrapping around me, pouring through me, holding me in something bigger than both of us.

Something beyond language passed between us in that instant. And I knew, right then, my life had just changed.

For the first time in my life, I felt what love truly was. And it cracked something open inside of me that will never close again.

It didn't come in a text.

It didn't arrive neatly scheduled on my calendar.

It wasn't something I could chase, check off, or perform.

It was only available because I was **present**.

And in that presence, I understood something I'd spent so much of my life rushing past.

Joy doesn't live in the "someday."

It doesn't wait at the end of the to-do list.

It isn't hiding in some far-off, perfect version of our lives.

Joy lives in this breath.

This second.

This heartbeat.

Right here. Right now.

All that mattered in that moment was him. Nothing else existed. No phone buzzing, no unfinished to-do lists, no world outside that room. A lifetime wrapped itself into that single heartbeat, and my whole world felt complete.

And here's the part that stops me in my tracks even now: if I hadn't chosen to be present, I would've missed it. The greatest moment of my life could've slipped by unnoticed.

Beautiful soul, I don't want you to miss it either. And so, this is where you stop reading my story and start living yours.

THE SPARK

In case you haven't figured it out yet, the secret to unlocking more joy comes down to one word. Presence.

But before we go any further, I'd love to clear up a common misconception about presence. It isn't just a woo-woo idea or some meditation buzzword, so if you're imagining yourself sitting cross-legged on a cushion for eight hours chanting "Om," or forcing your mind completely blank to reach some higher realm, that's not what I'm talking about.

Presence is really the radical act of showing up fully for the life you're already living. It's reclaiming the moments quietly slipping past you because you're distracted, stressed, or rushing from one thing to the next.

The ability to be fully there, to catch those sacred, life-altering moments—they aren't only reserved for people in hospice rooms or once-in-a-lifetime experiences. It's available to you right now. It's a skill. A practice. And when you learn it, life opens up in ways you can't imagine.

So how do you bring more presence into your life?

Here are four simple, surprisingly powerful ways to drop into presence right now:

1. The Door Reframe

Every time you walk through a doorway, let it be a reset button. As your hand touches the knob or you cross the threshold, ask yourself, "How do I want to show up in this next space?" Calm? Confident? Playful? Choose, then walk through as that version of you. Instant presence.

2. The Stoplight Game

Use every red light as an invitation. When your car stops, so do you. Feel your hands on the wheel. Notice your breath. Look around. What's one thing you see that you've never noticed before? This turns wasted time into a mini meditation.

3. Micro-Moment Anchors

Pick one daily activity, such as brushing your teeth, making coffee, or washing your hands, and make it sacred. When you do it, do only that, no phone, no rushing. Feel it. Taste it. Smell it. Practicing presence in tiny doses rewires your brain for more.

4. Joy Stamps

At the end of each day, "stamp" one moment into your memory. Ask yourself, "What's one thing today I'm glad I didn't miss?" Say it out loud or write it down. This trains you to notice life's gifts as they happen.

Let's try one right now.

Look up from this page and notice one thing in your space you've never really seen before. A color. A sound. A detail hiding in plain sight.

Breathe it in.

That's presence.

That's life, right here.

And here's why it matters: **presence is the doorway to every room where joy lives.**

FIVE PILLARS

Do you remember those five pillars I mentioned back in the introduction to this book?

1. Self-awareness

2. Nature

3. Creativity

4. Purpose

5. Community

Presence is how we get there, but these five pillars are where the real magic of sustained joy lives. Let me show you briefly how to access them, one by one.

NATURE: Step outside once a day and name five things you can see, four you can hear, three you can feel, two you can smell, and one you can taste. This grounds you in the here and now instantly.

CREATIVITY: Set a timer for five minutes and create something with zero expectation. Doodle nonsense, hum a tune, rearrange a shelf. When you create without an agenda, you land in pure presence.

PURPOSE: Ask yourself, "What actually matters right now?" Write down the first answer that comes. Let that answer guide your next choice instead of your to-do list.

SELF-AWARENESS: Place your hand on your heart and take three slow breaths. Ask, "What am I feeling?" Name it without judgment. Awareness opens the door to presence.

COMMUNITY: The next time someone talks to you, look them in the eyes and silently think, "I see you." Watch how it changes the connection in that moment.

Do this, and you'll start to feel the quiet, rich hum of life as it's actually happening. And that, my friend, is where joy lives.

*If you want to explore the five pillars more deeply, go to https://sharialyse.com/5pillars to download a free guide where I will guide you on a journey through each one of them.

JOY BELONGS TO YOU

For the record, I didn't set out to discover the five pillars of joy. I was just trying to survive. I was a young woman sitting in the rubble of Haiti, trying to understand how people with nothing could smile as if they had everything. And years later, I was just a daughter holding my father's hand as ALS stole his body but never touched his spirit.

In those moments, joy revealed itself, not as something to chase, but as something already here.

Joy is in the breeze through the trees (Nature).

It's in the courage to make something from your pain (Creativity).

It's in waking up with a reason, no matter how small (Purpose).

It's in knowing yourself enough to live truthfully (Self-Awareness).

And it's in letting others love you and loving them right back (Community).

These aren't just concepts, they're lifelines. They're how I keep standing when the world feels too heavy. They're how I find my footing when grief knocks me down. They're how I open my heart wide enough to catch the beauty in ordinary days.

And now they are yours for the simple fact that joy belongs to everyone. It isn't a luxury. It's not for the lucky few. It's a birthright.

Take these pillars. Use them. Build your life upon them. And watch what happens when you stop waiting for joy to arrive and start living as if it is already here.

Because it is, and so are you.

Shari Alyse is a TV host, bestselling author, and 2x TEDx speaker on a mission to help people reconnect to their joy. Known as *America's Joy Magnet*, Shari brings warmth, energy, and authenticity to every conversation, whether she's on stage, on camera, or coaching entrepreneurs and brands.

For over 30 years, Shari has been a trusted voice in media and entertainment, making 100+ appearances on ABC, NBC, CBS, and FOX. She is the host and executive producer of *Good Morning Joy*, a top-ranked talk show streaming on Amazon Prime, Tubi, Roku, and Apple TV. Her show has featured NY Times bestselling authors, spiritual leaders, U.S. presidential nominees, and celebrities, including Marianne Williamson, Dr. Joe Vitale, Neale Donald Walsch, and many more. Through these conversations, Shari brings heart, insight, and actionable inspiration to her audience. The show has been featured on a Times Square billboard and invited to India for an exclusive one-on-one interview with a world-renowned spiritual leader, cementing her global influence.

Shari co-founded one of the first wellness communities and directories in the United States, and has helped countless entrepreneurs and brands amplify their message through media strategy and PR.

Her latest project, *Good Morning Joy: Joy Drive*, is an 8-part docuseries that takes her across the United States, uncovering the secrets of joy and demonstrating how connection is the key to unlocking it. The show proves that, despite our differences, joy is accessible to everyone, no matter your circumstances.

Known for her infectious energy, magnetic presence, and real-talk wisdom, Shari Alyse is not just a voice in media; she's a movement. And joy is just the beginning.

Connect with Shari:

Love Yourself Happy is on Amazon here:
https://www.amazon.com/gp/product/1988645298/

Watch TEDx How Self-Connection Leads to Joy here:
https://youtu.be/DXdsngVZeNQ

Watch TEDx The Power of Perspective & Being Wrong here:
https://www.youtube.com/watch?v=rGb9gH_lRds

CHAPTER 2

THE JOYFUL INNER CHILD

A BODY-CENTERED APPROACH TO HEALING

R Scott Holmes

*"The basis of life is freedom. The purpose of life is joy.
The result of life is growth."*

~ Abraham Hicks

MY STORY

My entire perspective on life changed the day I fully embraced inner child work. Every day from that day forward was a new life, and it changed how I played in the world.

Love spills out of my overfilled heart like warm maple syrup. I watch my daughters squealing with delight as they open their last presents on Christmas morning.

"Oh my God, Santa got us Cabbage Patch Dolls!"

Yes, I purchased the not-so-pretty, oh-so-hard-to-get gift of the year just days before, from a friend of a friend who knew someone, after a desperate three-month search.

Joy fills me as I recall those ten years of Santa's secret and magic played out each Christmas morning on the living room floor. My wife was one of six kids and wanted to recreate her childhood Christmas chaos with our three daughters. She didn't celebrate Christmas so much as inhabit the Christmas spirit from Thanksgiving to Little Christmas on January sixth.

Christmas "threw up" in our house, touching every corner, shelf, doorway, and wall. That was her joy.

The feeling of joy is different from happiness. Joy lands deeper, is not as fleeting, lasts longer in our bodies, and provides everlasting memories.

"Mom!!!"

I run as though still being chased by the hideous monster in my dream, my feet never touching the floor as I leap into my parents' bed.

"What's wrong, honey?" Mom asks as she curls me into a warm hug.

"I had a bad dream, and I was chased. He almost caught me."

Warmth fills me as her reassuring hug allows my body to relax.

I don't have to run anymore, I'm safe.

The joy of comfort and safety.

New England August humidity drips down my back. My head is soaked in sweat as we play another game of kickball.

Ring-ring-a-ling!

Matt yells, "It's the ice cream truck!"

"Mom, Mom, can we get one?"

My mother hands me the precious dollar bill she keeps in the flowered sugar bowl over the sink.

My friends all line up to make the most important decision of the day.

"Hey, what are you guys going to get? I think I want a chocolate éclair."

It tastes better than I can ever remember.

The joy of anticipation.

There's a particular sound your bike tires make when you're riding full speed down the hill you pedaled so hard to get to the top of. The rubber tires sing as we race our banged-up, banana-seat Stingray bikes with the two-foot sissy bar in the back.

The baseball cards clipped to the frame are a staccato metronome to our city-wide adventures. Three, four, or five of us often ride to the other side of town, exploring in the easy fashion of kids looking for new escapades. We feel like a crew, always looking out for one another, pushing each other to be faster, stronger, and more daring.

There's a sense of togetherness. A sense of belonging. A sense that we can do this all summer long, and school won't sneak up on us.

The joy of camaraderie.

"Swing batter, batter."

"No hitting to right field."

"He was out!"

Shouts ring out throughout day-long neighborhood pick-up baseball games, from first thing in the morning until lunch, then all afternoon until dinner. If it's light enough, we stay out until the streetlights come on after dinner.

We share gloves, bats, and black-electrical-taped baseballs. The bases are trees, shrubs, or a hole in the dirt. Each of us bats twenty to thirty times a day, playing a game we love. Three to a side, four, five. We constantly change the teams to make it fair because being competitive is more important than winning.

The joy of competition and friendship.

"Dad, can I build a fort?"

There's a tree with three trunks in our yard. He says, "Well, we don't really have anything, but yeah, go ahead. Here's a hammer."

About four and a half feet up, I build a little platform with borrowed nails. It's about two by two by two, and I add a couple of rungs so I can climb up to it.

"Alright guys, come on up!" My friends come up, and only two of us can stand there at the same time. But it's a different perspective, and we can see further. We can see differently.

This must be how my dad sees life because he's so tall.

Brendan says, "We need more room. Why don't we build a treehouse—a real treehouse? Can we do that?"

Some of my friends bring two-by-fours, and another brings some old, used material, so we have a makeshift window. After a few months, we have an enclosed treehouse ten feet off the ground. We have walls and can fit six people.

"If we cut a hole, we could go up on the roof." We reinforce the roof, and now it's six by six by six. We can hold twelve of us on that floor. And when we stand, we're almost twenty feet up in the air.

By the time I turn fourteen years old, there are seven floors on this treehouse, about forty-five feet tall. When we sit there, we can see over the neighbors' houses. Once, we have seventeen kids in that treehouse at one time. You can always find somebody here, as it's now the neighborhood meeting place.

The joy and satisfaction of creative collaboration.

The fair rolls into town, seemingly overnight, every Fourth of July, with the smells of fried dough drowned in powdered sugar, brightly colored cotton candy piled high on white paper cones, oversized smoked turkey legs that taste like ham, and the nose-wrinkling smell of dried beer.

"Come see the Bearded Lady. The Snake-man crawls on his belly like a reptile. See amazing sights you've only read about."

I can hear the loudspeakers, the crowd noise, and the bells and whistles from my backyard luring me ever closer to spending my hard-earned money.

The Rocket, the Mighty Mouse Rollercoaster, the Tilt-A-Whirl, the Double Ferris Wheel, the Scrambler, and the Round-Up all pose threats to my stomach and boyhood.

"I'll bet you won't go on the Round-Up," says Ron, daring me to conquer my fear. The Round-Up goes super-fast, and then rises at a thirty-degree angle while it spins, keeping you in place. At least, that's the theory.

If all those kids can do it and not die, so can I.

I hand the older, gap-toothed attendant (he's probably eighteen) my pass and walk to an open space, as there are only a few other brave souls.

Great, maybe no one will hear me scream.

The ride spins faster and faster, then starts tilting upward. My death grip holds me in place until the giant hand of force and gravity holds me up. *Wow, this is cool.* The nausea I expected never shows up, and I start to relax and enjoy the ride, forgetting my fear. As the ride stops, I walk down the stairs, a bit shaky but triumphant.

I ride the Round-Up five more times that year, and every year after that.

The joy of conquering your fears through adventure.

She smells like wildflowers as I sit behind her in our steel and wood turn-of-the-century desks. Her long, flowing chestnut hair lands on my desk as she flips it. She will smile at me but won't talk to me.

Does she like me? I don't even know what to say to her.

My eleven-year-old self can't understand what's happening. I start looking forward to the school day, but can't concentrate on what the teacher says.

Valentine's Day comes along, and I think I can let her know I'm interested. We have to give Valentine's to everyone in the class, but hers is special. I wait all day after giving it to her. Wait. Watch. Wonder.

As we file out to go home, she turns and smiles at me. "Thank you for such a nice card."

My heart leaps, my stomach flips, and I feel like I'm walking on air. It's Friday and I must wait until Monday to see her again. I still didn't know what to do.

"Hi." She rides her bike up to my neighborhood on Saturday, hoping to catch me. In jean shorts, a cropped top, and bare feet, she looks like something from a movie.

"Want to take a ride around the block? I rode all the way up here."

I get on my bike and tell my friends I'll be back. As soon as we're around the corner, unseen, she stops, pulls me close, and kisses me full on the lips. Fireworks go off in my brain. I start sweating and don't know what to do with my hands.

She smiles and says, "Is that what you were looking for? I'll see you on Monday." And with that, she rides off.

I really don't know what to make of that or of her, but I think she likes me.

The joy of discovering romance, however it shows up.

The stories are true, but the names have been changed to protect the innocent.

In the moments shared, I didn't know or understand what I felt. It's only by revisiting those times in my life that I realize how much joy was imparted and imprinted on my soul—the joyful inner children I carry. Connecting with your childhood adventures through the lens of your grown-up self and finding joy is impactful.

THE SPARK

"The inner child is a source of wisdom, intuition, and creativity. By connecting with this part of ourselves, we tap into our true potential and live more authentically and joyfully."

~ Deepak Chopra

Joy isn't something we chase; it's something we remember. It lives beneath the noise, waiting for the stillness of being.

Joy arises when we return to ourselves; when we ground our essence in the body, clear the energetic clutter, and release what no longer serves us. It's the quiet radiance that emerges when presence takes the lead and the soul feels safe enough to exhale.

Joy is not performative or fleeting. It's rooted. It's sacred. It's the re-claimed voice of the inner child, the rhythm of the spirit, and the hum of life lived in alignment.

In this space, joy becomes more than a feeling. It becomes a way of being.

Let's explore how to return to that joy.

We remember the traumas of our childhoods, large and small, as they become triggers in our adult lives. We feel anger, loss, isolation, shame, and feelings of *not enough* as if they're on display today.

What if we replace those memories with times of joy, and allow *those* to manifest in our current, everyday life instead?

Here's a practice you can use to quiet the triggers your hurt inner child brings out:

Allow yourself to have a comfortable, quiet space. Taking slow, deep breaths, allow your mind to settle and come to a space of stillness.

Remember a time when you felt afraid, angry, or alone.

Do you have that scene clearly in your mind's eye?

How old are you? What are you wearing? What are you feeling?

Reach out to that child, whether they're two, seven, thirteen, or seven-teen. Connect with them. You know what they need.

Reassurance. Comfort. Permission. Someone to sit and hold their hand. Safety.

You are the person who can heal them. The only one.

Give them what they missed and asked for all these years ago. Allow them to know they're capable of being loved. That they're safe. That you love them unconditionally. Embrace them fully.

Don't let the connection go until that child knows you're there for them, as they've always come up to save and warn you. That's why you've seen them. Let them know the adult you are now has got this.

Another deep breath in and out to anchor this experience.

Now that your inner children are seen, heard, and acknowledged, the emotions that used to trigger you and cause chaos and misunderstanding will be quieter as you deal with life in your current, confident, grown-up self.

Another way to bring yourself back into your body is to use this meditation developed by Maysha from Akasa Living:

1. BASELINE ATTUNEMENT MEDITATION

(Face-to-Face with Your Heart)

Close your eyes. Take a slow, deep breath in through your nose, and let it out gently through your mouth.

Now imagine you're sitting across from your own heart, as if your heart is a dear friend. See it before you—glowing, pulsing softly, alive with light. Look into its eyes. Notice the warmth, the trust, the steady presence.

You may even see the eyes of your higher self, or not. It doesn't matter.

Feel its hum—steady, kind, unshakable.

Begin to breathe with it. Inhale, exhale, matching its rhythm.

Place your hand gently on your chest and whisper inside:

This is my hum. This is my steady joy.

Let yourself smile—a soft, private smile—at your own heart. It smiles back. You feel the bond, the friendship, the unbreakable connection.

When you're ready to close, whisper:

"I'll keep attuning to you. You are my baseline."

Take one more deep breath.

Open your eyes and return, carrying that hum with you.

2. PERMISSION TO SHIFT MEDITATION

(Flipping the switch doesn't mean leaving the essence of your baseline, but expanding upon it. Ascending does not literally mean "up"—it feels that way to us, usually. It means "shifting" your consciousness or frequency.)

Close your eyes.

Breathe in deeply, letting your shoulders drop as you exhale.

Before you, two screens appear.

On the left, you see your life as it is now.

Notice the habits, the feelings, the weight of it.

On the right, you see your life as you prefer it to be.

Bright. Expansive. Joyful. Creative. Effortless.

Take a moment to really notice the differences.

Especially how *you* move, act, and feel in each.

(The bigger the differences, the bigger the shift—and energy moves with less "resistance" when we embrace the momentum of the excitement of bigger shifts than when we try what the world has taught us, which is to baby-step everything. Small steps take more energy and create less change with more effort, more lag, etc.)

Now place your hand on your solar plexus, just below your ribs.

Say inwardly, or out loud if you wish:

I give myself permission to be this version of me, now.

Take a breath in, and as you exhale, step fully into the second screen.

Feel the first dissolve behind you.

You are in your preferred frequency.

Act in your imagination as this new you—walk, sing, create, love.

Notice how natural it feels.

End with a whisper:

"I am this vibration now."

Breathe in that knowing, and open your eyes when you're ready.

3. DAILY SPARK PRACTICE

(Excitement Generator)

Each morning, pause.

Take a single breath into your belly and ask yourself:

"What thing excites me today?"

It could be walking barefoot in the grass.

It could be brewing your coffee with intention.

It could be picking up your cards.

It could be singing, dancing, stretching, calling a friend, or sitting under the sky.

Whatever the answer, do that thing first.

No delay. No excuses.

As you do it, feel the spark inside you ignite.

This spark is your compass.

This spark is your permission slip.

This spark is your joy, reminding you:

Excitement is my baseline. Joy is my natural hum.

Let this practice weave itself into your rhythm,

until every morning becomes a quiet celebration.

These three, practiced regularly, will:

- Set your baseline hum (heart meditation).
- Clear resistors and shift you into alignment (permission).
- Build daily excitement momentum (spark).

Living your best 18-year-old life, where the world is a present you get to unwrap every day, is the freedom curious humans seek.

Are you curious enough to listen and ask the questions?

Feeling overwhelmed? We can find your happy place.

Braving isolation? Learn to love solitude on this journey.

Not being heard? You can embrace your true voice.

Contact me for a free 30-minute share to see if we can unravel the chains binding your inner child. See the resources section below for more information.

R Scott Holmes is a quantum healing practitioner and transformational coach. He has attained Reiki Master Teacher, Polarity Therapist, RYSE Teacher, Theta Healer, Universal White Time practitioner, Find Your Voice Coaching certification, and Amazon bestselling author.

He began walking in the holistic healing world when his wife of 39 years died after a 20-year battle with breast cancer. After years of caregiving for his multiply-impaired daughter and wife, the world of coaching, healing, and energy opened.

He has written and lived his healing journey through collaborations with Brave Healer Productions, chronicling the steps to finding his authentic self.

In holding space, he has helped countless professionals find meaning and understanding of who they are, how they can continue to heal, and the freedom and joy that brings to their lives.

His soul journey has been to help heal others through one-on-one sessions, teaching, volunteering with hospice, and his monthly podcasts. Writing books allows others to learn from the trials, pitfalls, choices, and understanding gained from the constant curiosity of this life we get to live.

Travel and all it entails is Scott's muse: museums, exotic food, history, sacred sites, majestic mountains, shamans, local guides, and the ever-changing beaches. Sharing life experiences with his wife, Patti, practicing Yoga, meditation, and learning Qigong daily are the tools he uses.

Connect with Scott:

Website: https://www.rscottholmes.com

Email: scott@rscottholmes.com

Facebook: https://www.facebook.com/Scott.Holmes.31105674

Podcasts:
Soul Empowerment with David McLeod, Gayle Nowak, Sara Jane, and Scott Holmes: https://yourlifemasterycoach.com

Today's Conversation with Sara Jane and Scott Holmes: https://youtube.com/todaysconversationwithsarajane

CHAPTER 3

STOP THE OVERWHELM

BREAK FREE FROM BURNOUT AND ACHIEVE LASTING CALM

Lolita Guarin

MY STORY

"It's good that you came today," the doctor said, his voice steady but uneasy as he flipped through the papers in his hands. "If you waited until tomorrow, I'm afraid it would be too late. We'd put you in the hospital."

I froze, not sure how to respond. *Surely, he means something else.* He avoided my eyes, scribbling and tapping his pen against the pad as if reluctant to say more. I turned toward my friend sitting beside me, hoping she heard differently, but her wide eyes and silence confirmed the truth.

I couldn't decide if I should feel relieved that I came just in time, or terrified that my condition was so severe it might have been fatal if I waited another day. "How long do you usually bleed?" the doctor asked.

Hesitantly, I admitted, "Sometimes it feels like as soon as one ends, another one starts. It can go on for three weeks at a time."

He finally looked up, his forehead wrinkled in shock, his eyebrows raised. That moment told me everything: This wasn't normal. I shrank back, guilt washing over me as if my body's condition was somehow my fault.

The ER was cold and eerily quiet. I pulled the blanket up to my chin, shivering. Of course, this happened on a weekend, when emergencies never politely wait until Monday. My gynecologist worked weekdays, but waiting would have been too dangerous. The surrounding silence made it feel as if the entire center opened just for me.

"We'll give you something to stop the bleeding," the doctor said before leaving, "but you need to see your doctor as soon as possible. One day it may be too late."

My friend turned to me. "How long has this been happening?"

"For a few years," I whispered.

Her jaw dropped. "And why didn't you go to the doctor sooner?"

"I thought it would just stop on its own."

The silence that followed was heavy. Then, she asked the question I dreaded: "So where's your husband?"

"He went for a bike ride."

Her expression shifted to disbelief. "He doesn't know you're here?"

"He knows. I told him I was going to the ER."

"Then why isn't he with you?" she pressed.

The truth cut deep. "He told me I was controlling. That I wasn't even allowing him to ride his bike alone, he said I was imagining things, that I only came here to get attention. He wasn't going to give in to my performance."

Her caring voice turned sharp with outrage. "You're not performing. You're bleeding to death. What kind of husband does that?

I stayed silent. I didn't need to answer. I already knew what kind of husband he was. As I lay there, countless memories surfaced of times I faced pain and fear completely alone, moments when the man who should have protected me became a source of harm instead.

But the more complicated truth was this: I abandoned myself. I wasn't just overworked; I betrayed my own body and soul. I pushed myself to exhaustion, piling on more tasks, saying yes when I meant no, and filling every space with productivity. I called it survival, but really, it was self-neglect disguised as discipline. I believed my worth depended on how much I produced, how busy I stayed, and how exhausted I looked. In fact, I wore stress like a badge of honor, as if my constant exhaustion proved I was valuable, needed, important.

We live in a society that glorifies exhaustion. Think about it; when someone asks how you are, how often do you hear (or say), "Busy. Tired. Overwhelmed," as if those words were medals of honor? Somewhere along the way, I absorbed the message that to rest was to be lazy, to slow down was to fall behind, and to prioritize myself was selfish. So, I pushed harder. I ignored my body's whispers until they became screams. I convinced myself I was fine—until my health scare proved I wasn't.

Lying in that hospital bed, I realized stress wasn't just exhausting me— it was killing me. That moment stripped away all illusions. I began asking myself questions I avoided for years. *Am I really doing work I love. . .or just the work that pays the bills? Are my relationships feeding my soul. . .or slowly draining the life out of me? Do I even remember what joy feels like. . .or am I just going through the motions, stuck in survival mode?* The answers were painful. But with that pain came clarity.

That was the moment everything began to change. I chose to stop living for approval, obligation, or mere survival, and to start living for truth, health, and peace. But I won't pretend it was easy. Learning to care for my own stress was stressful in itself. People-pleasing was my natural state for as long as I could remember. I lived with a constant hum of anxiety, and pleasing others gave me the illusion of safety. Letting go of that part of myself felt terrifying, because it meant letting go of the identity I carried my whole life.

Who would I be if I weren't the one always rushing, always saying yes, always taking on more than I can handle? Who would I be if I weren't the friend who showed up no matter how drained I am, or the coworker who stayed late while neglecting myself? In my family, loyalty was everything. The unspoken rule was that you showed up no matter how sick, tired, or overwhelmed you were; you never let others down. But looking back, I realized that loyalty was often one-sided. I poured myself out for others, believing if I worked enough, gave enough, or sacrificed enough, someone would eventually be there for me. The painful truth was, most of the time, they weren't.

Still, the fear of letting go ran deep. When I started releasing people who drained me instead of giving back, I was terrified of what would remain. Would I be left alone? Would I lose my sense of identity altogether? My past defined me for so long—my busyness, my loyalty, my constant survival mode. To let go of that felt like betraying not just who I was, but where I came from.

We hold onto the past as though it's sacred, even when it hurts us. We cling to traditions and patterns passed down through generations, as if breaking them will dishonor our families. But not everything handed down is holy. Some traditions are chains disguised as heritage. Out of loyalty and fear of abandonment, we keep repeating what harms us. That's why I stayed in a painful marriage far longer than I should have—because I believed loyalty mattered more than my well-being. I thought leaving meant failing, breaking a sacred vow, betraying who I was supposed to be. However, in reality, staying was self-betrayal.

So, I divorced the man who couldn't sit by my side when I fought for my life. I stopped forcing myself into obligations that suffocated me. And most importantly, I stopped abandoning myself. For the first time, I saw clearly how many years I ignored my needs, silenced my feelings, and sacrificed my joy to feel safe or accepted. It nearly cost me everything.

From there, I started small. I went to bed when I was tired instead of pushing through another hour of work. I ate when I was hungry instead of ignoring my body for one more project. I permitted myself to cry when the tears came, to laugh without guilt when joy bubbled up, to sip tea in my backyard without feeling I had to "earn" it. I cleaned out my closet, letting go of clothes that made me feel ashamed, and chose comfort over punishment. I practiced saying "no" without apology—and discovered the world didn't fall apart. In fact, it became lighter.

Every small act of honoring myself became an act of reclaiming my life. Each time I chose myself over the old patterns, I built a little more strength.

The more I allowed myself joy, the more resilient I became. The more I trusted myself, the less I needed the approval of others. Slowly, I discovered a truth that changed everything: loving yourself isn't selfish; it's a matter of survival. We can't pour into others if we're running on empty.

That health scare was my turning point. It forced me to face the truth about how I lived and gave me the courage to change. It also planted the seeds of what later became the CALM Process. Stress doesn't vanish from life. But it doesn't have to destroy us, either. CALM showed me how to face stress with clarity and compassion—controlling what was mine to control, accepting what wasn't, limiting what drained me, and multiplying what worked.

And here's the truth I want you to know: I'm not unique. My patterns came from childhood wounds, growing up with an alcoholic father and an emotionally unavailable mother. Stress and survival became second nature. I know many of you reading this carry your own versions of those wounds. But here's the hope: We're not powerless. We don't have to keep wearing stress like a badge of honor. We can choose differently.

We can reclaim our lives—not by pushing harder, but by honoring ourselves. I still believe I have a lot of life left to enjoy, and I'm deeply grateful for the wake-up call that forced me to see the truth. Now, I want to invite you to do the same. Look at your life. Ask yourself: "Where am I abandoning myself? Where is stress running the show? Where have I forgotten joy?"

Stress should not be stressful to manage, and that's precisely why I created the CALM Process: a simple, practical tool to guide you back to yourself. Step by step, it will help you honor your feelings, reclaim your peace, and finally live fully—not with guilt, not with shame, but with freedom.

THE SPARK

CALM PROCESS IN A NUTSHELL

Stress shows up everywhere: traffic jams that make you late, a child throwing a tantrum, a snarky email from your coworker, or even the quiet pressure you put on yourself to "get it all done." In these moments, most of us react automatically by snapping, shutting down, or worrying endlessly. But what if, instead of staying on autopilot, you had a step-by-step tool to guide you through the storm?

That's precisely what the **CALM Process** is designed to do. It's not complicated, it doesn't require hours of practice, and you don't need to remember a dozen rules. It's just four steps—short, simple, and powerful. Each step gives you a straightforward question to ask yourself, so you can shift from spiraling to steady.

C – CONTROL

Ask yourself: What here is actually in my control?

You can't control traffic, your boss's mood, or your child's reaction. What you can always control is your own attitude, your choices, and your next step.

Direction: When stress hits, pause and make two quick lists:

What I can't control: other people's words, the weather, the past.

What I can control right now: my breathing, my thoughts, my response.

Even this simple act grounds your nervous system and gives you a starting point.

A – ACCEPT

Ask yourself: What can I learn here? What can I appreciate, even if I don't like it?

Acceptance is often the hardest step because we confuse it with defeat. But true acceptance isn't giving up. It's choosing peace over obsession.

Direction: Try reframing the situation. Instead of, "Why did this happen to me?" ask, "What is this teaching me?" For example, a failed project may be teaching you about boundaries. A broken relationship may be teaching you about self-worth. You don't have to approve of what happened to accept it; you have to stop fighting reality.

L – LIMIT

Ask yourself: What am I doing that's making this worse?

Stress often multiplies because we keep feeding it with habits that drain us—overthinking, people-pleasing, saying "yes" when we want to say "no," or clinging to coping patterns that hurt more than they help.

Direction: Choose one thing you'll stop or reduce today. It doesn't have to be big. Maybe it's checking your email after 9:00 p.m. Maybe it's replaying that argument in your head for the tenth time. Limiting what doesn't work opens space for calm.

M – MULTIPLY

Ask yourself: What is already working for me—and how can I do more of it?

This is where momentum builds. Instead of focusing only on fixing what's broken, you also double down on what supports you.

Direction: Identify one habit, thought, or action that brings you calm—journaling, walking, breathing, celebrating small wins—and multiply it. Do it more often, more consistently, and more intentionally. This builds resilience faster than anything else.

QUICK CALM PRACTICE

Grab a notebook and pick one stressful situation. Write down:

C: What's in my control?

A: What lesson or value can I see?

L: What drains me that I can stop?

M: What already helps me, and how can I do more of it?

Even just this exercise shifts your perspective. Stress won't disappear from your life—but with CALM, you'll always have a tool to face it with clarity and strength. And the more you practice, the more natural it becomes—until CALM isn't something you "do," it's how you live.

Lolita Guarin is a renowned stress management expert, coach, speaker, podcaster, five-time Amazon #1 bestselling author, founder of *Be Amazing You*, and a passionate instructor on *Wellness Universe* who has helped countless people manage stress and reclaim their energy, clarity, and joy.

Her journey began after a serious health scare made her realize just how much stress ran her life. Instead of ignoring the signs or numbing the symptoms, Lolita chose to look inward. She began the hard but transformative work of facing her childhood wounds, unlearning people-pleasing, releasing perfectionism, and working through anxiety. Along the way, she discovered the power of forgiveness, not only toward others but toward herself. She learned to stop abandoning herself, to honor her emotions, and to treat her feelings as signals instead of weaknesses.

This healing became the foundation of her signature CALM Process, a practical and memorable four-step framework that helps release stress, stop burnout, and build inner peace. Through her books, podcast (*From Stress to Success Blueprint*), and coaching programs, Lolita brings compassion, humor, and real-world tools to people who are ready to break free from stress and step into their full potential.

When she's not coaching or writing, Lolita enjoys traveling, ballroom dancing, reading, and nurturing her own well-being so she can continue teaching others how to thrive.

Connect with Lolita:

Website: https://www.beamazingyou.com/

Facebook: https://www.facebook.com/LolitaGuarin

Instagram: https://www.instagram.com/lolita_guarin_stress_expert/

LinkedIn: https://www.linkedin.com/in/lolita-guarin-a069a811a/

YouTube: https://www.youtube.com/@BeAmazingYou/featured

CHAPTER 4

JOY BY DESIGN

A VALUES-DRIVEN BLUEPRINT FOR SUCCESS

Melissa Lewis-Stoner, MSW, LCSW-C

"The privilege of a lifetime is to become who you truly are."

~ Carl Jung

The journey to joy begins when you give yourself permission to pause, reflect, and return to who you really are. Healing doesn't start by doing more. It starts by choosing what aligns with your soul. True fulfillment isn't a reward for achievement; it's living in integrity with your values, noticing the small moments that remind you of who you were always meant to be.

MY STORY

I didn't plan to rebuild my life. I just knew I couldn't keep living the one that burned me out.

Burnout didn't happen overnight. For me, it crept in slowly. Exhaustion isn't a trophy, but no one could tell me that. I just worked harder and harder and kept pushing.

I felt myself disappearing inside the demands of a role that no longer fit. The environment I was in wasn't just unsupportive; it was toxic. There was little room for authentic connection and little tolerance for vulnerability. Add to this a constant pressure to overperform and be available and "on" every night and weekend. I felt unseen, unheard, and increasingly disconnected from myself.

One time, I had poured hours and weeks into providing documentation and rationale for budgeting, along with descriptions of every team task and its impact on the business and our customers, only to watch my work get picked apart line by line—so many questions about every sentence, every decision. Outwardly, I nodded and took notes. Inwardly, my dialogue was brutal.

Why doesn't he trust me?

Am I a horrible leader?

Did I let my team down?

Maybe this is not the right job for me.

Ultimately, my work was completely rewritten, our impact downplayed, and the department reorganized, adding to my negative self-talk.

Each day, I showed up wearing a mask, suppressing what my body screamed to share. I was exhausted, anxious, and overwhelmed. I pushed through meetings where I felt invisible, led initiatives that demanded more than I had to give, and endured performance cycles that measured my worth in metrics, not meaning. My nervous system was in a constant state of fight or flight until one day, it simply said, "No more."

November 4, 2021. The day began like any other workday. I walked into my home office with a Red Bull in hand and logged onto my laptop around 7:15 a.m.

A barrage of messages from my boss hit me immediately. Before I responded to one, another appeared. This went on for hours. And it was the norm. As I prepared for my fourth meeting of the day, I was already exhausted.

I needed to focus. I needed to be present. My next meeting was important. It was a one-on-one sync with a member of my team. As a leader, I know these sessions are sacred.

Listen. Just listen. Be present.

She shared concerns and asked for support. I tried to focus, but my Team's icon lit up again. Messages from my boss kept coming. Demanding answers, one-pagers, and justifications for decisions I made. On and on.

Suddenly, I felt light-headed. And different.

"Are you feeling okay?" she asked. "You're very pale."

I was not okay, and I knew it.

I ended the meeting and called my husband. "Something is wrong. I feel off, and my heart is racing." I found a blood pressure cuff in our linen closet and checked my pressure. It was high. Very high for me.

"I'm calling 911. I'm scared and feel like I might pass out."

He said he'd leave work immediately.

The next few hours are a blur. I ended up in the emergency room exhibiting symptoms of a heart attack, or so I thought. After scans, blood tests, and IV meds, the resident walked in, took a seat, and said, "Tell me about work."

I took a deep breath. My husband spoke first. "She is under a lot of stress," he said, explaining that I started working under a new boss a couple of months earlier. I nodded in agreement.

The resident leaned in. "You're going to have to do something about that. You didn't have a heart attack this time. This time, you had a panic attack. But you need to do something about this stress."

I was shocked and embarrassed. I'm a clinical social worker and a senior leader.

I should know better. Why didn't I recognize that the anxiety, stress, and emotional overload were this bad? Why didn't I listen when others expressed concerns?

After this episode, I pledged to do better.

I'm ashamed to say it took me another two years to make lasting changes. With the help of a coach and my husband's support, I began my burnout recovery journey.

I gave myself permission to pause and begin again. I showed up and listened. I shared my experience—what worked for me and what didn't. I set strong boundaries. I began a slow rebuilding of my life, rooted in nervous system care, soul listening, and presence.

I started a daily yoga and meditation routine. Again. I listened to music and went to concerts. Again. I reconnected with my garden. Again.

These small joys weren't distractions; they were breadcrumbs leading me back to myself. Every day pleasures reminded me that joy lives in the present, not in some distant achievement.

As I sifted through the rubble of burnout, I realized how much of my motivation was tied to external markers—titles, promotions, and accolades. I followed a path that looked successful from the outside but often felt hollow inside.

In this spacious season of recovery, I realized that what always drove me wasn't really the title at all, but the mission behind my work.

Joy isn't a reward for hard work or weekends. It's a practice of presence. The deep exhale comes when I let go of who I think I'm supposed to be and return to who I am. I'm mission-driven. I want to uplift, empower, and cultivate growth in others and myself. This clarity rekindled a joy that flows from alignment with purpose.

I did all this while still meeting deadlines, supporting a high-performing team, delivering on core metrics, and building award-winning educational products.

Then the news came: My leadership role was eliminated. Shock. Anger. Frustration. *What!? Why me?* The news landed like a blow.

Yet, if I'm honest, it was also an opening.

I was pushed out of a space that broke me, and it began a long time ago. In the stillness that followed, I began to understand something powerful.

I can't heal in the same place that broke me.

True recovery required not just rest, but removal from the environment that contributed to my burnout.

Suddenly unbound from expectations, deadlines, and leadership duties, I realized how tightly I clung to my professional identity. Without it, I felt untethered. But now I had space. A real pause.

This space became sacred. For the first time in years, I had time to reflect.

Who am I outside of my job? What do I actually want to do with my time? What really makes my soul shine?

These were the same questions I asked myself previously, but I always answered them the same way. I liked my team. I liked making an impact. I enjoyed creating products that enabled people to deliver better care. But really, I was just clinging to the status quo. It felt safe.

I had to define joy on my terms and return to the core of me.

We live in a culture that treats joy like a luxury. Like it's a reward to earn once the work is done, the emails are answered, and the laundry is folded. But joy isn't a reward for productivity. Joy isn't achievement or validation.

Joy is a state of deep contentment and aliveness that arises from being fully present and connected—connected to yourself, to others, to the moment—without needing anything to be different. It's the spark of inner light that exists without permission or proof, a signal of alignment. Joy emerges when we live in integrity with our values.

At first, joy felt foreign. I detached from my body and the present moment for so long. But then, I noticed joy moments in my day-to-day. You may know the moments I'm talking about: the warmth that rises when you act in alignment with who you truly are. The quiet peace of meaningful rest. The laughter that bubbles up when you feel safe to be silly and free.

I believe deeply that joy isn't random. It's relational. Rooted. Intentional.

FROM AUTOPILOT TO INTENTION

My old life was built on "shoulds":

I should climb the ladder, be grateful, and keep going.

The shoulds kept me stuck and sick.

Designing a joyful life meant slowing down long enough to choose differently. I rebuilt routines with intention, not obligation. I prioritized rest as a right, not a reward. I said no to things that drained me, even if they looked good on paper. I listened to my body, not just my calendar.

I returned to practices I abandoned in the hustle: yoga, meditation, and reading. I unrolled my mat not as part of a rigid wellness routine, but as a place to breathe again. Through yoga, I felt my body soften and reawaken. Meditation helped me become friends with silence and observe the racing thoughts I once drowned in at work. And, perhaps most quietly joyful, I finished a book from cover to cover—the first in ten years. It felt like reclaiming a part of myself that waited patiently all along.

In this stillness, something deeper surfaced: grief—unresolved, unspoken grief buried beneath the burnout. The loss of my mother. The loss of my grandmother. The death of my beloved dog. The sorrow was heavy, but it was also holy. Feeling it made room for compassion.

Joy became a compass, not a destination. Each choice became a design decision: *Does this bring me closer to alignment, or further from it?*

DESIGNING AS ITERATION, NOT PERFECTION

I had to unlearn the need to get it "right" the first time. Joyful living, like product design, is iterative. I tried things, changed my mind, started new practices, let go of others. Some days felt aligned. Other days, I fell back into old patterns. But I kept returning and beginning again.

I created a "joy audit," checking in with myself around what felt expansive versus constricting. I experimented with new ways of working, new rhythms, and new definitions of productivity. I gave myself permission to be in process while valuing progress over perfection.

I saw imperfections not as flaws, but as part of being human. Authenticity, I realized, fuels joy more than any polished facade. The more I showed up as myself —messy, real, and whole —the more joy I experienced.

I didn't escape responsibility. I created a system that supported my well-being without eroding it.

ANCHORING IN IDENTITY AND IMPACT

Perhaps my most radical shift was to decouple output from worth. For so long, I believed value came from what I produced. Joy doesn't demand performance. It invites embodiment.

While reclaiming my identity, my desire to make a positive impact on the world around me deepened. I no longer sought to prove myself; I wanted to serve others from wholeness. To create from overflow and not depletion.

Throughout my journey, my husband was my anchor. His quiet presence, unwavering support, and gentle encouragement became a refuge. He reminded me I was worthy of rest, joy, and rediscovery.

Joy became the foundation, not the reward. From this foundation, I began rebuilding my life while creating a legacy that's sustainable, soulful, and all mine.

You can do the same.

THE SPARK

PART I. LAYING THE GROUNDWORK

Before you embark on designing a life of joy, I invite you to create a safe, internal space to envision it.

If you've been in a chronic state of fight, flight, or freeze, you know how hard it is to access joy. Your nervous system is doing its job; it's trying to protect you. But when your body feels unsafe, joy can be hard to reach and even harder to sustain. That's why nervous system regulation is the foundation of my approach to joy by design.

In my own recovery from burnout, I learned to track my body's signals and ask:

- When do I feel most regulated and connected?
- Which people, places, or practices help me feel grounded and whole?
- What drains me, constricts me, or throws me into overdrive?

Your body holds this information. When your nervous system feels safe, joy becomes far more accessible.

PART II. VALUES MAPPING PRACTICE

I invite you to reflect on your top three values.

If you're not sure what they are, try these prompts:

- What moments in life made me feel most alive and connected?
- What makes me angry or frustrated? Which value is being violated?
- What do I want people to feel when they're in my presence?

Values examples: Integrity. Creativity. Connection. Rest. Justice. Curiosity. Joy.

Write them down. Keep them close. These are your design tools.

PART III. ALIGNMENT IN ACTION: MICRO-DESIGNING FOR JOY

Now that you know your values, ask: Where is there alignment in my life, and where is there disconnection?

You don't have to quit your job, move to a mountain, or redesign everything overnight. Start small. Small shifts can lead to big changes. Begin today, right where you are.

Below are some questions to guide you:

- Does how I spend my time reflect what I say I value?
- Where do I betray myself for approval or productivity?
- What boundaries would help me live in greater alignment?

- What rituals bring me back to my center?

Alignment is a practice. I invite you to make the conscious, daily choice to live in congruence.

PART IV. JOYFUL BOUNDARIES, BRAVE CHOICES

Designing a joyful life will ask you to disappoint others before you disappoint yourself. To say no to what drains you, even if it once defined you.

Yes, it's scary. And yes, it's liberating.

As you live in accordance with your values, some relationships will naturally shift. Certain roles won't fit. Old expectations will fall away.

You're not losing yourself. You're unbecoming of everything you're not.

Boundaries are sacred tools. They create the space where your truest self can breathe.

PART V. DESIGNING RITUALS OF JOY

Joy is sustained by rhythm, not rare events.

Rituals anchor you in what matters. And they don't have to be elaborate.

In fact, simple is often better:

- A morning stretch with music that makes you smile
- Lighting a candle before journaling
- A weekly walk with no agenda
- A Sunday evening "soul check-in"
- A few deep breaths before opening your laptop

These moments create micro-alignment, reminding your nervous system it's safe to feel joy. Joy isn't a detour from life. It *is* life.

PART VI. REDEFINING SUCCESS

One of the boldest acts is redefining success on your own terms.

For years, I measured success through titles, achievements, and proving my worth. Not until burnout did I realize I lived by someone else's metric.

Now, my success looks like:

- Rest without guilt
- Work in alignment with purpose
- Feeling safe in my body
- Living, leading, and loving from my values

That is joy. That is wealth. That is success.

I invite you to be curious and to ask yourself what it means for you to succeed on your own terms. Journal your responses. Revisit them often.

REMINDER: YOU ARE THE DESIGNER

You don't have to wait for joy to find you. You can create it—moment by moment, choice by choice, breath by breath.

This isn't about chasing happiness or forcing positivity. It's about shaping your days around what nourishes your soul. Joy by design isn't perfection. It's permission. Its presence. It's power.

And it's available to you now.

JOY DESIGN BLUEPRINT KEY TAKEAWAYS

Step 1: Identify Your Core Values

Write down your top three.

Step 2: Design Your Week with Intention

Detail:

- One daily micro-joy
- One weekly "no"
- One aligned "yes"
- One moment of sacred rest

Step 3: Reflect & Adjust

Ask:

- What gave me energy?
- What drained me?
- What felt aligned?

Repeat. Refine. Reclaim.

Reclaiming joy isn't a single event. It's a daily practice. A radical act of self-trust and self-acceptance.

I didn't plan to rebuild my life. But in choosing joy, I became the architect of something beautiful. A life aligned with who I am. A life where joy leads by design.

When joy becomes your blueprint, you don't just create a life that looks good. You create a life that *feels* good to live.

Melissa Lewis-Stoner, MSW, LCSW-C, is a licensed clinical social worker, product strategist, and behavioral health leader with more than 25 years of experience spanning clinical care, public health, and healthcare innovation. She began her career as a clinician in outpatient behavioral health and forensic social work programs, eventually guiding integrated care programs and public health policy initiatives.

Most recently, Melissa bridged the worlds of clinical expertise and product strategy. She has led teams in developing award-winning educational products and solutions that serve organizations across the healthcare continuum, guiding product strategy, roadmaps, and cross-functional collaboration. Along the way, she experienced firsthand the toll of burnout and the importance of designing a life aligned with values. This is a journey that informs both her professional work and her advocacy for well-being in leadership.

Beyond her professional achievements, Melissa is passionate about mindfulness, yoga, and cultivating daily practices that nurture balance and joy. She draws on her lived experience to help others create systems, programs, and products that are both effective and human-centered, emphasizing alignment, purpose, and sustainable impact.

She earned her Master of Social Work from the University of Pittsburgh and holds licensure as a clinical social worker (LCSW-C). Melissa is also a 200-hour YTT-certified yoga teacher.

Connect with Melissa:

Website: https://MelissaLewisStoner.com

LinkedIn: https://www.linkedin.com/in/melissalewisstoner/

CHAPTER 5

THE JOY THAT FOUND ME WHEN I STOPPED LOOKING

HOW A DOG AND KETAMINE SPARKED HOPE

Susan Wall Johnson

"Joy isn't lost; it's waiting to be remembered and invited back."

~ Susan Wall Johnson

I once believed joy had vanished from my life for good. Then grief hollowed me out—and love, therapy, and one very stubborn corgi sparked a light I thought I'd never feel again.

MY STORY

I didn't find joy in a gratitude journal.

I didn't manifest it with crystals or catch it on a full moon.

I found it after I went to hell and back—again, after losing the man who loved me every single day of my life.

After turning 50 and realizing I wasn't who I thought I was, but maybe that was the point. After a corgi named Banksy and a vial of ketamine cracked me wide open, but let me back up. Because before joy finally knocked again, I disappeared.

THE YEAR I WAS DADDY'S GIRL AGAIN

For the last two years of my father's life, I moved back in with my parents. He died slowly from pulmonary fibrosis.

The oxygen tanks hissed and buzzed day and night. His recliner—ugly, enormous, and lovingly dubbed The Manatee—became his command post. He watched sports. I made drinks. We swapped dark jokes and old memories. He was still my dad—still brilliant, witty, gruff, deeply kind. Still, the man who made me feel seen, safe, and solid in a world that never quite knew what to do with me. I was always his girl. From the moment I was born, I bonded with him.

He was my anchor, my protector, my favorite person.

And while I never wanted to be a doctor, I spent most of my childhood wanting to be just like him: smart, respected, funny, a soft heart hidden beneath a steady presence.

In many ways, I became that, just with more f-bombs and fewer scalpels. So when he got really sick, I came home. I stayed home.

I cooked his favorite meals.

Sat with him while he wheezed and coughed and waved off help with a stubborn smile.

I curled up next to him on the arm of his chair like a child in a grown woman's body, memorizing every sound of his voice, every story he repeated, every grumble, every laugh. But I wasn't just living with my father.

I was also living with my mother, the narcissist.

And if you've ever met a Southern woman who perfected performance but never quite mastered warmth, you get it.

Living with her felt like trying to grieve inside a pressure cooker. I tiptoed. I translated. I tried to be everything to everyone, yet again. But I didn't care, because I was there for him.

My Daddy. I would've walked through fire just to make his last days better.

THE MORNING THE OXYGEN MACHINE WENT SILENT

"Susan!"

The minute I heard my mom call my name, I knew something was horribly wrong. The tone in her voice sent a shiver down my spine; I went numb. All I could do was turn into a robot, completely void of emotion, because I knew I had to be strong for my family. It was a moment I dreaded for two years, yet knew was inevitable. I turned into a soldier for a split second, bracing myself. But then I saw him—the only man who had ever seen me and loved me completely—sitting there, gone. A wave of fire ran through every cell in my body. I dropped to the floor, pulling him toward me, placing his head in my lap. I held him and repeated, "I love you, Dad. I love you so much!"

Immediately, I wished I had hugged him tighter and kissed his cheek harder the night before. As we waited for the funeral home to come, I lay next to him, trying to get one more hug, one last moment before I would never see him again. Tears filled my eyes, but before they could fall, my mom's cold presence snapped me back to reality.

And then, after the funeral, silence fell—and with it, the hardest year of my life.

THE YEAR THAT BROKE ME

People talk about grief like it comes in waves.

This was a tsunami that swallowed me whole. For the next year, I didn't live. I survived. Barely. I was still in therapy, still on antidepressants and anxiety meds. But nothing could reach me. I rarely left my bed, let alone the house. Hired help walked the dogs. I had groceries delivered. I canceled appointments, turned down invitations, and quietly unraveled behind closed doors.

I was in the deepest depression of my life—and no one really knew. Because I still smiled when I had to. Still sent thank-you texts. Still knew how to sound "fine." But inside? I was done. My father was gone. My nervous system was fried. My will to live flickered like a dying bulb in an old Southern porch light.

Even two years later, on my 50th birthday, I couldn't celebrate. Couldn't post the cute "I'm fabulous at 50" selfie. Couldn't fake joy that wasn't there. What do you do when the person who always believed in you is no longer breathing? You fall apart. And then, one tiny miracle at a time, you begin to find joy again.

My joy arrived in the form of a stubborn, squatty, and ridiculously handsome corgi named Banksy.

At first, he was just cuddly company. Someone to feed. A reason to get out of bed, even if it was only to let him out to pee. But he didn't just fill the silence; he disrupted it. Loudly. He barked at delivery drivers, squirrels, and occasionally the wind. Sometimes it drove me crazy. But even when he made me mad, he made me feel something. And in the deepest depression, feeling anything—even irritation—is a step toward living again. Banksy had a way of pulling me back into life whether I wanted it or not.

On sunny afternoons, he flopped belly-up in the middle of the rug, paws splayed like he owned the place. Sunlight spilled through the window, landing on his fur in gold streaks. I found myself sitting on the floor with him, feeling that warmth seep into my own skin for the first time in months.

Not long after Banksy came barreling into my life, I began ketamine therapy. I heard it described as a "reset button" for the brain, but I wasn't chasing a quick fix. I was desperate for any chance to feel joy, to feel different. What I found wasn't just glimpses of joy; it was transformative joy. The sessions were calm, quiet, almost dreamlike. For the first time in years, my brain stopped replaying every loss, every mistake, every harsh word from my mother.

It was like someone opened a window in a suffocating room and let the light in. And then, almost without trying, joy snuck back in through my senses. The first time I bit into a fresh summer peach, juice dripping down my chin, I laughed out loud—because Dad loved peaches. The same goes for the first forkful of strawberry shortcake, sweet and tart, piled high with whipped cream. Or the day I made speckled butter beans with white rice, his absolute favorite, and the kitchen smelled exactly like the Sundays we used to spend together. Sometimes joy arrived on the couch, too—watching a sports documentary and making comments out loud to Dad, as if he sat right there. I caught myself laughing, not just at the TV, but at the thought of what he would've said.

It felt like sharing something with him again, even if it was only in spirit. These weren't just meals or moments—they were portals. Each one brought him closer, but instead of aching, I smiled. I didn't suddenly become a different person. But I started to like the person I already was. I laughed more. Took longer walks. Called friends back. I started dreaming again—about traveling, about writing, about finally moving to Italy.

And that's when I realized:

Joy doesn't always come looking like your typical definition. Sometimes it shows up in a dog who won't stop flopping on you, a therapy that makes you feel like you're rewiring your own brain, a perfect peach on a hot afternoon, or a golf documentary you "watch together" in the quiet. Sometimes it tiptoes in so quietly, you don't even notice it took up residence in your chest until one day, you catch yourself smiling for no reason.

THE SPARK

THE SPARKBACK METHOD

How to Reclaim Joy Through Sensory Memory

Step 1: Choose a Sense

Start by taking a slow, deep breath. Hold it in for a four-count and release it on an eight-count.

Now, pick the sense that feels most alive for you right now—or the one that feels easiest to connect to. For many people, smell and taste are the most powerful joy-triggers because they're wired directly to memory. That's why the scent of perfume or the taste of a sweet, fresh peach can transport you instantly to a summer afternoon with someone you love. If you feel stuck, pick the sense tied to the strongest positive memory you can recall. For example:

If you remember dancing in the kitchen with your grandmother, start with sound and play that same song.

If you remember the warmth of your childhood dog curled against you, start with touch by holding something soft and warm.

If you recall the smell of marinara simmering on the stove, go with the smell and recreate that aroma in your kitchen.

Your brain doesn't need a huge event to reawaken joy—it just needs a cue that feels familiar and safe.

Step 2: Recall a Joy Memory

Close your eyes and let yourself drift toward a moment—big or small—when you felt comfort, connection, or delight. Don't overthink it. The memory doesn't have to be picture-perfect or free from all sadness; it just has to contain one clear point of joy. If you're having trouble, start with moments connected to people, places, or even pets that made you feel loved or at peace. Maybe it's the quiet clink of silverware at Sunday dinner, the sound of ocean waves, or the smell of your dad's aftershave. Pro Tip: If sadness sneaks in, imagine you're pressing "pause" on the rest of the memory—just hold the part that feels good, like isolating one note in a song.

Step 3: Recreate the Cue

Now, bring that sensory detail into your present moment. If it's taste, cook or buy the food. If it's sound, play the song, even on repeat. If it's tactile, find a texture or object that feels similar to the original. And if recreating the exact cue isn't possible, get creative:

Can't go back to that beach? Play an ocean sounds playlist.

Missing your grandmother's biscuits? Find a bakery with something similar and breathe in the scent.

Longing for the feel of a beloved dog's fur? Wrap yourself in a thick, soft blanket and imagine the weight against you.

The brain responds to the essence of the cue, not just the exact replica.

Step 4: Stay With It

This is the part most people skip—and it's where the magic happens. Instead of rushing past it, pause. Take a deep breath. Let your shoulders drop. Notice how your body feels: warmer, looser, softer. Allow the joy to wash over you without forcing it to be bigger or longer than it is. Even 30 seconds of truly being in the moment can shift your emotional state. If tears come, let them. If a smile comes, let it spread. If that funny laugh happens, let it.

Pro Tip: Try placing a hand over your heart or belly as you breathe; physical touch can deepen the body's memory of safety and joy.

Step 5: Repeat Often

The more you practice, the easier it becomes for your brain to find joy in the everyday. Build this into your week; maybe you light a candle with a scent you love every Sunday night, or eat your favorite fruit on the porch every Thursday morning. Think of it like keeping a pilot light on in your heart—always ready to spark a flame when you need it most. Sometimes joy isn't about chasing something new; it's about remembering what already lives within you, and choosing to spark it back to life.

Susan Wall Johnson, MBA, is a Southern-born storyteller, speaker, and intuitive guide whose life reads like a plot twist you didn't see coming. A graduate of Davidson College and the University of Kentucky MBA program, she's navigated careers in real estate, fashion, and events while surviving addiction, chronic illness, and sexual assault.

Her upcoming memoir, *Why I'm Finally Saying It All Out Loud*, blends gallows humor and raw vulnerability to show how even the messiest seasons can lead to extraordinary transformation. After losing her father to pulmonary fibrosis, ketamine therapy and a stubborn corgi named Banksy cracked her open to joy again.

Susan is the founder of Still Sovereign™ and Susan Wall Speaks LLC, where she helps women reclaim their voices through coaching, retreats, and her forthcoming podcast *Holy Shit, Now What?!* She plans to relocate to Florence, Italy, with her two corgis, Banksy and Brody, where she'll write, speak, and host transformational retreats that remind women that even their darkest chapters can become their greatest comeback stories.

Connect with Susan:

Website | Instagram | Facebook | LinkedIn | Linktree | YouTube

@SusanWallSpeaks

CHAPTER 6

A LOVE LETTER TO THE JOY FLOWERS BRING

HOW FLOWERS SHAPE MEMORIES, MOODS, AND MOMENTS

Melinda Bourg

MY STORY

"I don't know what kind of flower that is, but we had it at our wedding," he said from the other side of my desk, closing his eyes with a small smile. My coworker was instantly taken back to one of the happiest days of his life by the Stargazer Lily scent.

At that moment, flowers became my love language.

Flowers create joy because they connect to us on multiple levels. Personally, I recall my mother's rose garden, a wrist corsage from my crush at my first school dance, and a moment of solace at my father's wake. My mother appreciated the flowers I picked for her on my walks home from grade school; however, she had to teach me not to "pluck them from the gardens" I passed along my journey.

I can still see it like an old, grainy movie in my head. During the spring of 1973, I was five. My mother and I visited the Norfolk Botanical Gardens for the Azalea Festival. Small enough to hold her hand without thinking about it, I let my fingers curl into hers as we walked, surrounded by pink and coral blooms. Everywhere, azaleas flamed in shades I never imagined: blush, fuchsia, and deep magenta. It seemed as though nature decided to celebrate itself.

I vaguely recall my mom wore a pale-yellow dress with a wide-brimmed hat. I remember her laughing as she bent down to show me how each petal was soft and papery. But what I remember most is her kneeling beside me near a giant pink azalea bush. She wrapped her arm around my shoulders and whispered, "Look at this beauty, Melinda."

As I looked up at her, I understood flowers weren't just pretty. They meant something to her. *I* meant something to her. This moment meant something to her. Flowers make it possible to hold happiness in your heart.

Flowers have been woven into the human story for millennia. Their presence transcends geography, language, and time. They appear in the earliest cave paintings and ancient burial sites, where blooms like cornflowers and lilies rested with the dead as tokens of love and remembrance.

In Ancient Egypt, the lotus embodied rebirth and divine creation. The laurel and roses symbolized victory, honor, and passion in Greece and Rome. Across Asia, cherry blossoms capture the poignant brevity of life. In Mexico's Día de los Muertos, marigolds commemorate ancestors with vibrant offerings.

Regardless of culture, flowers speak a universal language in rituals, celebrations, healing, and art. They console us in grief, heighten joy at weddings, affirm care, or convey a simple "I'm sorry." Their power lies in evoking what words can't: beauty, impermanence, hope, and connection. Whether painted on temple walls, carried in bridal bouquets, or grown in home gardens, flowers remain enduring messengers of human emotion and meaning.

CONNECTIONS

Flowers blend beauty with memory, linking us to key moments. Unlike most gifts, they fade quickly, making their impact linger in our minds. On my sixteenth birthday, while in class pretending it was just another day, a delivery arrived: pink roses and white daisies from my dad. He was in the Navy and usually away, but that year, he was home. *Wow, Dad's thinking about me no matter where he is.* Those flowers meant more than just petals; they embodied love, pride, and a connection I didn't realize we had before.

To this day, seeing pink roses and daisies brings me back to that birthday and hugs my heart. Flowers have a unique way of conveying joy, comfort, and cherished memories. They brighten our lives and become part of our stories. Studies show that just looking at flowers lifts our mood and gives us energy. Sometimes, a single flower in a vase makes a whole room feel happier and turns an ordinary day into something memorable.

Scent enhances this effect. Fragrances from flowers such as lavender, jasmine, and roses stimulate the limbic system, the part of the brain responsible for processing emotions and memories. That's why the smell of lilacs evokes childhood memories. Gardenias may bring back memories of a loved one. The brain links the flower with the feeling, forming lasting connections between beauty and experience. Physiologically, flowers help calm us. Studies show they lower blood pressure and reduce stress hormones such as cortisol, a chemical released during stress. Flowers also improve focus and healing. Hospitals with floral arrangements often see faster patient recovery. Workplaces with plants report greater creativity and less fatigue. Flowers do more than decorate. They interact with our biology, quietly shaping how we feel, think, and connect with the world.

Flowers bear our deepest emotions, acting as silent messengers when words fail. They speak a universal language that transcends culture and time. No flower is more linked to love than the rose. Across centuries and continents, roses have meant passion, devotion, and romance. In ancient Rome, they adorned garlands; today, they fill Valentine's bouquets. Love appears in many blooms: tulips embody perfect affection, orchids show admiration, and forget-me-nots stand for enduring love that doesn't fade.

In times of loss, flowers offer solace and comfort. White lilies represent a soul's purity at rest. Chrysanthemums on graves in Europe and Asia signify remembrance. Marigolds guide loved ones home during Mexico's Día de los Muertos. Flowers soften grief, surround sorrow with beauty, and remind us that love continues beyond death.

Flowers are nature's promise of new beginnings. The lotus grows clean from muddy water. Daffodils signal spring's arrival. A dandelion growing through concrete shows strength and hope. Good times follow bad ones. These are real-life examples of perseverance and believing in what's possible.

Flowers mean more than just beauty, and each one seems to send its own message. This concept, known as floriography, is a symbolic language of flowers. People throughout history used flowers to express feelings difficult to articulate out loud.

In ancient Greece, violets stood for fertility. In Japan, the chrysanthemum represents the imperial family and long life.

The strict social rules of Victorian England made it challenging to express love or grief openly, so flowers became a secret code. There's something deeply romantic and personal about receiving a handpicked bouquet that shows how someone feels about you.

Red Rose	"I love and want you."
White Rose	"I am worthy of you."
Blue Violets	"I am faithful to you."
Daisies	"I will not share the secrecy of our love."
Sunflowers	"I only have eyes for you."
Forget-Me-Nots	"True love and remembrance when parting."

Today, flowers' meanings still shape our traditions. We give lilies to show sympathy, roses for romance, leis to celebrate, and tulips to honor mothers. Flowers let us share our feelings without words. Each petal holds a story, a tradition, or a memory, making even a simple flower feel full of emotion.

What's a memory you hold close to your heart?

THE CREATIVE SPARK

Flowers inspire people across centuries, their fleeting beauty giving rise to creative works that endure far longer. Their shapes, colors, and meanings encourage us to interpret and express complex feelings. Painters choose flowers as subjects and symbols across generations. Georgia O'Keeffe painted close-up views of flowers, turning them into bold and provocative scenes.

I once visited Claude Monet's gardens at Giverny, which inspired his famous *Water Lilies* paintings—a special memory with my mom. She told me, "This is such a beautiful and special garden. No wonder it inspired him during his career."

Through art, flowers live on, their short lives captured in paint. Their influence extends beyond visual art, shaping stories, poetry, and music.

Wordsworth's daffodils dance beside the lake and under the trees, Emily Dickinson's poems open like pressed petals, and songwriters often use roses to convey love. In all forms of writing and music, flowers symbolize emotions such as happiness, sadness, longing, and hope. One song about a flower that resonated with me as a tween was Bette Midler's "The Rose." I remember thinking, *This is the prettiest song I've ever heard.*

Flowers' influence extends into our everyday lives, not just art. Floral designs on textiles, buildings, and jewelry exist worldwide. From lotus patterns in ancient Egypt to embroidered flowers in high fashion, their impact is everywhere. Flowers inspire us to create and decorate our surroundings. They remind artists of beauty and how quickly it fades, pushing them to capture special moments.

Have you ever looked at a flower in a piece of art, knowing the artist captured it at its peak of beauty?

Nature's delicate gifts often lead to bold artistic choices. I enjoy keeping flowers close in my daily life. One of my favorite pieces of jewelry is a gold locket with a floral design my mom gave me for Christmas.

Working with flowers, whether tending the garden or putting them in a vase, feels special. It helps us slow down and notice things more clearly. Each step is calming. You might feel the stem in your hands, hear the sound of cutting, or see how the colors and shapes go together.

In the garden, it feels as though time stands still while we tend to the plants. By planting, watering, and trimming, we feel a deeper connection to nature. We relax as we smell a rose, hear the buzzing of bees, and see a seed grow. Gardening teaches us to be patient and thankful, showing us beauty takes time.

In her documentary TV show, *Gardens of the World with Audrey Hepburn*, the actress famously said, "To plant a garden is to believe in tomorrow."

Arranging flowers is another way to pay attention. Picking flowers, matching them to how they feel, and arranging them together is a careful process. Each choice is a small way to enjoy color and life. When we're done, we have more than a bunch of flowers; we have a reminder to feel calm and creative. It helps us slow down, breathe, and enjoy the moment. In a busy world, this simple act is a gentle way to find happiness, one flower at a time.

THE JOY OF ANTICIPATION

Each bloom arrives in its own perfect moment, carrying the thrill of anticipation and reminding us that life is always unfolding.

Flowers are nature's quiet timekeepers; with silent fanfare, they mark the year's passage.

The first tulips of spring are like a breath of hope after winter's long slumber. Their vivid cups of color break through the lingering chill, heralding renewal and possibility. As tulips awaken us to what's fresh and just beginning, summer follows. The garden explodes with life: sunflowers rise, faces turned to the sun, radiating warmth and boundless energy. They capture the spirit of long, golden days and the joy of being fully present in this season of abundance.

Each October, I plant my sweet peas and daffodils that become the first flowers I pick in the new year. There is a sense of excitement I feel while waiting for them.

When autumn arrives, a tapestry of rich, deep hues emerges. Dahlias reach their peak—their intricate petals and jewel tones whisper of harvest and gratitude, urging us to savor beauty before winter's hush returns, and to celebrate all that has blossomed. As we notice flowers throughout the seasons, we learn to move in harmony with the earth. Gradually, we look forward to the joys ahead and treasure the fleeting wonders of the present.

Pause when you spot the first tulip, the tallest sunflower, or the last dahlia; these moments invite us to connect deeply with the world around us.

Giving flowers is one of the simplest and most meaningful ways we show affection. A single flower for a stranger, a bunch left on a doorstep, or a vase for a friend in need all say a lot.

During COVID, I would create flower arrangements for my friend's mother. She lost her husband the year before and I wanted her to know she wasn't alone. Flowers are more than just gifts; they show we care and help us feel connected.

We give flowers in times of love and loss, to celebrate important moments, and to comfort others. No matter where you are in the world, their message is clear. You matter. There's something very human about giving flowers. Their beauty is meant to be shared. When we give a part of nature, we give a part of ourselves. Because flowers are delicate and beautiful, they encourage kindness and remind us we're not alone.

Next time you see a bunch of flowers, a wildflower, or a flower in your garden, stop for a moment. Think about how it quietly makes someone's day better.

Every flower that grows is a quiet act of kindness.

By offering flowers, you foster connection. You join a timeless tradition of generosity and love, expressing without words: *You are seen, valued, not alone.* Give them to friends, neighbors, or strangers. Let them remind us beauty is for everyone.

Flowers are my love language because they connect with who I am in a quiet and beautiful way. They remind me of my mother's laughter among the azaleas, my father's pride as he arranged a bouquet, and how a single bloom brightens an entire day. Flowers weave together memory, science, culture, and the wild beauty of nature. They show me love doesn't always need to be loud; it can be gentle, like smelling the first sweet pea of spring, cutting a rose for your window, or offering a daisy to someone just because.

Flowers remind us that joy lives in small, intentional moments, and we choose beauty and connection every single day.

THE SPARK

I'd love for you to try to bring flowers into your life with a simple, joyful action today. Pick up a single stem at your local shop, start a pot of seeds on your windowsill, surprise someone you care about with a bloom, and place a flower by your bedside or in your child's hand.

Using flowers in hands-on projects connects us to nature. We turn short-lived beauty into lasting happiness. Pressing flowers saves the delicate look of a bloom and keeps a special memory. A daisy tucked between book pages takes you back to a sunny summer afternoon. Pressed flowers become special keepsakes, perfect for decorating journals, cards, or framing as gentle pieces of art. Each one is a tiny time capsule.

PRESSING FLOWERS

Supplies:

- Fresh flowers or leaves (small, flat ones work best)
- A few sheets of paper (parchment, printer, or blotting paper)
- A heavy book (like a dictionary)

Steps:

1. Pick your flowers. Choose blooms that are not too thick (pansies, daisies, ferns, and rose petals press beautifully).
2. Prepare them. Pat gently with a paper towel to remove extra moisture.
3. Arrange them. Place the flowers between two sheets of paper.
4. Press. Slip the paper inside a heavy book and close it. Add more books on top for extra weight.
5. Wait. Leave for 1–2 weeks until completely dry and flat.

Making wreaths is a centuries-old tradition that inspires great happiness. Imagine making a wildflower crown for a child or hanging a sweet-smelling lavender wreath on your door. Stringing a garland to celebrate the holidays adds your own tradition.

LAVENDER STRING GARLAND

Supplies:

- Dried lavender stems (fresh lavender can be used, but dries more fragile)
- Twine, string, or thin ribbon
- Scissors

Steps:

1. Cut your string: Decide how long you want your garland to be, then cut the twine to length.
2. Prepare lavender: Trim stems to about 6–8 inches. Gather into little mini-bundles of 3–5 stems.
3. Attach bundles:
   - Tie each mini-bundle directly to the twine with a knot.
4. Space them out: Place bundles every few inches, all pointing in the same direction for a flowing look, or alternate directions for a fuller style.
5. Finish: Leave a bit of extra twine at each end for hanging.

Tip:

- Dried lavender will keep its fragrance for months. Give it a gentle squeeze to refresh the scent.

The inspiration flowers provide goes beyond crafts and enters the kitchen. Edible varieties, such as nasturtiums, violets, and calendula, add bright colors and flavors to your table. Bake them into cakes or freeze them in ice cubes for a playful touch, and suddenly, everyday dishes feel like a party; this makes eating healthy more enjoyable. Nasturtium leaves and flowers have a nice, peppery taste that goes well when added to salads. Besides being rich in vitamin C, they help reduce swelling, clear mucus for easier breathing, contain iron and potassium, and fight germs. Imagine sipping rosewater lemonade on a hot afternoon or enjoying a lavender gin cocktail.

NASTURTIUM SALAD

Simply add a small amount of nasturtium leaves and flowers to your salad. Add more as you become accustomed to the peppery undertones they bring.

As you weave these little gestures into your routines, celebrations, or moments of healing, notice how flowers quietly enrich your days. You might find, as I have, that flowers don't just decorate life; they infuse it with love, meaning, and a touch of everyday magic.

Within us lies a simple truth: We're made to love nature.

Biophilia, a term popularized by E.O. Wilson, describes our innate attraction to living things. It's why we stop for a sunrise, relax in the woods, or smile at a flower. This connection isn't something we learn; it's part of us, shaped over millennia.

Flowers show this bond clearly. Their colors once guided us to food and marked the seasons, vital for survival. Their scents warmed or reassured us. Today, even without needing flowers for food, they nourish our hearts and minds.

Seeing a garden or a single flower awakens a sense of belonging. In a world that keeps us indoors, flowers remind us of that link. They invite us to slow down and reconnect with the patterns that always sustain us. With them, we remember we're part of nature, not apart from it.

Let flowers be your love language, too. Speak it. Live it. Be the reason something blooms in someone's heart today.

For a free companion pamphlet to this chapter, please visit her website in the Contact section below.

Melinda Bourg is an entrepreneur, floral enthusiast, wellness advocate, and a collaborating author of *Joy Unleashed The Ultimate Guide to Living Your Best Life*. She's the founder and CEO of Fleurmagination, a global online community for people who love flowers. A passionate public speaker, Melinda shares the health benefits of gardening and the joy of living in harmony with nature.

Drawing on her background as a senior technical recruiter, she connects with diverse audiences through warmth, insight, and real-world experience. Whether on stage, in the garden, or online, Melinda inspires others to find beauty, peace, and connection, one bloom at a time.

Beyond flowers, Melinda is a sought-after speaker, sharing insights on how gardening enhances mental and physical well-being. With a background as a Consulting Rosarian, a previous board member of the San Diego Rose Society, membership in the SoCal Flower Collective, and an alumnus of Floret Farm's small-scale flower farm training, she brings deep expertise in floral cultivation, breeding, and design. She partners with wellness organizations like the Integrated Wellness Collective as a Board Advisor and health educator on Nest Earth, an online community for modern parents focused on making eco-conscious changes for living easy.

Connect with Melinda:

Website: https://www.fleurmagination.com/

Facebook: https://www.facebook.com/fleurmagination/

Instagram: https://www.instagram.com/fleurmagination/

Threads: https://www.threads.com/@fleurmagination?__pwa=1

YouTube: https://www.youtube.com/@melindabourgfleurmaginatio4241

Fleurmagination Global Online Community:
https://fleurimag.mn.co/sign_up

Work with Melinda: https://www.melindabourg.com/

Amazon Products: http://bit.ly/47JjW3y

LinkedIn: http://bit.ly/41l66AA

CHAPTER 7

THE JOY OF STRESS

THE ART OF SHIFTING YOUR PERSPECTIVE

Jenny Tasker

MY STORY

I don't remember coming to the emergency room.

The familiar smell of alcohol tickled my nose. I heard beeping and faint whispers of people rushing around me, but I couldn't make out anything they said. A baby's cries were so loud my ears hurt, and I remember thinking, *That poor thing sounds so terrified.* Suddenly, alarms rang, and my chest felt heavy. Someone shouted, and then everything went quiet.

I couldn't see anything except a vibrant glow that felt like a hug. I was overcome with joy unlike anything I'd ever experienced before. I remember thinking, *This is it. I'm crossing over.*

It felt warm and calm, and I heard a woman's voice whispering. I tried to sit up, completely unaware of the doctors working on me, helping me breathe. I felt someone's hand on my heart, gently urging me to lie back down. That's when I caught a glimpse of long, bright-red curls before she transformed into a blinding, bluish-green light that completely encompassed me.

Wait—do I know you?

I heard a familiar voice in my head. *Everything's okay now; you're safe, I'm right here. It's not your time.*

I felt tears escape my eyes, overcome with gratitude for being alive. She went on to remind me that I'm not this body. I'm not my circumstances, or the things that have, or haven't, happened to me. What powers me is a brilliant spark, my true essence.

I know this soul path is hard, full of many twists and turns. Just remember, it's okay to feel frustrated, afraid, or even angry. Allow these feelings, knowing you don't have to carry them forever. You can also choose to release them. Our time here is brief, and it's a privilege to feel and experience life fully.

Remind yourself to let go when something no longer serves you. There's much power in that surrender. Trust yourself to know when it's time to tune in and be still, or when to spread your wings and shine.

A long night of ups and downs passed before they figured out the right cocktail of medicines to stabilize me. Several days and many tests later, the doctor said I could finally go home.

"Woohoo!" I yelped, jumping up. "I'm already packed! I can't wait to see the kids."

The aftereffects of almost dying, coupled with a cocktail of medications surging through my veins, made me feel invincible. One thing was for sure: beating death was invigorating. As my husband, Shawn, closed my door and walked around to get into the van, I shouted, "Let's stop for hamburgers on the way home, I'm starving!"

I've dealt with these scary reactions for so many years, but this time felt different. This experience gave me a whole new perspective on how I can choose to look for joy, even in the most difficult moments.

It took four more scary years of emergency room visits, many perplexed specialists, and a whole lot of research before I finally received a diagnosis.

"Well, what do you know; you're right!" said the doctor I'd waited six months to see. He read from his computer without looking at me. "There's no cure."

Even though I already knew—my research was extensive—my ears roared.

He went on. "From what I can see here, the suggested medications can cause many unpleasant side effects, some quite dangerous." The doctor finally looked up at me, blinking a few times, "I think it's safest for you to keep doing what you're doing. It's our best chance to keep you stable."

After years of research, we finally had an answer. I have mastocytosis, a rare condition that causes my body to produce an overabundance of mast cells, a type of white blood cell that plays a crucial role in my immune and nervous system responses. Mast cells are concentrated in our skin, blood vessels, nerves, lungs—pretty much everywhere—and are best known for their involvement in allergic reactions and inflammation. Their purpose is to protect and warn our body against invaders. In my case, they sit all over me like little soldiers, always at high alert, ready to fire into a flare at any given moment. It's unpredictable, scary, and almost anything can become a trigger and send me into anaphylaxis.

I must have walked out of the office and found my way to our van, because the next thing I knew, Shawn was running around to open the door for me. "What happened, babe? Are you okay?"

I told him what the doctor said. "I need to do some more research to see which course of action is best for me." My eyes teared up as I looked out the window.

Why do I always have to be right? Am I going to die?

I felt stressed, validated, and a little numb that evening when I pulled out my laptop. I was glad to have a diagnosis finally, but to say there's no cure and my future looked dim was impossible to comprehend. I frantically scoured the internet using every resource I could think of. The rarity of this condition created roadblock after roadblock.

As panic set in, I felt that familiar flushing as my body responded to the stress. I thought, *well, this isn't working. I'm driving myself bananas in this rabbit hole. Deep breaths, Jenny. How can I make this easier? How can I support myself?* As I continued to breathe, I tuned into my body's rhythm.

Moments later, my fingers flew across the keyboard. Instead of looking for a cure, I searched for support groups and resources—anything to help me navigate this journey more easily. I researched high-histamine foods, artificial dyes, and fillers—anything that could contribute to inflammation in my body.

This simple shift helped create forward momentum, something positive to focus on. I learned so much that I educated my own healthcare team. It felt empowering as I continued to trust my gut and make those bold choices. I wasn't going to die, not yet anyway. I was determined to thrive.

Being put on disability in my 40s gave me a lot of free time. One morning, I woke up inspired to create a Facebook page to share my musings. I thought it would be healing to share some of the poetry and quotes I've written over the years.

Whenever I get ready to write something new, my mind wanders back to a life-changing day in grade nine.

I was attending the Davis School of Performing Arts, a private school that taught dancing, singing, and acting, all while immersing us in the world of the arts. It was an amazing experience where I met the most inspiring and talented people, while gaining the confidence to explore my own passions.

On a surprise class trip, we were invited to spend the afternoon with Bryan Adams, a renowned Canadian musician, at his home in North Vancouver. We hung out around his pool like old friends, snacking on grilled cheese sandwiches, fresh fruit, and bottomless lemonades. He shared some of his writing process—how it can be healing, and a lot like poetry. We spent the afternoon singing as he casually strummed his guitar. I can still see him so vividly, sitting on the edge of the pool with a big grin on his face, feet kicking the water as he sang his newest release, "Summer of '69."

No recorded version will ever sound as good as that special moment.

Brian lit a spark in me, and I began to write every day. I found it cathartic and fun to challenge myself. Sometimes I'd share my writing with family or a few special friends over coffee, but mostly those words were just meant for me.

It's been just over a decade since I started Living Your Best Life with Jenny Tasker, and I'm so glad I did. Thanks to the magic of the internet, I'm surrounded by an amazing community of beautiful souls from all over the world, helping one another live their best lives despite life's sometimes scary and unpredictable circumstances.

Just a few weeks ago, I woke up to another flare. "Are you okay?" Mom whispered as she came into my room and put down a fresh glass of water. It was 6:00 a.m., and I hung over the side of my bed with my face in a bucket.

"I'm sorry I woke you." My voice echoed as she rubbed my back. "I'm supposed to be helping you," I mumbled, getting sick again.

"I'm fine," she said. "I don't think there's anything in that bucket I need." We both chuckled, sharing a moment of joy in the stress.

"You're going to hurt your arm."

This was the last thing Mom needed. She went through a heart attack, surgery for her seven-month-old hernia we'd nicknamed Herman, and a bad fall that broke her arm, all within the past year. Yet here she was, rubbing my back and tending to me through yet another flare-up. But truth be told, as hard as it all is sometimes, I'm so grateful we have each other to lean on when life sends so many curveballs.

"Okay, enough of that; you have nothing left in you!" Mom said, commanding the nausea to stop. "Come on, time to sit up!"

"Okay," I grunted. *Enough is enough, time for the big guns.*

As I reached for my rescue meds, Mom asked, "Do you know what got you?"

"I have no idea." I shrugged as I swallowed my pills. "I woke up with a bad headache, and the room was spinning."

"Do you want an ice pack? Your face is all swollen."

I didn't have a chance to answer her as she darted out of the room. *Man, that woman can move when she wants to.*

"You've barely eaten in two days; do you want me to make you some toast?" she called worriedly from the kitchen.

"I don't think I can eat. I need to give these meds some time. I can't even keep my water down."

"Okay," Mom said quietly, handing me the ice pack. "I'll be back to check on you in a little while." She slipped out of the room.

A short while later, Shawn poked his head around the door. "You okay, sweetheart? Can I get you anything?"

"I'm okay at the moment," I said. "I just need to rest for a bit and let these meds do their thing."

As I drifted off, I thought: *What a blessing to be surrounded by so much support and love.*

I woke up five hours later feeling like I was hit by a train, but I'd improved. Pulling myself together, I changed my clothes and went outside to sit in the sunshine with my family. I took in a few deep breaths of fresh, salty air, and my body began to relax. I looked from my mom to my husband, as I listened to my son and daughter laughing together in the kitchen, and thought, *How on Earth did I get so lucky?*

Learning to find joy, even in the most stressful times, gives me the ability to embrace and make the most of every moment I'm gifted. As I flow in and out of flares, alternating good days and bad, I focus on the small blessings and remind myself that even in my darkest times, if I focus on my light, it will always guide me through.

THE SPARK

Things get chaotic when we're caught up in our stress. Those are the times to allow grace, reminding yourself that you're not alone. It's okay if this doesn't feel good; it will soon pass.

We all must go through things that are scary and hard as we grow and evolve through our learning process.

The following are three ways to live a happy, joyful, and fulfilling life, despite your struggles.

THE ART OF SHIFTING YOUR PERSPECTIVE

Stress is impossible to avoid. As soon as that hormone begins surging, our brains are already off to the races, calculating all possible scenarios.

Learning to shift my perspective helps me navigate even the most difficult situations.

When I start to feel tension in my body, that's my signal to shift my thoughts and look at things from a different angle. It's a skill that quickly became an ongoing daily habit, helping me adapt to my life's ever-changing circumstances.

The other day, as my husband and I were caught up in some unexpected traffic, frustration kicked in, and he started muttering under his breath. I looked over at his scowl. "It'll be okay, love. Trust there's a reason we're not supposed to be on the highway yet."

After a moment, he released the breath he held. "Yeah, you're probably right." As the traffic slowed again, we had a rare opportunity to take in the incredible views from the highway bridge, making us both smile.

Looking at things from a different point of view doesn't just help me feel better; in a condition like mine, it's a lifesaver. Even the smallest amount of stress can trigger a flare. This practice helps keep my body safe and takes me out of fight-or-flight mode.

If you have trouble shifting your thoughts, try reaching out to people you trust, such as friends, family, neighbors, or perhaps a support group. Making these connections, even if only on the phone or through social media, made a huge difference to my well-being.

STAYING TUNED IN

Being mindful of the signals our body gives us can be immensely powerful. Whenever I'm unsure of a situation, I always ask myself two questions:

- How do you feel about what is happening?
- Is this serving my purpose?

Then I remind myself to slow down and tune into my body, quietly waiting for the answers to come—and trust me, they will. Our body loves to tell us how it feels.

If I'm in danger, my heartbeat slows, and I get a high-pitched ringing in my ears. I can instantly feel the alert my gut sends, and the friction in the air as the little hairs on my arms stand up with dread. This is my body warning me to leave or get help.

When something brings me great joy, my heart races with excitement, and my stomach does somersaults. I get a giddy, playful feeling that bubbles up, even a little breathless. This is my body feeling energized by this high vibration.

In overwhelm, my ears will roar, and my heart beats rapidly. I feel pain in my stomach, and the nausea creeps in. I might feel scared and unsure, wanting to retreat inward, to curl up, and hide until I feel safe again. This is my body telling me to shift my perspective and give myself a rest from this situation.

Sometimes the answers require a more mindful approach: slowing right down, becoming aware of my breath, my very being. Tuning in to your body in this way allows you to listen to its frequency, enabling it to tell you what it needs. Find the volume button and turn it up to full blast! Learn to depend on this compass as if it's your closest ally, because trust me, it is.

LETTING IT FLOW

When I feel out of sorts, I go outside and take in a few deep, cleansing breaths as I shift my focus to my surroundings. The seagulls soaring in the wind overhead, as the crows try to get my attention, hoping for a peanut. Life is in full bloom all around me, ever-moving, ever-changing. Nature constantly flows freely with its environment.

Have you ever noticed how a tree behaves in a storm? It allows itself to bend and flow as it bathes in the wind and rain, washing away any dust or debris. Once the storm passes and the sun breaks through the clouds, the tree gently sheds the rain as it reaches for the light, growing taller and stronger with each new storm. This reminds me that all things can and will adapt to their environment, in their own time. We just need to allow ourselves to trust in our unique rhythm and flow.

Give yourself the time and grace your body needs. Allow yourself to feel all the feels. Let all of it flow. It's cleansing for the soul and an important release of energy in your body. When we fight against something, we're using force. This gets exhausting very quickly. There will be times when force is necessary, which is why we experience surges of adrenaline in emergencies, but force is hard work and very tiring. Allowing and surrendering to help bring balance and flow back to my body are an integral part of my healing process.

Living your best life doesn't mean everything is always going perfectly; it means you're choosing to live it fully, embracing all of it–the joys and the imperfections–and allowing limitless possibilities for happiness.

Jenny Tasker is an empathic energy worker, writer, and mental health advocate.

Using intuition coupled with the boundless optimism gained through living with a rare disability, Jenny instinctively sees things from different perspectives, finding solutions, viewpoints, and opportunities others overlook.

Her passions include chilling with nature, exploring the world with her husband, hanging out with her family, and empowering and uplifting others through her Living Your Best Life with Jenny Tasker community.

A positive inspiration, Jenny represents all she shares with the world. She approaches each day with authentic, heart-based energy, allowing everyone to feel seen, heard, and supported. For Jenny, every new day is a gift to be opened, explored, and lived to the fullest!

Connect with Jenny:

Instagram: https://www.instagram.com/jennydtasker/

Facebook: https://www.facebook.com/bepositivewithjennytasker

LinkedIn: https://www.linkedin.com/in/jennifer-tasker-7a1187112/

CHAPTER 8

THE ME-SET BUTTON™

REBEL AND END YOUR NEED FOR EXTERNAL VALIDATION

Susan Throop

"The quieter you become, the more you are able to hear."

~ Rumi

I know what it's like to feel swallowed by doubt and anxiety. To feel like your joy is just out of reach, always slipping past you. I've been there—the couch sinking beneath me, steam rising from my teacup, heart racing with a thousand "shoulds," trying to meet everyone else's expectations while the noise of the world, and my own mind, drowned out what truly mattered to me.

MY STORY

When you're always scanning the room for disaster, joy feels like a luxury you can't afford.

I didn't always trust joy.

For a long time, I saw it as something I didn't earn—or worse, didn't deserve.

And when my imposter syndrome gets loud, I still stumble through the trust walk.

It whispers doubts when I'm least prepared, making me question whether I'm worthy of happiness. *Is joy just a mirage meant for others, and not me?* Some days, that voice is louder than my own heartbeat.

As a child of divorce, I always braced for the next letdown from my biological father. I remember falling asleep in the picture window, waiting for him to pick me up—and he never came.

As a wife, I lived in constant tension, anticipating the next narcissistic demand from my (now ex-) husband, doing emotional gymnastics to maintain the illusion of peace.

Every day felt like walking a tightrope, where one wrong move could trigger an explosion. I became an expert at hiding my own feelings to maintain the fragile calm. But in the process, I lost touch with who I was beneath the fear and exhaustion.

As an employee, I operated in survival mode under a boss who was a taker—quick to explode, slow to listen, and always expecting me to over-explain what he was too arrogant to ask.

When you grow up learning good things don't last, vulnerability gets punished, and worth must be earned, joy doesn't feel like a gift.

It feels like a trap.

It was like living behind a glass wall, watching happiness happen to others while barred from entering. Joy wasn't safe. It was a promise that always broke.

And yet, when I finally let myself consider asking for a divorce, something shifted.

I began to wonder:

What if joy isn't light and fluffy?

What if it's a fierce, grounded choice to reclaim meaning—on your terms?

That question stayed with me, quietly, even as I walked through some of the biggest moments of my life. Moments that, on the outside, looked joyful, but on the inside told a different story.

When I married my ex-husband, we had the traditional church wedding—the tuxedos, the dresses, the flowers.

I wasn't a bridezilla. I was numb.

I have almost no memories of the day.

I do remember one thing:

We released butterflies outside the church. Of the 60 that took flight, my dad got the only one that didn't make it. Dead in his palm.

He thought the whole idea was silly—and of course, he got the one that proved his point. Not joy.

But then, there was the father-daughter dance with the man who chose to be my dad. Just two minutes. But in that moment, I dropped the mask.

My dad, who survived cancer three times, lived long enough to make it to this moment.

His hands were steady and strong as he held me while we danced. His smile reached his eyes, like he knew something I didn't. For two minutes, I let go. I felt safe. The rest of the room faded into a blur.

Joy, I realized, *is presence*.

And then, the music stopped.

I suddenly missed his warmth and strength.

I slipped back into the performance, pushed the feeling away, and powered through the rest of the day.

When the photos came back after our honeymoon, my favorite picture wasn't from the ceremony, the kiss, or the grand production.

It was from that dance.

Just one fleeting glimmer of joy—one I barely held on to.

That wedding wasn't a celebration.

It was a performance.

A well-executed plan, not a moment of presence.

And the truth is, it wasn't just the wedding.

I've felt that way in boardrooms, too—big wins, promotions, public praise.

Moments I worked hard for, and all I mustered was a brief exhale. Not a celebration; just relief it was over, followed by a breakneck sprint to the next task.

Because you can't feel joy if you don't feel safe, and for some of us, trusting joy is the hardest part.

For all the high-functioning perfectionists, trauma survivors, over-achievers, caretakers, and fixers:

You know who you are.

You're the ones praised for being *so strong*, but never permitted to be soft.

Early in life, we write stories based on what we see. We learn how love works in our families: what's safe to say, and what gets shut down.

If you grew up in a chaotic or unstable environment, you likely learned to seek control, leaving joy far behind. Because control feels safer than trust, but that need for control? It's an illusion.

You can only control yourself—and, at best, influence others.

Still, we cling to it. Because loosening our grip, even just a little, feels like free-falling. But people don't need us to bulldoze our way through life. They don't need another know-it-all in the room.

What they want—and what they remember—is someone who listens with intention, who responds instead of reacts.

Gentle doesn't mean easy.

Soft is not weak.

It takes real strength to stay grounded in a chaotic room.

To choose curiosity over control, to admit, "I don't know," and still walk through it with you.

That's not a lack of power.

That's leadership—the kind rooted in clarity, confidence, and compassion.

And leadership isn't just for the workplace.

It's how you show up in your own life.

To feel joy, you have to loosen your grip—even just a little.

That's terrifying—a body-tightening, heart-pounding, claustrophobic kind of fear.

And that's also where the healing begins.

It's where you pick up the pen and start rewriting your story.

You don't have to erase the past to find joy—you just have to reclaim what it means.

Like the photo of me and my dad at my first wedding.

That image hasn't changed. But I have.

I learned joy wasn't an exception; it was something I could choose, even in the messiness.

I'm capable of joy when I feel safe.

And I can create that safety for myself.

It's no longer a reminder of a failed marriage.

It's a moment between a father and daughter—not tied by blood, but by love.

Two survivors who saw each other like no one else could.

When I asked for my divorce, there was no dramatic betrayal. No explosive fight. I remember feeling suffocated by the weight of everything. I needed to get outside. I laced up my running shoes. *Time to pound the pavement.* Tunes blasting, I ran, my legs vibrating with every step, my heartbeat echoing in my ears. My sneakers slapped the asphalt, each thump a tiny rebellion against the weight I carried too long.

Am I brave enough to choose myself? Am I ready to step into the unknown?

Every "what if" raced through my mind—the loneliness, the judgment, the fear of failing again, the weight of breaking my vows—and beneath it all, a quiet certainty began to grow: *I can't keep losing myself for someone else's comfort.* The cold wind whipped against my cheeks, and I let out a shaky breath I didn't realize I was holding.

It wasn't sudden clarity. It was the slow unraveling of years of excuses: *It's just stress. It's just a rough patch. Maybe it'll get better.* Each step grounded me in a raw ache. I felt smaller, quieter, tethered to a life that wasn't mine. I blinked away my tears, smiling at the sharp reminder I was still here—still moving.

By the time I reached the park, my legs were burning, and my lungs felt like they were on fire. I sank onto a wooden bench, letting the sun warm my face and the wind tangle my hair. A calm clarity overtook me. I allowed myself to grieve the man I married—the life we built, the promises that no longer held meaning, the dreams that quietly slipped away long before this moment. He was already gone, in ways time and distance made clear. And yet, in grieving, I felt the first spark of permission to reclaim myself.

I closed my eyes, breathed deeply, and for a fleeting moment, a tiny voice whispered: *This is the moment you choose yourself.*

I let the tension drain from my shoulders, let the racing thoughts settle. He moved away for work, and I realized this was my moment to let go, to reclaim myself.

I leaned into the quiet ache, letting it coexist with my longing. The bench beneath me grounded me, my lungs expanding with each breath. Each heartbeat seemed to drum a new rhythm into my chest, a soft, steady reminder: *I'm strong and brave, I can do this.*

Letting go wasn't about abandoning someone; it was about finally walking toward me. I felt alive, and for the first time in years, I felt a little of that life inside me.

I just missed me more than I loved him.

I can't rewrite the early chapters of my story, but I can choose how the next one starts.

Choosing to leave wasn't just about walking away; it was about finally walking toward myself.

I moved across the country on faith and hope that something better, *someone* better was meant for me. That leap wasn't just a change of address; it was a declaration that joy was within reach.

I'm now married to my last husband—and I'm *not kidding*.

He's good for my soul.

He's my safe place to fall apart and my biggest supporter.

His laugh, his smile, the way our home feels—that's what brings me joy.

Our life is peaceful.

It's calm and quiet in the best way.

And now that I have this joy, I protect it fiercely.

I can breathe again.

Joy didn't erase my past—it rewrote what it means.

And that's where I reclaimed my leadership:

In my life. In my work. In my voice.

I know authentic leadership isn't for everyone, and that's exactly as it should be.

But are leaders ready for this kind of joy?

They'll hear it because it speaks the language they've been waiting their whole lives to understand: their own.

You're not broken because joy is hard for you.

You're not late. You're layered.

Your lived story lives in your body, mind, and soul.

And sometimes, joy feels like a wild dog jumping onto your walking path: unexpected and kind of terrifying.

But joy isn't all-or-nothing.

It's more like training for a 5K run.

You don't go from the couch to a winning time on day one.

You show up. You practice.

You don't have to trust joy all at once.

Just trust yourself enough to let it visit.

A birthday party.

An anniversary dinner.

A belly laugh on vacation.

Try it. It gets easier.

Get out of your head. Find your safe people.

Let them help you rebuild your joy muscle.

My goal? To get back to the fierce five-year-old girl who was ready to take on the world on her terms.

I'm getting there.

I strive every day to make her proud.

To let her joy out.

You can, too.

I'll leave you with this:

Where have you made space for joy in your life recently?

Not because everything was perfect, but because you were finally ready to feel again?

Joy doesn't show up just because we hope it will. It shows up when we tune back into who we truly are—and that takes practice, patience, and permission to be real.

Over the years, through boardrooms, burnout, and personal break-throughs, I noticed a pattern in the moments I felt most like myself. A way to check in, realign, and come back to the *me* I actually like.

I started calling it my ME-Set Button because, like resetting your phone, it clears the noise and gets you back to your original settings.

It's the same tool I use with leaders, teams, and changemakers who are tired of chasing success they can't feel—and are ready to build it from the inside out.

THE SPARK

Pressing the ME-Set Button™ feels like stepping into a quiet room after hours of noise. The world pauses just long enough for you to notice yourself again. Your thoughts settle—not perfectly, but enough to see what truly matters. Anxiety softens, doubt loosens its grip, and for a fleeting moment, you remember the rhythm of your own heartbeat—not anyone else's expectations. A gentle clarity spreads through your body, calming your nerves and creating a sense of alignment that lets you breathe, reset, and step forward, grounded in your own truth.

The ME-Set Button™ is a simple three-step reset that checks your alignment and reconnects you with the version of yourself that's been waiting quietly under all the noise.

It's made up of three parts: Calm. Curiosity. Choice.

PART 1: CALM

Can you sit in a silent room and not reach for noise?

Try this: Close your eyes for 45 seconds and simply *be*—no music, no scrolling, no distractions.

What do you feel? Is calm even on the list?

If not, don't judge it—just notice. Then give yourself one minute a day that belongs only to you.

My favorite? An extra minute in the shower, just letting the water run while I breathe. Sometimes I add a drop of essential oil to my palms and inhale deeply.

It doesn't have to be big, but it has to be yours.

The closer you get to yourself, the less you need external noise.

Calm isn't the absence of chaos; it's the presence of *you*.

PART 2: CURIOSITY

Start to observe your body's response to life gently.

I discovered I curled my toes into my shoes every time I felt tension or uncertainty—and I only noticed when I got quiet enough to be curious.

That simple awareness showed me I was always bracing. Always ready.

That's *not* character—it's a trauma response.

But curiosity isn't about blame. It's about gathering data without judgment.

Your body remembers everything. Let it teach you, not shame you.

You can start rewriting those responses—or reshape your environment so you no longer need to brace at all.

PART 3: CHOICE

Once you notice, you can choose.

Not perfectly, not always, but more often, and with more ease.

Choose to take a breath before reacting.

Choose to rest without earning it.

Choose to speak up—or stay silent—with intention, not fear.

The biggest shift I've made is asking: "Is this decision coming from fear or freedom?"

Processing isn't a destination. It's a return to yourself, again and again.

You can start small: one smile, one breath, one moment you don't rush past. Those choices stack. They soften the fear.

And over time, joy feels less like a risk and more like a right.

I'll leave you with this:

Choosing joy isn't naïve; it's a rebellion. And every small choice to feel again, laugh again, breathe again is how you take your power back.

When you learn to trust joy, you stop outsourcing your worth.

You realize joy isn't a reward for perfection or approval.

It's not something you earn; it's something you reclaim.

You stop waiting for life to be less messy or for people to be more validating.

Joy becomes your compass, not your finish line.

It's the thread that reconnects you to *your* truth—

your voice, your values, your unrepeatable rhythm.

And when you trust it?

You lead differently.

You love deeper.

You live freer.

Not because everything is fixed, but because you finally are.

If this spoke to something in you—the part that's ready to stop waiting for permission and start living from your own settings—this is the work I live for.

If you're ready to press your own ME-Set Button™, to clear the noise and lead with your true joy, know you're not alone—and there's a way forward.

In my work, whether it's one-on-one coaching, speaking to teams, or leading workshops, I help leaders and changemakers clear the noise, tune back in, and lead in a way that feels unmistakably theirs.

Joy isn't something you chase; it's something you carry. Your next chapter doesn't begin when life is perfect. It begins the moment you press that ME-Set Button™ and say, "I'm ready to come back to me."

If these words stirred something in you, good. That tug you feel? It's your own ME-Set Button™ waiting to be pressed. Don't let it gather dust. Reach out, and let's walk this next stretch together.

Susan Throop is the founder of House of Evolura™, a leadership and consulting company dedicated to helping leaders rewrite their stories and unlock the power of authenticity.

With over 20 years of experience leading leadership development and strategic initiatives at three Fortune 500 companies, Susan blends corporate expertise with a deep passion for empowering leaders to lead with confidence, clarity, and humanity.

Through her signature framework, The ME-Set Button™, along with dynamic workshops and transformative keynotes, Susan equips high-performing professionals and changemakers to break free from the exhausting need for external validation, reconnect with their core values, and lead in a way that is both effective and unapologetically authentic.

Known for her empathetic approach and a gift for turning complex ideas into simple, actionable insights, Susan inspires leaders to embrace calm, curiosity, and courage—creating teams and cultures where people feel seen, valued, and capable of thriving.

Fun fact: When she's not empowering leaders and helping people heal, Susan enjoys accidental adventures with her family abroad and crafting homemade chocolates to share with those she loves.

Connect with Susan:

Website: https://houseofevolura.com/

Instagram: https://www.instagram.com/houseofevolura/

Facebook: https://www.facebook.com/houseofevolura/

LinkedIn: https://www.linkedin.com/company/houseofevolura/

CHAPTER 9

YOUR JOY JOB

IGNITE ALIGNED ABUNDANCE

Michelle Pecak

MY STORY

I don't want to do this anymore.

I sat cross-legged on the beach, feeling the soft sand between my toes, eyes closed. Shallow breathing. Exhaustion. Brain fog.

The thought was so loud, it startled me—as if it came from someone behind me. But it was just me, drenched in 20 years of corporate fatigue, the heat of gaslighting, and the stench of unrealistic expectations drifting into the crisp, salty October air.

A warm tear slid down my cheek, and I didn't stop it. Instead, I breathed more deeply, as though letting the ocean convey this message through a channel of subconscious love. It was like tuning into a radio frequency, one I had ignored for far too long. My voice cried for help, and yet—paradoxically—I never felt so free. Overwhelming emotions washed over me like the waves that washed over the beach.

As I pondered my next corporate role, the calmness of that statement—*I don't want to do this anymore*—felt so right. But then came the panic: *Now what?* How do you walk away from two decades of relationships, reputation, and knowledge? How do you start over with 20 years invested?

Did I pick the wrong career? The wrong spouse? The wrong company? I was so sure then, so certain my visionary brain knew. So, why does it all feel wrong now?

"Fuck." The word left my lips, sharp and unfiltered. "You just said that out loud."

How did I not notice before? Why didn't I see this career wasn't fun or fulfilling? My inner critic was ruthless: wrong career, wrong company, wrong life choices. It echoed like a gavel, judging every decision I once celebrated.

But here's the truth: in those pivotal life moments, I was so sure. Every cell in my body screamed with delight when I made those decisions. My visionary brain *knew*. But now everything felt like it was crumbling.

That moment in the sand was the first crack in my corporate armor. I wore it so long and so well, it convinced me I was invincible. But my armor was heavy. I was strong until I realized I didn't want to live on a battlefield anymore. I didn't want life to feel like warfare, staying several moves ahead to survive. I was empty. I was exhausted.

The rules were simple. Follow "the right path": go to college, get a "good" job, get married, have kids, and eventually earn the right to retire to do what you actually want to do. I followed the rules, but the outcomes weren't what I planned, anticipated, or expected. But this is what I was taught. I followed *the right path*.

College taught me belonging. My corporate career taught me the importance of being valued. Marriage and divorce taught me healing. Having kids taught me the importance of building community. But there didn't seem to be any retirement in sight to allow me to do what makes me happy.

Do I really have to wait till I'm over 60 to do what I actually want to do?

I followed the "right path." I did what I was supposed to do, and I was successful. If I achieved the goals, earned the titles, and checked the boxes, why did I feel so empty on that beach?

Crap, what if the right path forgot to include joy?

Fast-forward 1,000 days—a little shy of three years later—and I can now look back and see what I couldn't see that day. Those life decisions weren't failures; they were "blessons"—blessings wrapped in lessons, preparing me for what was to come.

Success without joy is hollow.

"Fuck. I missed that memo."

This wasn't failure. This was a reset. A recalibration. The soul's way of stripping me bare so I could be reborn. This salvation shaped me and prepared me for what was to come.

If you're between the ages of 40 and 50, you may know this feeling well. It's the deep ache for something more meaningful—the craving for purpose beyond a paycheck. Some call it a midlife crisis. Others call it burnout. I call it a soul's recalibration back to alignment. This is the call back to your authenticity. Your inner voice.

The spark comes quietly at first, then ignites like wildfire. Once you feel it, you can't un-feel it. There are no take-backs.

I chose joy as my word of the year, the same year I heard "the voice" at the beach. That was the beginning of my surrender.

Joy isn't a milestone to achieve—it's a lifestyle you choose. Joy is your soul calling you to its highest purpose, urging you to activate your deepest impact. If joy is the spark, then the journey is the human experience. The invitation is to surrender to the *how*, live in alignment, and activate your center of abundance.

What blessons are you here to learn as the journey unfolds in divinely perfect timing?

That day on the beach, I didn't know it yet, but this was where my journey to my joy job began. The surrender to the *how* was the moment I gave myself permission to be curious—and where my courage began.

My mantra became, "This is happening for me, not to me." Every experience was a blesson preparing me to activate my joy job, which led to my aligned impact.

WHAT IS A JOY JOB?

Your joy job is your transformational guide from surviving in your day job to thriving in your joy job—where passion, purpose, paycheck, and superpowers create aligned abundance.

This isn't necessarily about quitting your day job. For some, yes, that may happen. But for many, it's about shifting from the world validating your worth through external output to turning inward and living aligned with joy.

When you do this, your energy transforms into a magnet that attracts abundance. This is how you redefine success—not by what you achieve externally, but by who you become internally. This is how you become the magnet, not the machine.

Yes, you still need a paycheck, but don't miss out on your purpose in the process. Whether you're ready to leave corporate, start a joy job on the side, or simply crave more fulfillment and flow, your joy job is your permission slip to step into your brilliance—and get paid for your passion. Yes, you can monetize your joy. Money increases your impact potential.

So, you might be asking: *Okay, I want my joy job, but where do I start? Once the spark ignites, how do I know what's next?*

For me, this is where Human Design entered the story.

I stumbled on Human Design through a wellness event I was hosting for executive women. The theme was Body / Mind / Spirit, and we brought in a Human Design reader for the "mind" piece. That day, I learned I was a Projector.

The first time I saw my chart, I said, "What the heck is this?" It's a bunch of numbers, symbols, and a few key words—as if I'm magically supposed to know what all of it means, but someone forgot to give me the decoder ring. No thanks; I don't want to pay someone every time I want to learn more about myself. This seems like a scam.

But then something unexpected happened.

The information about Projectors made me feel seen. My *soul* craved more insight. For the first time, I had words to describe *me*—why I operate the way I do, why I feel different than others, and why I burn out faster in systems that aren't built for me.

When I shared what I learned with my communities, people responded instantly: "Of course you bring people together—that's your gift."

That stopped me cold. I never considered my ability to connect people and resources (Channel 37–40 in Human Design) to be a *gift*. It came so naturally, I assumed everyone could do it.

Huh!

If these were my true gifts and superpowers, then no wonder I was burnt out; I didn't use them in my corporate career. I built billion-dollar supply chain pricing models, but ignored my natural genius for building people and community.

That realization changed everything for me.

That's where the joy journey really begins.

WHAT IS HUMAN DESIGN?

Let's take a quick step back. At its core, Human Design is simply one doorway into self-awareness. I like to think of it as the treasure map of your inner gems, hidden in plain sight if you know where to look and how to get into alignment. Here's the real message: Until you know yourself deeply—your strengths, your patterns, your natural energy—you can't fully monetize your gifts. When you're blind to what makes you magnetic, you undervalue yourself, hustle in misaligned ways, or try to copy what worked for someone else.

Self-awareness is the currency that turns talent into income.

When you see yourself clearly, you can finally package, position, and price your brilliance with confidence and clarity. Human Design was my shortcut to awareness, but the tool doesn't matter as much as the courage it takes to look inward.

If Human Design isn't your tool, then use whatever works for you to know your mission, values, decision-making, motivation, and how to articulate who you are, what you're good at, how you do it, and why you do it better than anyone else. That's where the "Joy Job for Me" formula kicks in.

Warning: If you're up for a fast side hustle, instant money, and a quick fix, this formula isn't for you. Your alignment will determine how quickly you can monetize your joy. That's why I recommend you *don't* quit your day job while you find and build your joy job—because it's work. Inner clarity and aligned action may sound easy, but it's a process to discover your true Human Design and purpose in this lifetime.

There are many paths on your own personal treasure map. You may be able to quit your day job, and your joy job will become full-time; good for you! Or, you may build a side gig that lights you up inside and funds your slush fund, vacations, and the luxuries in life that are important to you. Some people may not figure out how to monetize, but their happiness and joy are enough to pay them in the dividends of a fulfilled life.

Your joy job can be whatever it needs to be in your life, as long as it brings you more joy and increases your impact.

If this treasure map concept hasn't scared you away, then your soul may be ready to find your inner gems, and every step along the way will lead to more joy as you ignite your VIBE: Voice, Impact, Boldness, and Energy to aligned abundance. These steps can help you navigate your own map.

THE SPARK

THE FOR ME FORMULA

Your joy job is built on the For Me Formula (M+E):

M's → Mission, Mapping, Monetizing, Momentum

E's → Essence, Expertise, Execution, Empower

Step 1: Mission + Essence

Define your essence. What lights you up so much you'd do it for free? What's your MVP: Mission, Values, Purpose?

Anchor your purpose. Create a simple statement: *"My mission is to help [who] do [what] so they can [result]."*

Step 2: Mapping + Expertise

Here's where your day job comes in. Yes, you need it! Your day job skills are the building blocks of your joy job.

Audit your skills. List three to five things you do well in your day job or past roles. Circle the ones that bring you the most joy.

Define your ideal client + problem. Who do you naturally help? What problem do you solve for them? What transformation do they experience?

Step 3: Monetizing + Execution

Money is essential. It's energy, it's exchange, it's impact potential. But here's the shift: You charge for your value, not your worth. You build a model that sustains your joy job while enabling your impact.

Design your offer ladder. Create at least one offer (product, service, etc.) in each ladder tier (free, low, mid, high-ticket, VIP). This creates entry points for your ideal client at every level.

Test and refine your offer. Try different combinations to see what resonates with people.

Step 4: Momentum + Empower

This is where play enters. Play until it pays. When you're lit up and aligned, your energy does the attracting. You can't predict where the money will come from—but that's the beauty of surrender. Your joy job will empower others as much as it empowers you.

Thought leadership. Share your voice consistently (social media, podcasts, writing, speaking). Build community and connection around your message. Find your VIBE Tribe.

Fuel with fun and flow. Stay in your zone of genius. Pick projects that feel light, energizing, and exciting; your joy is magnetic. Others will be drawn to it.

Momentum is where curiosity meets courage. Keep showing up with consistency, and your joy job will expand beyond what you can imagine.

If you need some extra clarity, tools like Human Design have insights unique to *you* and can help you define your inner gems.

LIVING IN ALIGNMENT

Here's the hard truth: The work is internal.

You may have traumas to heal. Identities to shed. Conditioning to break. Childhood imprints to release.

Your VIBE isn't for everyone. Alignment means attracting and repelling in equal measure, just like a magnet. People are with you for a reason, a season, or maybe even a lifetime. Some people will fall away, and that's part of the journey. To find your joy job, you must first *find yourself and get into alignment.*

Alignment isn't just about healing. It's about finally living from *joy*, not from obligation.

Once you're aligned, you'll become magnetic.

MY JOY JOB – SAMPLE MAPPING

What is my joy job?

The launch came when I created MY VIBE Community: A Conscious Marketplace.

It's the integration of my corporate superpowers—two decades scaling billion-dollar companies with my soul gifts: connecting people, building systems, and creating containers of reciprocity.

In Human Design, it looks like this:

- **Channel 37 → 40** | Community and Reciprocity
- **Channel 19 → 49** | Connecting People to Resources
- **Channel 18 → 58** | Judgement and Visionary Discernment
- **Channel 26 → 44** | Influence and Surrender

Together, they form my life's work: building communities that CARE (connect, amplify, reciprocity, elevate) through the implementation of better systems for the benefit of all.

YOUR INVITATION

If this chapter sparked something in you—if you've heard that whisper, *"I don't want to do this anymore,"*—this is your call.

Your joy job begins when you choose alignment over armor.

This chapter can be your guide, your treasure map, and your permission slip—not to quit, but to align.

Your joy job isn't just about feeling good—it's about creating aligned abundance.

Your joy job is waiting.

Michelle Pecak's day job is the founder and CEO of Simple Smart Consulting, a supply chain consulting firm that created Quantum Operations, an assessment of how people, process, product, and pricing are all connected by strategy.

Michelle is a Six Sigma Black Belt who has worked for some of the largest billion-dollar-plus B2B distributors and manufacturers in the world, scaling companies through strategic pricing and heart-centered leadership.

Michelle is a master connector who believes in holistic wellness as an internal luxury that helps you become the best version of yourself, reach your highest potential, and make your own quantum leaps!

Michelle's joy job is the founder and chief vibe officer of MY VIBE Community. In this conscious marketplace, healers, organizations, professionals, entrepreneurs, and executives come together with the heart of reciprocity and collaboration. The MY VIBE Members commit to CARE: Connect, Amplify, Reciprocate, and Elevate. Welcome to the new paradigm of commerce.

Michelle is the creator of MY VIBE Human Design, Human Design Reports, and Action Plans for Executives and high performers. This unique approach to Human Design provides leaders with a high-level, tangible understanding of their Human Design, enabling them to incorporate insights for immediate impact. Choose your own adventure through the treasure map and find your inner gems. Align with your VIBE: Voice, Impact, Bold, Energy.

Michelle is a 5/1 Projector who's here to integrate her corporate superpowers—two decades scaling billion-dollar companies—with her soul gifts: connecting people, building better systems for all, and creating a community of reciprocity. She does all this through her life's work of bringing people together.

We're stronger together when we're aligned with our higher purpose, and when surrounded by people who have "MY VIBE."

Connect with Michelle:

Websites: https://www.myvibecommunity.com
https://www.myvibehumandesign.com

Instagram: https://www.instagram.com/michellepecak
https://www.instagram.com/myvibehive

LinkedIn: https://www.linkedin.com/in/michelle-pecak/
https://www.linkedin.com/myvibenetwork/

Linktree: https://linktr.ee/MYVIBECOMMUNITY

YouTube: https://www.youtube.com/@myvibehive

CHAPTER 10

THE JOY PORTAL

INSTANTLY FIERCE, FABULOUS, AND FUN

Jean Voice Dart, M.S., Expressive Arts Therapist

*"The joy portal awaits you, not beyond your pain, but through it.
With your creative imagination as your guide,
you can reclaim joy as your birthright."*

~ Jean Voice Dart

MY STORY

When chronic pain touched my life, a shadow fell upon my heart until I joined the joy warriors and discovered a magical portal.

I've known my body was different since early childhood. My dreams showed me a future of pain and dependence on wheelchairs and braces. I often fainted and fell. Yet in early adulthood, I discovered the limitless joy life brings.

MY HEROES—THE JOY WARRIORS

Stephen smiled, his body rocking gently in his powerchair. Light caught his cheeks as he reached toward me. I entered the room carrying something precious to both of us. Dressed in a green and brown polo shirt, jeans, and classic tennis shoes, he welcomed me with wordless, heartfelt sounds. Though cerebral palsy limited his movement, his warm greeting needed no words.

"Good morning, Stephen."

Our shared love for music was raw and sincere. I placed the black case on the counter, opened the brass latches, and set the autoharp on Stephen's wheelchair tray. Our eyes met while I attached an assistive strap to his wrist. "Let's make music." We began.

Looking around, I saw fearless joy warriors.

Plastic tubs, labeled with braille tags, carried yarn sorted by color. Despite her severe visual impairment, Betty's fingers danced upon the knitting needles, moving the pale pink yarn and flawlessly completing a perfect row on her crocheted blanket.

The atmosphere buzzed, charged with determination and creativity. Sandra painted with limited mobility, using adaptive brushes. Her canvas bloomed with bold strokes of crimson and indigo, delighting onlookers. In the corner, a fellow coworker gently guided a passionate group of individuals with upper-body challenges in dance and movement. Everyone giggled and moved to the sounds of "Stayin' Alive" by the Bee Gees.

Thomas, though legless, used his arms to navigate and assisted Monica as she built a wooden birdhouse for the garden. Many lived with labels related to mental or emotional challenges. I had labels too, but I chose a different one for all of us: joy warriors. Our laughter filled the room, creating a warm and welcoming atmosphere.

Each managed emotional, sociological, mental, and physical pain and trauma daily. These were my heroes.

FINDING THE DOOR TO THE PORTAL

I knew a joy portal existed, but it wasn't always easy for me to find the door.

Surrounding myself with inspirational people became my haven as I managed daily pain. I wore braces and bravely navigated HSD, hypermobility spectrum disorder, a misunderstood and incurable condition. Daily migraines, fatigue, and complications challenged my mobility, but I lived my dream job as a creative arts teaching aid and earned certification as an expressive arts psychotherapist.

Since childhood, I loved writing, storytelling, drawing, dramatic arts, dance, and music, but I didn't delve deeper. Something was buried within me. I needed to fiercely face it to find peace with my life.

As I looked around the room at my heroes, I saw we each tirelessly sought the same goal in life—joy.

"Jean, can you please talk to Taylor? I can't understand what he needs."

"Yes, of course."

Taylor sat near an open window. The pleasant fragrance of lilac bushes filled the room, and the wind gently blew my hair. I immediately felt a deep connection to the earth.

Having lost most of my hearing years ago, I straddled the hearing and deaf communities. I watched Taylor communicate using basic ASL and noticed the poetic dance of his hands and face, expressing his feelings—pairing joy with pain.

Taylor expressed his frustration, yet laughed at his humanness, candidly asking for help. I opened the cabinet, gathered the craft-making supplies, and accompanied him to a wooden table scattered with beads, sequins, glue, textured paper, paint, and clay. He lived, loved, and laughed at life, embracing all its dramas.

His sincere, raw expression of emotions resonated deeply in my heart, like a tuning fork. I attuned to this rhythmic vibration and vision. It felt like home.

As we sat together, creating a montage of mixed-media art, my pain melted away, filling my heart with joy. I visited this otherworldly place through my imagination. I was no longer different, weird, less-than, or weak. I was fierce, fabulous, and fun.

I silently spoke to God. *Can joy and pain harmoniously coexist? Yes, they can, and they do.*

Looking around the room, I saw these joy warriors knew this secret. They weren't perfect, and neither was I. I breathed in this truth.

Life is beautiful, and joy is here, now and always.

I fully accepted this divine wisdom, yet there was something dark buried within me, something that triggered pain and shame and blocked me from joyful living.

I stood in front of the portal.

Should I fearlessly open the door? No. It frightens me.

WHIPPING AND DODGING IN FULL PURSUIT

Each day, I chased after joy. I saw it around me, but it seemed impossible to snatch for more than a moment. It was here and gone. I felt like Harry Potter, engaged in a magical game of Quidditch, riding my broomstick, whipping and dodging Bludgers, in pursuit of the elusive Golden Snitch. I was fully engaged, beaten, bruised, buried in havoc, yet learning.

So, what is this sparkling ball of joy, and how can I keep it in my heart?

I didn't want a ticklish moment of amusement. I wanted a full-on, Holy Mother of God experience. That's what I ached for, and life provided the answer.

I walked away from the creative activities and approached our office cubicles. Our assistant, Jenny, put a file on my desk.

"I typed up your grant proposal, Jean. Let me know if you need anything changed."

She smiled and tossed her hair while leaning over the adjacent cubicle. "Hey, Brian. I'll deliver that report to you in an hour. No problem."

Brian worked for weeks on a proposal to bring more jobs to physically challenged citizens in our community. We shared a common goal.

I carefully sat down, feeling my body inflamed with nerve pain, and instantly shifted from basking in joy to wanting to chop off my head and legs.

I resented my body and yearned for love.

Ugh. I hate this.

God, please make it stop. Please remove my pain.

I dodged life's challenges while searching for that golden spark, investing my energy in work with passionate, purpose-driven colleagues. Their radiance and joy inspired me as they dedicated themselves to health and happiness.

Like the clients, these caseworkers, therapists, and teachers were also joy warriors, carrying a secret spark that illuminated the room. Some, like me, carried trauma, tragedy, and turmoil, but true joy warriors don't toss aside painful life experiences, nor do they hide them. They dance with them, embrace them, and celebrate them.

Can a person living with chronic pain be fierce, fabulous, and fun? Can it be me?

RECOGNIZING THE SPARK

I always recognized this spark in others. I felt it in my mother, father, grandmother, aunts, and uncles. They knew how to be silly, let go of pride, doubt, or fear, and have fun. I saw it when my dog rolled and pranced in anticipation, when the birds waved hello, and the squirrel scampered in delight.

I heard it among my friends, in their raucous celebrations of life: shouting at the wind, picking apples to bake a pie, dramatically breaking into joyful song, making silly faces, telling jokes, and laughing until their sides hurt. They replaced power, false pride, anger, and fear with a passionate zest for life, community, creativity, and compassionate care.

This spark is a fiercely bold, joyful love for life. It's a divine, selfless desire to serve without doubt or hesitation. The moment one walks hand-in-hand with pain is the moment the joy portal opens, the spark is ignited, and the heart is aflame with a passion for life.

THE AWAKENING

Often, we know the truth, but we need an awakening—a magical moment when time stops, and everything aligns with universal truth. It's that moment when we're ready to embrace our life passion and purpose. The universe knows when it's time for a change, and we simply must answer the call.

I looked over at Brian, writing his proposal. I looked down at my creative arts grant. I looked at Jenny, selflessly flitting around the room. I looked at our brave and joyful clients, and then I stopped. I stopped to talk to God.

God, please help me be a channel for divine love. Please help me face, embrace, and replace my angry reaction to pain with gratitude and joy.

Tears welled up in my eyes as I heard these comforting words.

Trust your heart, my spiritual guide whispered. *There's nothing to fear. You're ready to fly free, and I'm here to fly with you.*

The universe knows when, where, and who must answer the call.

I answered.

THE EXPERIENCE

The workday ended. I exited the building and walked to my car. My lungs expanded with gratitude as I inhaled the fresh, cool air, approaching my wheeled freedom machine. I stepped in, turned the key in the ignition, and headed home, ready to purge myself of useless chatter, senseless doubt, and frantic fear.

I flipped on the radio and instantly heard the opening lyrics to Lynyrd Skynyrd's "Free Bird," fueling the flame and empowering me. As I neared my home, the five-minute wailing, unapologetic guitar riffs channeled grief, longing, and defiance, transforming these emotions into motion and sound.

The repetitive guitar phrases brought me tension and release. The layered harmonies spiraled upward like a prayer shouted in the wind. My heart pounded against my chest in anticipation of facing my nemesis, Pain.

I was ready. "Let's do this!" I shouted above a relentless cascade of pentatonic licks, hammerings, and bends that felt like a bird breaking free from its cage mid-flight. I watched the bird fly, and I flew with it, beating my wings against the cold air, pounding against me.

I was ready. It was time to clean house. Being happy wasn't good enough. Yes, I had a happy life, but I wanted it all. I wanted to be drenched in joy, purified, and free.

I dropped my belongings, picked up my journal, and began writing my feelings—feelings deep inside of me, old feelings about this pain that haunted me throughout my life, feelings about being criticized, misunderstood, assaulted, abused, abandoned, feelings of doubt and hatred for myself and my pain.

I closed my eyes. There in the innermost part of my being, I saw it. Pain stood there in front of me, humped over in the shadows, cloaked in darkness. Pain was my caged bird. I saw it, felt it, and readied myself to speak to it honestly and lovingly. Truth whispered to both of us.

Pain is not your enemy. It's your partner, telling you when you've stretched yourself too far, telling you to stop, shift, and adjust. Pain is your friend, yet you abandoned it, ignored it, hid it, gossiped about it, denied it, blasphemed it, and hated it. It's time to love it.

I embraced my partner, Pain. We wept together, receiving truth in silent communion. I no longer hated it; I adored it, and it was time to set it free.

With tearful words, in a raw, honest voice I'd never heard before, I spoke aloud. "Thank you, Pain. I hear you, see you, and love you. You're a devoted friend. I'm sorry for abandoning you, ignoring you, and hating you. I'm sorry for not appreciating your efforts to save me from injury or harm. Thank you for loving me, helping me, and blessing me. I love you."

Instantly, Pain, once a caged bird trapped behind iron bars, broke free from its prison and transformed into something beautiful, a flying, radiant being of Sound and Light. We flew together, bonded with love.

I released heartfelt tears of joy, then spent the evening safely and creatively expressing my newfound emotions through art, music, and writing. I drew my experience, designing a beautiful joy portal—a safe space to return to anytime.

Later, I wrote a few lines of poetry, softly singing to myself, taking the words into contemplation before nodding off to sleep. The sweet simplicity spoke to my inner child, healing old wounds and bringing comfort.

Open. Open.
Joy, Pain, and me.
The portal is open
And we're flying free.

Open. Open.
Joy, Pain, and me.
We partner together
In harmony.

Joyfully
Sharing,
Declaring,
And caring.

Open. Open.
Joy, Pain, and me.
The portal is open
And now I am free.

After chanting these simple, repetitive words, the dark cloak covering my heart disappeared, and the loving sounds of this rhythmic lullaby cradled and rocked me into a peaceful sleep.

I am a joy warrior. Now it's your turn. Are you ready?

NEXT STEPS

If my story resonated with you or sparked a sense of recognition, I invite you to take your next step using the tools and techniques below. You have the power to enter your joy portal and begin the journey toward your best life now. I'm here to support you every step of the way. Let's do this together.

THE SPARK

THE WORLD AWAITS

You are a joy-driven, courageous, creative conqueror, persevering, resilient, and unbroken by life's fiercest storms. We've all been hurt, more than anyone will ever know. Yet, through life's blows—whipped, thrashed, and knocked flat—you rose, bruised and battered, declaring, "Get ready, world. Here I am, and I'm not giving up." And here you stand, radiant with strength, ready to embrace joy.

Your joy portal is unique. It's brimming with everything that makes you smile and fills your heart with delight. The moment you begin to imagine and create it, you open the portal and instantly transform. So, why not start now?

A. CONNECT TO THE BODY

Let's begin by connecting to the body.

1. Ground the body. Sit or stand comfortably. Let your spine lengthen. Place one hand on your belly, one on your heart. Take a slow, deep breath into your belly. Exhale gently. Feel the Earth support your body's weight.

2. Breathe with intention. Choose your words. Inhale: *gratitude*. Exhale: *peace*. Inhale: *courage*. Exhale: *perseverance*. Think the words as you breathe. Let them echo inside you.

3. Feel and acknowledge. Let your breath guide you inward. Notice your body—its temperature, tension, rhythm. Notice your emotions without judgment. Feel your pain, your joy, your longing. Whisper silently: *I acknowledge myself. I accept myself.*

4. Presence check-in. Ask yourself gently: "What am I feeling—mentally, emotionally, physically, socially, spiritually?" Let the answers arise like ripples. There's no need to fix. Just witness.

5. Open and begin. Take one final breath. Exhale with a sigh or sound. Open your eyes slowly. You're here. You're whole. Let the creativity begin.

B. CREATING THE JOY PORTAL

1. Name the Pain

Begin by naming the physical, mental, emotional, sociological, or spiritual pain you wish to partner with. If you like, use a metaphor, color, or sound to express it (for example: grief as fog, anger as crashing cymbals). This will guide your creative flow.

2. Create the Portal

Using drawing, collage, sculpture, crafting supplies, or your limitless imagination, create a symbolic doorway. A simple pencil sketch might be a good place to start. However, you can choose to include textures, colors, music, or fragrances to create a feeling of transformation.

3. Embody the Passage

You can also choose to incorporate movement. Stand before your portal, whether it's a paper drawing, a physical structure, or an imaginary doorway. Move (or imagine moving) through the portal, slowly expressing pain with gesture, breath, or sound. Shift into movements of release—opening, rising, or flowing. Let your body enact the movement of crossing over.

4. Reveal the Joy

On the same page or in the same creative space, partner joy with your life challenge. Creatively and spontaneously express yourself through dance, poetry, painting, music, etc., in a way that embodies both joy and pain. Let it be intuitive, vibrant, and emotionally true. Allow joy and pain to embrace one another.

5. Witness and Reflect

Sit with your portal and joyful creation. Journal or record: What happened when I partnered joy with pain? What surprised me? What does joy feel like now? Share with a trusted friend, therapist, coach, or other professional, if desired.

6. Ritualize the Return

Close your eyes, review, and remember. Keep your artistic creation whether it be a permanent structure, music recording, wearable trinket, or photograph of the experience. Recognize your expressive arts creation as an open doorway to the threshold of joy. Embrace this sacred space within your heart. Keep the portal open. Once you have entered, imagine you have removed all darkness from your heart. Trust your spiritual guidance. Accept yourself as fierce, fabulous, and fun. Revisit your portal as needed.

C. USING THE HEALING FORCE

Remember, when using the expressive arts (whether through writing, rhythm, sound, imagery, voice, drama, or movement), the process is the healing force. You don't just describe pain; you move through it, sing with it, paint it, weep it, and release it. That's the gift you offer your world: not just courage to endure, but courage to express and transform.

Thank you for your courage. You are a brave, brilliant joy warrior. The world eagerly awaits your life-changing miracles, selfless actions, and soothing words. You can ignite hope and uplift weary hearts by incorporating a joy portal into your life.

Please learn more about me below and request a complimentary session to take further steps. I'm happy to support you on your journey to joy.

Jean Voice Dart, M.S., RMT, is a multiple international bestselling author, expressive arts psychotherapist, coach, and teacher who navigated through grief, trauma, and chronic pain, upleveling her life from stressed to blessed. She has witnessed a lifetime of miraculous transformations, helping others feel, reveal, and heal through the arts. Those working with Jean spark creative flow, fine-tune skills, and gain effective strategies to manage life challenges through the expressive arts (art, music, writing, movement, and drama). She currently lives near the Pacific Ocean with her husband, Matt, and their dog, Pumpkin.

Credentials

- Certified Expressive Arts Grief and Trauma Coach (CCF)
- Certified Art Therapy Practitioner (CATP)
- Credentialed adult continuing education teacher (music, fine arts, creative writing)
- Credentialed Teacher K-12 (MS, in Special Education)
- Group and private music, art, theater, and writing teacher, primary and secondary
- Registered Music Therapist (RMT)
- Nearly fifty years' experience as a therapist, teacher, performer, presenter, coach, and speaker

Connect with Jean:

Website: https://www.jeanvoicedart.com

Contact: https://www.jeanvoicedart.com/contact

Facebook: https://www.facebook.com/jeanvoicedartauthor

Instagram: https://www.instagram.com/jeanvoicedart

LinkedIn: https://www.linkedin.com/in/jeanvoicedart

YouTube: https://www.youtube.com/jeanvoicedart

CHAPTER 11

THE QUIETEST JOY

FINDING LIGHT
IN THE SHADOW OF CANCER

Felicia Rangel

"There is always a wellspring of joy beyond what you can see."

~ Phillip Rangel

MY STORY

During the darkest season of my childhood, I discovered joy isn't always loud. Sometimes, joy whispers. My dad's cancer diagnosis washed away the world as I knew it. Growing up in Southern California, where the sun shines brighter, the skies are endlessly blue, and the ocean waves carry away every worry, I looked at the world through rose-colored lenses. Life felt light and full of promise. My world was safe, uncomplicated, and inherently good. My dad, Phillip, was unshakeable, a steady presence of certainty woven through every part of my life. In late December of 1990, he was diagnosed with "the silent killer," pancreatic cancer.

Pancreatic cancer was an unfamiliar stranger in my world. It sounded abstract, like a character flaw in a distant story—not something that touched my world, my hero, my dad. I dedicated myself to understanding what exactly this cancer was. Here I was at 13, with parents in their 30s, experiencing the shock of learning what this disease was capable of.

Suddenly, my world of nonstop tennis practices, beach days, and time with friends didn't matter the way it used to. The facts were sharp, unforgiving, and as real as a turbulent storm at sea. This cancer has the highest mortality rate of all major cancers. Hirshberg Foundation for Pancreatic Cancer Research says, "For all stages combined, the five-year relative survival rate is 13%."[1]

Our family's world shrank. The energy in my house shifted from warm and predictable to tense and fragile. I ruminated on a continuous stream of fearful thoughts and images.

Will my dad's broad shoulders that always envelop me in the biggest bear hugs shrink?

Will his laughter, so loud and infectious, grow quieter?

Who will tuck my siblings in at night?

Will our daily dad-and-daughter chats turn into days, weeks, or months spent in hospital waiting rooms?

For me, there was a loss of innocence. Barely a teenager, I suddenly navigated an adult world that felt heavier, darker, and far more fragile. Our home, once wrapped in a rose-colored bubble of my dad's laughter, love, warmth, and music, grew quiet and forlorn. The comforting routine of my youth gave way to cold uncertainty.

How can I help my mom? Who's going to be her solid rock now that Dad's sick?

How will my younger siblings be affected by Dad's diagnosis?

Who will be my biggest supporter at tennis matches?

What about our beloved Akita Champion? Who'll take him on his favorite walks around the neighborhood?

---

1   Hirshberg Foundation for Pancreatic Cancer Research: https://www.pancreatic.org

Mom and Dad sat me down, apart from my younger siblings, to share the news that one of the best pancreatic surgeons in California would operate and remove the cancer. In that moment, my world no longer felt upside-down. It felt as though a million pounds had been lifted from me, and a new lightness replaced the heaviness that weighed so heavily on my heart.

Will Dad survive?

Will he be healthy enough to continue his daily runs?

How long will he be hospitalized?

When will his laughter fill every room in our house again?

In January 1991, my father finally underwent surgery. What should have been a six-hour procedure culminated in 19 grueling hours. It was scary then, and it's still scary now. My mom said during his procedure, Dad "flatlined" for fifteen minutes.

Flatlined? What does that mean?

How could this happen?

The surgeon was supposed to save him.

Dad quickly lost so much blood; he needed two emergency blood transfusions to save his life. It's why I choose to donate blood each year—to give another dad, mom, child, or perfect stranger the same chance he had. His fight wasn't just about survival; it was about living.

Post surgery, my dad had a six-month recovery stay in the hospital. The surgeon said realistically, Dad would live between 18 months and three years, maximum.

Will my dad live another day, to see the sun rise and set?

Will he get to see me graduate?

Will we have to spend our family holidays without him?

Our family spent every free moment we had driving back and forth from San Diego to Los Angeles in our trusty silver Volvo station wagon to be with Dad. Sometimes, we snuck in his favorite dessert, rainbow sherbert—anything to make him feel like it was all going to be okay. I remember watching my dad, once strong and invincible, resting often in a hospital bed. My mom and I made sure to surround him with his Bible, meditations, encouraging get-well cards, fragrant flowers, and the sounds of his favorite music to give him a sense of home.

Even in the murkiness of recovery, Dad's presence still managed to give me a sense of warmth and safety. His recovery was unpredictable, but there he was, asking about my day like any other healthy dad, with a smile that said, "It's going to be better than just 'okay.'" Those moments near his bedside allowed me to understand the quietest joy in presence—not in grand gestures or loud celebrations, but in simply being there, together.

Against all odds, he recovered and dedicated himself to healing, rather than just surviving. Experts used the word "miracle" more than once. What I remember most clearly isn't a single moment of celebration. It's the slow return to a new life. Making Sunday pancakes in the kitchen with my mom. Early morning meditations in the quiet hour. The sound of my dad's laughter filling each room of the house. The light in his eyes as he read something funny in the paper. In those small, ordinary moments, joy quietly settled back into our lives.

During my dad's battle with pancreatic cancer, my world shifted, slowed down, and narrowed. The everyday distractions fell away. What remained was real: our fears, our unconditional love, our hope. From that space, I learned how to hold joy gently, even in uncertainty.

For anyone navigating a life-changing diagnosis, whether for themselves or a loved one, it's easy to feel swallowed by fear. I've been there. And yet, here's what I learned from walking through that fire and coming out the other side, not untouched but deeper, softer, and surprisingly more joyful.

THE SPARK

My dad's recovery wasn't instant. It was slow, full of setbacks, and cautious hope. But gradually, he grew stronger. He no longer had to lie by himself for months in that hospital bed. The vibrant color began to return to his face. When he was finally released and able to come home, I remember one afternoon, we sat in the family room having our father-daughter chats, like we did countless times before his diagnosis.

I must have said something funny, because I remember him laughing. It wasn't the loud, booming laugh I remembered from before. It was quieter, gentler. But it was enough. That's where I discovered it: the quietest joy, not in dramatic announcements or celebrations, but in the ability to sit beside him on our cozy family couch, with the sunlight streaming through the windows and the gentle breeze blowing inside the room. Just breathing. Just being.

I once blindly believed happiness came from moments of excitement, success, or recognition. Yet, we find the deepest kind of joy in stillness and resilience. It's holding the hand of your hero when every day feels like it could be his last, while also being grateful that life is a gift to experience for all it brings. We can uncover meaning, beauty, and the quietest joy, even in the face of something as terrifying as pancreatic cancer.

This experience didn't just mark a chapter in my life; it redefined who I am. It taught me resilience isn't loud. Love isn't always found in grand gestures, but in quiet companionship. The hardest moments often reveal the most tender truths. It gave me an emotional fluency I wouldn't trade for anything.

When someone you love is facing a life-altering diagnosis, it can feel like the ground has shifted beneath you—especially when you're still finding your own footing. This section offers gentle, grounding support. Here, you'll find mindful, heart-centered practices to help you breathe through the hard days, stay connected to yourself and your loved one, and carry hope forward—even when the path is uncertain.

Ask Questions, Even When You're Afraid of the Answers

It's natural to feel scared, but seeking the truth can help you feel more grounded and in control. Here are some ways to approach those tough conversations with care.

- Knowing the truth will help you feel more in control.
- Don't be afraid to ask doctors what's happening, even when you're young.
- Write down what you don't understand in a journal or notebook. Get clarity from someone you trust.

Let People Help You and Don't Feel Guilty About It

Support often comes from unexpected places. Learning to accept help is a vital part of the healing journey.

- Extended family, friends, and neighbors often want to help; they just don't know how.
- Let them bring you food, run errands, or simply sit with you.
- Accepting help isn't a weakness; it's love in motion.

Make Space for Both Sadness and Joy

Embracing your full range of emotions creates room for healing. Allow yourself to grieve and find moments of happiness; both are a part of healing and hope.

- Joy doesn't require you to deny sadness. In fact, they often arrive hand in hand. Cry when you need to. Laugh when you can. Sometimes, both happen in the same moment; make space for both. There's no "right" emotional timeline.
- Life doesn't pause for cancer, and finding moments of joy, however small, is vital.

Stay Present, Even If You Don't Know What to Say

Presence and companionship can speak louder than words. Here are simple ways to show your love through being there.

- You don't need the perfect words. Just being present matters.
- Sit beside your loved one. Hold their hand. Read them their favorite story. Play their favorite music. Watch a movie together.
- Sometimes, the quietest presence is the loudest kind of love.

Build Mini-Rituals of Light

Creating small, consistent moments of calm and connection can bring peace and grounding amid uncertainty.

- Start by carving out just five minutes a day to be still; no phone, no agenda. Sit outside. Breathe deeply. Let silence introduce you to what you've been missing.

- Have a morning cup of coffee, tea, water, or fresh-pressed juice.
- Take morning or evening walks, even if they're short.
- Read together. These moments become anchors in the storm.
- Listen to music together. These simple acts become sacred.
- Practice noticing one beautiful thing each day. Write it down. Let it be small.
- Joy loves repetition, ritual, and the quiet consistency of shared time.

Take Care of Yourself, Too

Your well-being matters. Nurturing yourself helps you stay strong and present for your loved one. It's how you keep your strength and compassion alive for the journey ahead.

- You can't support someone else if you're running on empty.
- It's not selfish to get rest, eat well, or take breaks; it's necessary for your well-being.
- Talk to an expert, board certified psychologist, licensed life coach, or counselor to help you process the journey.
- Journal, meditate, or take quiet time to recharge.

Where in your life might quiet joy be waiting for your attention? Is it a conversation you've been too busy to have? That big solo trip you keep meaning to take? A moment of stillness you're avoiding? You don't need perfect conditions to find joy. You only need to notice what's already there.

Even now, years later, when life's good and full—I find myself seeking out those same quiet moments. The feel of sunlight on my face. A joy-filled pancake breakfast with my family. An unexpected laugh. They remind me of a time when I learned what mattered most.

While I wouldn't choose that path, I now understand that within hardship, there can live an extraordinary depth of meaning. That joy carried me through my dad's illness. That joy taught me how to live.

Felicia Rangel is the co-founder and Chief Communications Officer of Fabularis Entertainment and Media, a boutique agency with over 30 years of experience serving the global health, wellness, and transformation communities.

Fabularis provides a comprehensive range of services, including public relations, media relations, brand strategy, strategic partnerships, social media curation, and communications.

Felicia is committed to leveraging the power of clear, authentic communication to build trust, foster meaningful connections, and drive impactful change. Through strategic storytelling and public relations, she ensures that her clients' messages not only reach their audiences but also resonate deeply and inspire action. Her work consistently aims to elevate voices, uphold integrity, and highlight the nuanced moments that shape the human experience.

For organizations and brands seeking to enhance their narrative and achieve measurable results, Felicia and the Fabularis team offer strategic expertise and a dedicated partnership to communicate with clarity, purpose, and impact.

Connect with Felicia:

Website: https://fabularismedia.com

LinkedIn: https://www.linkedin.com/in/feliciarangel

X: https://www.x.com/feferang

CHAPTER 12

THE JOYOUS MAGIC OF LIVING "INSIDE-OUT"

VITAL INGREDIENTS FOR KEEPING CONTACT WITH YOUR SOUL

Ilene Dillon, MSW, Emotional Realignment Developer

MY STORY

The first time I lived on the farm, I didn't recognize joy.

I only knew I was there by myself, staying with grandparents who hugged me and talked with me a lot. I felt so good.

Because I was almost five, I didn't consciously recognize I was treated like a regular child for the first time in my life—loved, protected, bathed, and fed regularly. I was, for the moment, an "only child" instead of "little sister," ordered around and hit if she didn't obey. My sister, merely 22 months older than me, was also neglected during my first two years of life. With no adult protecting me, she hit me to get me to obey. With no escape, I became very compliant!

I'm going to school, just like my sister! I miss her so much. We were always together, and now she goes to school every day. I'm going to school, too, just like my sister!

We lived with my dad and stepmom. Every day I "went to school," copying letters next to pictures I recognized: "ball," "baby," "cheese," "curtain." I opened the Children's Dictionary and found a picture of a ball. Repeating its name out loud, I noticed letters beside it. Laboriously, with my untrained, four-year-old hands, I copied the letters.

"Ball," I proudly said aloud.

Twenty-three years later, I discovered why I was so driven to learn to read. Because of early neglect (my dad was in New Guinea in World War II, and my mother was very young and alone), the person with whom I bonded—attached to for my survival—was my barely-older sister. I was desperate to keep our connection, which I discovered I could do by "going to school" on the days she went.

I'm going to school, too! I'm learning to read.

Staying connected to my sister that way gave me peace. I didn't want her to go away from me, so I found a way to keep her near. Could I start first grade at age five? My dad said, "No."

But teaching myself to read is how I got to the farm, too.

My grandparents lived on a 500-acre farm. They raised cows, chickens, pigs, cotton, turkeys, tobacco, peanuts, cantaloupe, and watermelon, and grew a massive family vegetable garden.

My grandmother cooked on a wood-fired range, starting it each morning with dry kindling. Somehow, she got the temperature to support her cooking without burning the food. My grandfather farmed the land, milked the cow, and fixed the machinery.

Every morning, my grandfather took me along when he milked the cow.

I love this! The cow is eating her breakfast; her food smells sweet.

Each morning, my grandfather washed the placid cow's udder with water heated at home in the kettle, then used a clean cloth my grandmother gave him to dry it.

The milk makes a funny noise when it hits the bottom of the bucket. Papa makes Beauty's milk stream into his bucket. Beauty is so warm; I want to lean against her forever.

When his bucket was full, foam puffy on top, Papa carried it to the smokehouse, pouring some milk into a bowl for the mother cat and her continuously renewing litter of kittens. I picked them up, loving their soft little bodies and sweet mewing.

When we returned to the house, my grandmother called out, "Ilene, you dust yourself off and wash your hands and face. I don't want a hair in my kitchen." Every day was the same.

Papa drew water from the well, dropping a big bucket hung on a chain and drawing it up full of cold water. I searched for the catfish that lived in the well, whose job it was to eat algae off the walls. I wanted warm water to wash my face, like Papa took for the cow; the well water was cold.

In the kitchen, my grandmother had warm, freshly made biscuits, ham from a recently butchered pig, and eggs I collected myself from the bantam hens, half the size of normal chickens. The eggs I ate were small and special. I *felt* special.

After years of being the beaten-up little sister, unsupervised and unloved by adults, then staying in boarding schools run by stern, strict women, I was the only child. I got *all* my grandparents' love and attention. If I missed my sister, I don't remember it. That's how powerful being loved by two adults was for me. It was like being back in Heaven.

I never want this to end. I want to stay here forever.

And still, I didn't recognize joy.

When I rejoined my family after that blissful, loving year, people didn't notice I'd been away! My stepmom said I went with the family to George Washington's estate, Mt. Vernon. I didn't, and I knew it. She insisted I was wrong. After that year of being seen and cherished, the pain of my misremembered absence was agonizing.

Our military family began moving. We lived in three locations in Germany, Paris, France, Georgia, and five places in Virginia. Then, we moved on to Montana, Oklahoma, and back to Virginia—all before I was 20 years old. I attended multiple school districts; friends stayed behind, and I never saw them again. Joy receded from my awareness. I no longer knew how to find it. I didn't feel it, didn't expect it, and didn't think about it.

In the subsequent decade, I married, moved cross-country from my family, finished six years of self-funded college, went through years of psychotherapy, and had a child. My husband divorced me. I knew how to face challenges, how to do things on my own, and how to work hard.

Still, I didn't recognize feeling joy.

Gene referred to himself as an "aging hippie." He was a naturalist who led nature hikes and survived by selling psychedelics to friends and acquaintances. During the time we dated, he invited me to the Pygmy Forest, where he planned to introduce me to LSD.

Mt. Tamalpais predominates Marin County, north of San Francisco, California. It's a friendly mountain, sister to Mt. Diablo, rising 35 miles across the San Francisco Bay. In addition to its famous annual Mountain Play and cross-country race, The Dipsea, Mt Tamalpais has a Pygmy Forest. Mountain winds keep the trees stunted. There, Gene introduced me to a specific strain of LSD that enhanced my visual abilities.

For an entire day, we sat and looked into the sky, where I clearly saw air currents *before* hawks and crows entered to ride them in lazy circles. Amazing! It was a gentle day of mentally soaring with the birds, sweet conversation, and basking in nature's beauty and magnificence.

Leaving, we faced a steep downhill roadway. I started running, going faster and faster. At the bottom, where a small creek crossed the roadway, I threw myself to the ground, surprised to hear myself crying deep, loud sobs I made no attempt to control.

"Ilene, are you okay?" Gene caught up to me, concerned I hurt myself.

"I'm fine!" I said, smiling through tears. "I just realized I made it. I got back home, back to myself! After all the detours, losses, pain, and changes, I made it back to my *self.*"

At last, joy! The tears I cried were tears of joy.

That day on the mountain, at age 32, seeing deep into nature, allowing myself to feel amazed and supported, I got back to my self—for the first time since I was five years old!

Being with my self *was* joy!

THE SPARK

For me, joy is about being part of something larger, including nature. As a single parent, I chose backpacking and snow skiing as our "family sports." We filled our home with cockatiels, rabbits, dogs, a pony, cats, and a parrot. In the summer, my children fed themselves dinner by "grazing" in our annual organic vegetable garden. They grew up on a hillside of open space. Back then, I thought I safeguarded my sanity. Now, I can see I held the door to real joy open for us!

I discovered I was most often unaware of joy. Two things were missing, and one thing was in my way. I lacked love and my sense of self. Anger I held onto was in my way.

Prior to age three, I was a bubbly, always-dancing little girl. Without adult protection, I lost my self and became a compliant little sister. Love was absent from the beginning. Our neglect was so great, I remember making scrambled eggs for myself on a gas stove. I was removed from that home just as I turned three.

In adulthood, realizing the absence of self and love, I no longer saw the pathway back.

I had self and love in my year on the farm. They relentlessly eroded afterward and took me decades to find again, robbing me of internal peace for years.

As a therapist, I helped others reconstruct their fragmented pieces. I learned how to progress toward restoring self, and regained love by creating both for myself.

My decades-long progress ultimately led to my return to joy.

Here's what I did.

FINDING "SELF," SUPPORTED BY PERSONAL BOUNDARIES

Many people, fearing ego domination, attempt to reduce the self. Knowing the soul occupies our body and our body operates as our "home base" through which we orient, protect, and enjoy our lives, *we must develop, maintain, and protect our self.* It's not selfish; it's necessary. It keeps us from living disoriented, lonely, frightened, and deadened lives.

Childhood is designed for us to occupy, explore, and develop our personal sense of self. Before we can fully connect with others, we must occupy "home base." If we don't complete this job early in life, we're constantly drawn to go back and finish it. It's not selfish or egotistical; it's foundational. We can't connect with others or our world in healthy, successful ways until we complete this.

I first found my self by setting personal boundaries. On a driving trip through Europe in the 1980s, I decided to take one hour each day entirely to myself. I was 45. During my hour, I sat in parks, took walks, enjoyed watching people and sights, meditated, or took a luxurious bath.

What happened surprised me. I noticed I felt myself draw energy up from deep in the center of the Earth, through my feet and legs, and connect with all of me. I allowed myself to feel and listen to my own self, *experiencing* myself individually, separate from all others. At last, I recognized and felt my own soul.

To uncover my self, I needed to face fears of abandonment, rejection, disorientation, and nothingness—all terrifying. I went for it, replacing these with personal power, strong self-esteem, happiness, and joy.

STEPS TO RECLAIM YOUR SELF

1. Become aware of your current sense of self. If it's incomplete, *decide* to reclaim it. You don't have to know how; just decide.

2. On three-by-five cards, write, "I am worthy," and "There is nothing wrong with me." Spread them around where you live. When you notice one, read the statement aloud in a firm voice. The subconscious mind can't resist repetition. Hearing what you say aloud, your brain will accept this "truth" and make it a belief.

3. Take inventory of who you are—not of what you *do*, but who you *are*. Impatient? Kind? Smart? Hesitant? Pretty or handsome? Who are you? Be as honest and clear as you can be. Make a list of who you see yourself to be, not what others tell you. To cement your progress, practice saying "no" when pushed to do something you don't want to do.

4. You're now ready to set boundaries, a process of identifying where you begin and end in relation to others. Make another list about how you want to live and be treated: left to yourself, or frequently invited? Hugged by friends, not touched, or a handshake? Do you allow others to critique you without asking if you want to hear it? Take time alone daily to identify what you want and don't want for yourself. Put a star next to your non-negotiables, highlighting those things you don't want to have in any part of your life. Give yourself permission to walk away.

5. Manipulative people have difficulty spending time alone. Since we all begin life by being manipulative and need to grow out of it, chances are you may still manipulate. It's your prison, not something "bad." To break out of it, develop your ability to stay totally alone for a minimum of three days—72 hours. You're setting boundaries with yourself so you get clearer about who you are and separate from others.

6. With these steps, you choose to be a "grown-up." To help with this, frequently ask yourself: "What decision would a grown-up make?" Hanging back out of fear, shyness, avoiding criticism, etc., aren't grown-up. Grown-ups take up space and have opinions, expressing their full self. As we grow up, we move from being *dependent* to *independent* to enjoying *interdependence*. We're all here to live the life that feels best for us, which offers us joy.

CHANGE DIRECTION!

Few people learn to approach their lives from the correct direction. Most of us were taught to live from the "outside in," but life works best by living from the "inside out."

If we want more love, for example, we learn to "go looking for love." Love is *outside of us*, and we need to find the person who has ours. Our divorce statistics show this isn't a reliable method.

Instead, *create the love you want inside yourself!* Doing this takes work, yet it fills us with love that belongs to us, that no one can take away. It's not as difficult as we learned. And, once you build love inside of you, two things happen: 1) You get so filled with love that it spills over onto others, and 2) it gets reflected back to you from outside.

The principle is this: *What you have inside of you, you tend to attract from outside of you.*

I decided to love myself, reasoning that if I did so, at least I had *some* love! Now, I don't have just *some* love, I have a *constant and deep flow of love coming to me!* Once someone who believed herself to be *unlovable* for 45 years, I can attest to the power of this revision. In my life, I went from crying myself to sleep nightly because I had no friends, to having people close to me *and* those I just met telling me how much they love and admire me, showering me with invitations and gifts!

I want this for you, too.

DEVELOP AND GROW LOVE FOR YOURSELF

Loving yourself isn't "ego." It's restoring whatever love you "lost" as you passed through life. Almost all of us lose the incredible, unquestioned love that filled us when we first started life. See this in any child who doesn't hesitate to expect love and care, even in the middle of the night! Loving yourself means you *know* you're loved and meant to expect and enjoy it.

If, like me (formerly), your self-love is almost completely drained out, how do you fill yourself up again?

USE THIS SIMPLE EXERCISE

Sit quietly in a safe space where you're alone and won't be interrupted. Close your eyes. Envision either a human baby or a baby animal that appeals to you. Keeping your eyes closed, allow yourself to feel the love you have for the baby you envision. Take time to feel the love everywhere you can inside yourself, focusing on the love you feel for a precious baby.

Now, release the baby's image and continue feeling the same love for yourself.

Be gentle with yourself. This may be difficult to do. When I began, I held onto the love I felt for myself only five to 10 seconds!

As frequently as you can, for three weeks, transfer the "baby love" to yourself. Your brain will accept your love. You'll start to believe you're lovable. What we believe, we create. We change our life experiences by changing our beliefs.

Furthermore, the principle "once the mind has grown to a new place, you can't return it to the past," assures you the more love you feel for yourself, the greater the amount of love you'll have.

LET GO OF HELD-ONTO ANGER

"To forgive" means "to let go." The person who gets most hurt when you hold onto anger is you.

Anger is the most active emotion we feel. Since anger is energy, it behaves like water, which builds into a reservoir when its stream is blocked. Anger builds up when held onto. Held-onto anger is now proven to be part of the etiology of diseases, including diabetes and cancer. Held long enough, anger can kill you.

I call continuing to feel angry toward another person "allowing them to get me twice." Once, as part of the angering situation. Then twice, because the anger I'm holding onto can hurt or kill me. *Twice.*

Let go of anger. Heal yourself and move on. You'll make room for happiness and joy.

Dear reader, I hope joy isn't as far away from you as it was from me for so long. Even if it is, you can regain, nourish, grow, and live with joy, starting now. Stay aware of developing your self, loving that self, and releasing held-onto anger. You'll *automatically* move into joy.

Awareness creates the path to joy.

Ilene Dillon, therapist, coach, podcaster, international professional speaker, multiple bestselling author, solver of deep problems, and developer of Conscious Parenting and Emotional Realignment, is determined to change human consciousness for the next 2000 years!

This is no joke.

She's prepared her entire life by becoming a recovered angry person, then helping thousands of people to recover emotionally, too. Her system defines what emotions are, what they're for, and how to work with them to create life-enhancing processes, with long-lasting and successful outcomes.

A practical and impatient person, Ilene questions our usual "mental health" approach, which promotes "getting through" emotional experiences. She prefers addressing "cause," which leads to complete learning and issue resolution. Ilene's interested in discovering how things are designed to work, how to work definitively with anger and human energy, then get things done and finished! To those struggling with life problems, Ilene inevitably says: "When I went through that issue, I discovered. . ." She leads not by pointing to signs, but by inviting others to follow.

Since early childhood, Ilene's life has been full of variety and change. She continues living in unusual places in adultood, including a Seattle houseboat, on Texas leased hunting land, at the end of the Golden Gate Bridge, and in her 24-foot RV. In 2015, she went ocean swimming with a full-grown Jaguar.

She's been the wife of a psychotherapist-turned-minister, a brilliant high school dropout-turned-carpenter, and a brilliant neurosurgeon, who allowed her into his operating room to watch brain surgeries first-hand. She parented three brilliant children and five amazing grandchildren as a married, single, step-, adoptive, and grandmother.

Ilene's book (2019) is *Emotions in Motion: Mastering Life's Built-in Navigation System.*

Connect with Ilene:

Websites:
https://www.emotionalmasteryforlife.com
https://www.thewellnessuniverse.com/world-changers/ilenedillon/

Email: ilene@emotionalmasteryforlife.com

Instagram: https://www.instagram.com/ilenedillon/

LinkedIn: https://www.linkedin.com/in/ilenedillon/

CHAPTER 13

LIFE PISSED IN YOUR CHEERIOS

FINDING SUNSHINE ON THE DARKEST DAYS

Deanna Cotten

"Living with joy isn't about escaping the storms of life;
it's about finding a pocketful of sunshine when the clouds roll in."

~ Deanna Cotten

MY STORY

THREE SECONDS FROM THE LAST GOODBYE

Did I appreciate today like it could be my last?

It was the most normal, bone-chilling winter day in Wyoming. I dropped my girls off at school, rushed through the drive-thru of my favorite local coffee hut, peeled into the parking lot, and promptly sat down in my padded teal chair at the office. The schedule was back-to-back with clients, as usual. I had 15 minutes to review my calendar and prepare for my first meeting.

Time slipped by. Before I knew it, my girls were piling into my office to reflect on their drama-filled day at school. My husband often dropped by when he got off work at 3:30. We usually spent a chaotic 30 to 45 minutes discussing the evening plans and tasks that needed to be done, such as appointments, grocery shopping, and meal planning.

My husband told our girls they couldn't stay with me; instead, they needed to get home safely before the storm rolled in. We were under winter weather advisories, which are typical that time of year. As always, he gave me a kiss, told me he loved me, and instructed the kids to head out to the truck. I watched my youngest stomp out the door, arms crossed, with an attitude. *She's going to hold this against me all evening.*

I needed a couple of hours at the office to finish projects with deadlines that couldn't wait. *Just breathe, Deanna. It will work itself out.*

Anxious to beat the storm, I hit send and gathered up everything I'd need to work from home, should the roads close the following day. I tossed my laptop bag over my shoulder, closed the office door behind me, and started scrolling for a brainless podcast episode to detach me from the long day's work. Arriving at my car, I tossed my bags onto the front seat, slammed the car door shut, and buckled up—just *another normal day in the books.*

As I approached the interstate, bright flashing signs overhead warned, "Black Ice, No Unnecessary Travel." *Unnecessary? I've done this drive a thousand times. Icy roads are just another typical Tuesday in Wyoming. I'll be fine.*

Life doesn't stop amid Wyoming's extended winters or icy and dangerous roads. It's like a game of Russian roulette out there. But you never think it can be you, so you take your chances until one day, the barrel spins your way.

A State Highway Patrolman sped past me on the right, lights flashing and sirens blaring. In a few short seconds, he was out of my line of sight. It was a slow, but peaceful drive home. Soon, I discovered myself on a runway I never asked to be on, ending without a money-back guarantee.

As I came around the last mountainous bend, my tires hit a patch of black ice. My car began to slide. Through the fog, I caught a glimpse of the highway patrolman's flashing lights. He was parked next to a jackknifed semi on the right-hand side of the road.

My heart skipped a beat, adrenaline coursing through my veins, but I somehow felt a strange sense of calm. *Deanna, don't panic. You are in control. Plan your exit.*

My tires glided seamlessly to the right. I had time to think about what was happening. There was time to avoid the accident. I remained calm, believing I was in complete control. *If I just throw my car into the median, I can avoid impact. It's life or death. Go left. Left. . .NOW!*

The highway patrolman was helpless, waiting with the wreckage I spotted through the fog just seconds ago. *Stay calm. I can do this. Just a little left, a little left.* My hands clenched the steering wheel tighter, my stomach twisting, my mind racing through every what-if.

My car failed to obey my thoughts. As I spun in circles on the two-lane interstate, my car inched closer and closer to the wreckage in front of me. I came to a stop. I was facing head-on traffic. A second semi hit the same patch of black ice that sent me into oblivion. He headed right for me.

"No, no, *nooooo*," I screamed as the headlights stared me square in the face.

I plowed my foot into the gas pedal, begging my tires to move, the smell of burning rubber so strong I could taste it. I went from calm to screaming so loudly, my lungs felt like swallowing fire. My hands clenched the steering wheel as I pleaded for my life.

My husband, my children, my parents, sisters, nieces, nephews. Is it too late to run? I looked away from the headlights and peered into the distance.

The snow-covered field was glittered with a safety net I couldn't reach. The young highway patrolman looked at me with fear and sadness in his eyes. *We are all going to die.*

I let go of the steering wheel and took my foot off the gas pedal. *What I can't see won't hurt me.* Bracing for impact, I surrendered in silence. *This is it. This is how it ends.*

I wasn't scared to die. I was pissed I didn't get to say goodbye.

I had zero control over the outcome. The worst time to have no control is when it means life or death. There is no turning back. I've never felt so helpless.

My family is going to get the worst call of their lives tonight. I want to protect my husband and children's hearts. Can I just tell them I love them one more time?

Unable to close my eyes, I watched the headlights close in on me. A split second later, the headlights were gone, and the box end of the truck was swinging towards me. The sky turned gray, tricking me into believing it was daylight. A gust of wind stood between us. My car began to shift towards the median.

The sound of the snow bank barreling underneath my car was the shelter I pleaded for all along. I came to a sudden stop in the tire tracks of the semi that spared my life. I panicked as every vehicle came around the bend, not knowing the destruction awaited them.

My car was at a rest. I peered out my driver's side window. The truck driver was climbing down from his truck, only to discover we were stuck in three to four feet of snow, preventing him from safely walking towards me. We landed about 50 yards apart. I rolled my window down and yelled as loud as I could, reassuring him I was not physically injured. The emotional whiplash was too much to describe as I yelled across the median.

In the last three seconds of my life, that truck driver made a split-second decision to flip his own truck into the median, risking his own life and career to spare mine, the patrolman's, and the other semi driver who was awaiting a tow.

In a state of shock, my body was convulsing uncontrollably. I did not know where my phone was. I pushed random buttons on my dashboard screen to call for help, somehow finding the emergency line.

"911, can you state your emergency?" said the dispatcher.

"A semi almost killed me. I'm in the median. I'm on I-25. Please close the roads, please, everyone coming around that turn is sliding everywhere," I replied hysterically.

"Please, you have to close the roads!" I pleaded with everything in me.

"Ma'am, help is on the way. We are working to close the roads. Stay in your vehicle and keep your seatbelt on," the dispatcher instructed.

For the next 35 minutes, my heart sat in my throat until the roads were closed, allowing emergency personnel to safely come into the wreckage.

"You got lucky tonight," the officer said to me as he approached my car with a flashlight.

Lucky? Cashing in at the slot machines when you are $60 ahead is luck.

"Can you please tell that driver thank you for sparing my life?" I asked the officer. I kindly declined emergency services that arrived on scene. My husband and his best friend located me on our Life 360 app. Although the roads were closed, officers allowed them to come down to assist me. My husband and his friend paved a path through the snow bank, helped me out of the car, and we all held tightly to each other as we shimmied across the interstate.

I was less than five minutes from home. I almost made it. I almost didn't make it. I sensed confusion setting in amongst the shock as we approached the driveway.

As I walked in the front door, still gasping for air, I promptly told my kids, "Never take another day for granted."

SURVIVING WAS JUST THE BEGINNING

This marked the beginning of a lonely and isolating journey. It turns out nobody can experience your trauma the same way you did. They simply were not there.

I wanted everyone to know how short life is. I wanted everyone around me to close their office door for the last time, knowing the headlights were coming. I'm usually filled with words that inspire and encourage, but I simply couldn't find the words.

I was thankful to be alive. At the same time, I was pissed I had to live through this nightmare to recover. Although strong in my faith, I was angry at God. He rejected me at Heaven's gates. *How could He let me experience this trauma and pain if He's a good God? Why didn't He let me die?* There was no source of reasoning for me.

Every morning, I woke up thankful to be alive and angry that I was alive at the same time. Getting behind the wheel again felt like a molehill

I turned into a mountain. It took every ounce of energy to get behind the wheel. I obsessively watched the Wyoming Department of Transportation's app, justifying the need to stay home every day. When I did leave, I would tell everyone in the car not to talk to me. In my mind, I was preparing my exit at every turn, just in case.

I went to work the following Monday. I was sure I shut my office door for the last time three days prior, yet here I was staring at that blue door, unable to make sense of how I was supposed to meet deadlines that didn't care about my trauma. *I can't shake the numbing pain. I can't wake up from this nightmare I'm trapped in.* The headlights taunted me when I was awake and haunted me in my sleep.

I was always the life of the party, a little over the top, and filled to the brim with more energy than most. Overnight, my light faded. I usually power through the darkest times with a great attitude. Living felt like a complete and utter distraction, adding fuel to the fire.

As the week closed in, I woke up believing my family would bury me that day. *I can't live this way.*

I lived in a continuous state of shock. I was here, but I wasn't present for the things that still vied for my attention. My doctor suggested I find a trauma counselor. I didn't have time for another appointment on the calendar, but I had no other choice. Life had to go on.

"Listen, I have a lot going on, I am super busy, and I really don't have time for this mess. What do I need to do?" I asked my new counselor at my intake appointment. She chuckled under her breath; she knew I was a project, and it would be a long road ahead.

Trauma counseling allowed me to mentally and emotionally recover.

Unexpectedly, counseling revealed past traumas that were stumbling blocks in my life. Over the course of that year, my testimony stood strong. I wasn't scared to die; I was pissed I didn't get to say goodbye.

While navigating the aftermath of this trauma, I experienced physical symptoms that were affecting my quality of life. My right hand was weak, making it difficult to write or type. I slept sitting up, and for some reason, I could no longer hold myself up in my chair at work.

After a year of trauma counseling, I jumped into the new year empowered, with a vision board covered in sunshine, glitter, and rainbows. Just 12 days later, my hopes and dreams would shatter again. Before the new year had a chance to ring in, my vision board went up in flames.

"Deanna, do you want me to shoot straight with you?" my doctor asked.

I spent years suffering from multiple autoimmune diseases. *Everything is Figureoutable* as Marie Forleo had taught me. *There's a treatment for everything. Write me the prescription and let's keep moving.*

"I'm 95% sure you have ALS." He stated matter-of-factly. "You'll need to advocate for yourself harder than you ever have before. This is a debilitating and fatal disease."

Is this a joke, God?

Amyotrophic Lateral Sclerosis, also known as Lou Gehrig's Disease, is a motor neuron disease that causes the body's voluntary muscles to die. These are the muscles that affect the ability to walk, talk, eat, swallow, and eventually breathe, leading to death. There's no cure, and treatment options may only prolong life by up to three months. The additional three-month extension on life was less likely than death itself.

There's a 5% chance, I thought. I survived the headlights barreling in at full speed, so clinging to that 5% seemed realistic.

Two weeks later, the final test confirmed the terminal diagnosis.

A RAY OF SUNSHINE

As the headlights closed in on me once again, God asked, "Do you still believe what you said you believed?"

I knew what this meant. *Do I still believe I'm not scared to die?*

I couldn't help but wonder, *did it become easier to believe I wasn't scared to die because I got to live?*

"I'm still not scared to die," I muttered out loud.

"Then I showed you favor. This is your opportunity to say goodbye," God said.

A Bible verse I've known for many years hit close to home. Psalm 90:12 says, "So teach us to number our days, that we may apply our hearts unto wisdom." My time was being cut short.

Although ALS will likely be the reason I exit this life, I may get struck by lightning or hit by a bus instead.

In the face of terminal disease, I get to see life through a new lens—one that reminds me life is short, and each day should be filled with sunshine. Don't live like it's your last day, though; the house payment won't live on a wing and a prayer.

I'm still not scared to die. I'm honored I get to say goodbye!

THE SPARK

Life's darkest moments have a way of humbling the soul and reminding it who's ultimately in control. Life's darkest storms have a way of making one crumble in the face of the impossible. Naturally, we want to control the fiery darts life throws our way. I've learned that I can't control the outcome, but I can control how I respond.

We'll all face the headlights. Maybe they're already staring you in the face today. Not one of us makes it out of here alive. I just glimpsed that my time will be much shorter than I expected. I'm not trying to scare you, but life is going to take a piss in your Cheerios someday, too. Maybe you will get a warning like I did, or it will be unexpected.

Regardless, shall we make mimosas and get on with the party?

FINDING A POCKETFUL OF SUNSHINE ON THE DARKEST DAYS

A fake smile can hide the pain, but it won't heal the wound. Everyone has unresolved trauma serving as a stumbling block.

I know you don't need another appointment on your schedule, but past life events may be holding you back. You have previous trauma preventing you from achieving your life goals and dreams.

Don't wait for a death sentence to start healing. It will feel like a day late and a dollar short, I promise. Investing in your mental health now is like investing in sunshine for life's darkest storms ahead.

Step one: schedule that appointment! Then, cultivate the following habits so you have the tools to discover a pocketful of sunshine, even when life pisses in your Cheerios.

- **Daily Routines**–There is comfort to be found in your normal. Having a morning and evening routine becomes an anchor when your world turns upside down. Simple pleasures like coffee on the porch, going for a walk, or journaling are affordable ways to reflect on life and find your calm.

- **Thankfulness and Gratitude**–Practice thankfulness and gratitude daily. Choose to see what you are thankful for and why you are grateful. This isn't avoidance or denial; it's armor for your soul. Intentional reflections allow you to reach into your pocket and find a glimmer of hope.

- **Discovering Faith, Community, and Connection**–Whatever your faith or grounding beliefs are, anchor yourself in them while it's sunny out. It's harder to build a shelter in the middle of the storm. Let people in, even if it feels too heavy. Surround yourself with others' light. The darkness is louder when you isolate.

- **Make Memories on Purpose**–There is never going to be a perfect time. Book the trip even if you aren't sure how to pay for it. Fight the fatigue and show up to the party. Say I love you one more time. Send that text. The smallest memory you create today might be the pocketful of sunshine you need for tomorrow's storms.

Deanna Cotten is the author of *Embracing the End*, honored with Amazon's "Therapist Approved" badge. After a brush with death leading to a terminal diagnosis, she decided if life was going to end, she'd at least remind others they are dying too. With her signature dark humor, Deanna normalizes death and dying by equipping others to discover purpose and peace at the end of life. She is living proof that not even dying can steal your joy. As an inspirational writer, speaker, and guest podcaster, Deanna has a growing online community of 44,000 fans and followers, generating more than 40 million views across her social media platforms.

Connect with Deanna:

Facebook: https://www.facebook.com/deanna.cotten.2025

TikTok: https://www.tiktok.com/@d.anna.cotten

CHAPTER 14

WE BUILD THE FUTURE WE WANT TO LIVE IN

KINDNESS HELPS US DEFEAT OVERWHELM AND CREATE JOY

Michael G. Neece

MY STORY

"I want a separation," my wife said nervously.

Five days later, I drove my white minivan up the coast with two dogs, a cat, and everything I needed to work and live. Nobody budgets for a surprise marital separation, so six hours of driving would get me to a free place where I could wait it out.

I'll figure this out. For now, just drive.

As I drove north into Delaware, a close family member, Teddy, made an attempt on his life.

Only my wife knew about Teddy's crisis, and she thought she could keep it under control without me, so she didn't tell me for four days.

By then, I had settled into my new living situation. I ate healthy meals, exercised, worked, talked with my therapist, and journaled. I figured out how to carry my heavy dog, Toffee, down the icy steps into fresh snow so she could pee. She had been weakening slowly for two years, and now she quivered and stumbled at random moments. It meant I had to prop her up carefully as she relieved herself. As we locked eyes each time, I prayed silently, *Hang in there, girl. You'll be okay.*

After my wife finally told me about Teddy's suicide attempt, I cleaned the borrowed home in a frenzy, packed up, and again drove the white minivan for six hours with the dogs, the cat, and all my essentials.

I'll figure this out. For now, just drive.

Back home, I sat at the kitchen table with my now-estranged wife and made plans to help Teddy, whose only support was the two of us. Keeping a still-packed bag and leaving the pets, I drove to Teddy's, where I spent eight days figuring out how to get him into a medical care facility, sleeping on his couch each night so he felt safe. We flew 2000 miles from home to get him into a great recovery center, and my return flight got me back to his apartment, where he said I could live for a while.

At Teddy's, I crammed my essential items into already-stuffed drawers. *I wonder how Teddy's doing*, I thought each time I reached for my socks. Teddy's roommate and I knew each other well before this, so while it was weird for both of us, we bonded most evenings over missing Teddy and watching movies.

As the days grew into weeks, I journaled, ate carefully, and walked tens of thousands of steps each day around a nearby lake. *How did I get here? How can I fix things? What's my next move?*

A few weeks into that new, awkward life, my wife texted me, asking me to come home.

It wasn't to reconcile, though. Instead, my beloved Toffee had taken a turn for the worse. My wife wanted me to come home, sleep on the couch near the dog for the next few nights, and take her to the vet. I drove home, thinking yet again, *I'll figure this out. For now, just drive.*

Three days later, Toffee died in my arms.

How will I ever find joy again?

THE SPARK

Earlier in my life, any one of those things—a flailing marriage, a suicidal family member, or a dying pet—would've knocked me over. In addition to that, I was a new business owner, focusing on startup efforts and worried about my next paycheck. Perhaps a few years earlier, I would've felt powerless.

What saved me? What can I teach you that will spark your joy?

Simply put, I've worked on my kindness practice in recent years, making me resilient in a way I never dreamed possible. The strategies I teach corporate leaders, human resources executives, frontline workers, and even friends and family—those very things kept me alive, sane, and even *joyful*, if you can believe it.

I'm going to share three sparks for building your kindness practice. When you strengthen your focus on kindness, it builds trust, innovation, and productivity in the workplace. You'll build a healthier personal life. Having this strong, reliable kindness practice helps you face life's biggest problems while building stronger family relationships. Even when it comes to love and romance, these strategies help. And, as I'm sure you're anticipating, they help you find more joy and reduce stress across all parts of your life.

A kindness practice is a regular habit of giving grace, compassion, empathy, and curiosity to yourself and others as often as possible, even in the most trivial moments. Most people use the phrase *in kind* to mean trading similar things with others. The way I rebrand that phrase is this: living *in kind* means doing the kindest thing you can think of in any situation. Your kindness practice consists of your efforts to live *in kind*.

What's the opposite of living in kind? It's fighting fire with fire because your ego is bruised. Your instincts make you want to strike back or curl up in a ball, but that's just allowing your emotions to rule you instead of you ruling your life.

With a strong kindness practice, you respond from a place of values and beliefs instead of relying on knee-jerk reactions. When that feeling of righteous indignation bubbles up because something didn't go right, a good kindness practice means you don't have to yell, hide, or try to sabotage someone.

Imagine a team leader at your workplace sending you *that* email—the one with 50 people on copy, insisting you're to blame for a mistake. "You did this to all of us with your carelessness! We missed the deadline because of YOU!"

If you let your emotions take over, you'll fire off an angry *no-I'm-not-and-you-stink!* Email response. That never, ever goes well.

The alternative?

THE FAVORITE PERSON PRACTICE

Stop for a moment, close your eyes, and envision your favorite person. You might pick your mother, cousin, or best friend since grade school. Whoever you choose, get a really clear image of them in your mind. Remember their hug, how they move, or the pep talks they give right when you need them. Find joy in your heart, and envision the kindness you hope everyone gives them because they deserve it. Keep your eyes closed until you really have a good image of them—their smile, their hand in yours, how they smell, their tone of voice—and hold onto your compassion and love for them.

Now, with eyes wide open, consider the sender of that angry email and pretend they're your favorite person.

Instead of being offended, angry, sad, or scared, now I bet you're curious. *Why is my best friend so angry? Why did she blame this all on me? What's going on with her that she's so upset?* And usually the essential question comes up: *How can I help make it better?*

When my wife told me she wanted a separation, it was easy to engage in the Favorite Person Practice because she *was* my favorite person. I felt deep curiosity about her state of mind, her pain, her desire to be alone, and what I could focus on to make things better for both of us.

Every morning, think about your favorite person. It's a wonderful thing to do, no matter why you do it. As you think of them more often, you're prepared to bestow forgiveness, kindness, and even love onto complete strangers in the name of this special someone in your life. And that brings you great joy, partly because you think of someone you care about a lot more often. But also because you realize you're a kinder, more forgiving person, and you are!

But what about kindness to yourself?

FOCUS ON YOUR THREE-FOOT RADIUS

In the Navy SEALS, a high-performing elite military strike force, they think strategically about how to control their personal three-foot radius. When in a battle situation, focusing on distant yelling or sounds of gunfire just distracts you from what's immediately in front of you. In your three-foot radius, there could be a child to save, a piece of equipment to hand off to someone, or an attack from an enemy who is close enough to touch.

Why focus on distant things when we have critical situations right in our grasp?

As I planned the first actions of my marital separation, I followed this strategy. I knew I needed a place to stay, so within moments, I knew where to go. My wife said she needed to focus on self-reflection and that pet care would drain her time and attention, so I agreed to take all three pets with me. If I had instead focused on her reasons for the separation, the righteous indignation I felt, the hurt, sadness, or anger that wanted to take control and direct my actions, my focus would've been on things outside my three-foot radius.

The three-foot radius idea got me focused on finding a place to stay, packing, coaxing pets into the car, and then driving.

When Teddy's crisis came up, I could've collapsed. I could have spent my energy being angry with my wife for not telling me quickly. Instead, I thought through the steps of closing the house down, packing, and driving home. The three-foot radius was forefront in my mind. *What's in my control? What can I do right now? How can I be near Teddy so I can help?*

We usually think of kindness as actions we take for the benefit of others. Maybe you envision helping someone get an item from a tall shelf, buying coffee for the person behind you in line, or holding a stranger's baby on an airplane while they rest for a few minutes.

But kindness has to be focused inward, too. You deserve love, kindness, and attention. Neglecting yourself doesn't earn any points, bragging rights, or accolades except with people who don't have your best interests at heart.

By deciding on your priorities using the three-foot radius concept, you're being deeply kind to yourself. And, as it turns out, it's also kind to anyone who relies on you. When you decide what's in your three-foot radius and honor those things, you're undistracted, productive, efficient, and more deeply in a flow state. And ask any joy expert—if you can find a flow state, you feel joyous, fulfilled, or even euphoric. Research clearly shows that those in a flow state reduce their anxiety, stress, and even self-doubt.

Imagine taking up this practice and suddenly breezing through emotionally-charged situations, accomplishing more than usual, and feeling a sense of satisfaction at the end!

As each new challenge appeared, knowing what was inside or outside my three-foot radius allowed me to keep trudging forward, making progress toward solutions, and calming my nervous system, even as I handled it all.

Imagine a workplace where everyone thinks this way. Just like with the Favorite Person Practice, the Three-Foot Radius strategy pulls the ego out of the way, so you make value-based decisions rather than emotionally reactive ones.

And the last spark I want to share with you is just as vital as the first two.

ALWAYS LOOK FOR THE SILVER LININGS

For so many people in the United States, you can envision a life filled with advantages and great privilege, and you'd likely be correct. Many of us are not wealthy, but so many of us have great parents, amazing mentors, and a thriving network of loving family, friends, and colleagues. I certainly do.

Asking someone with a lot of privilege like me to list gratitudes turns out to be easy. There is a highly effective way of doing this that most people don't teach, but for now, I'm going to give you a different spark. It's even more magical: Silver Linings.

When you focus on gratitudes, you think of easy things like the taste of your favorite food, a great hug someone gave you, or a promotion you got at work. Finding silver linings involves examining your painful situations and struggles to identify what was good about them.

My wife wanted a separation. That has since turned into a divorce. What is the silver lining here?

If she were a terrible person, horribly abusive or cruel in some way, the silver lining might be the thought, *good riddance!* And voila, that's it. But she's not a terrible person. She's strong, smart, committed to family, and great at her job. What's the silver lining?

Knowing that someone is done with a relationship is good information to have. She could've tried to fake interest in me, contorted herself to try to fit that lie, become deeply resentful and angry, and it could have spilled out into our family.

Instead, she was honest. Powerfully honest. Letting me know she was done with the relationship meant we could each move on—a kindness to her and, ultimately, even though it felt horrible at the time, to me.

What's the silver lining in Teddy's emotional distress and near-death experience?

He's still with us. I can still give this man a hug, tell him I love him, and he can still enjoy a good, fulfilling life. Getting the treatment he needed means he now has a better life. He has even found joy!

And what about my dead dog?

I was immensely sad losing Toffee. Most of us would jump to the obvious silver lining that she's no longer in pain, and yeah, that's a good one. But there's something less obvious that I'm thankful for. I got three days with her at the very end. I stroked her fur and told her, "You're such a good dog. You're doing a good job." I snuggled with her and got to show her my love in those final days.

What are your silver linings? If someone gets a promotion that you wanted, it's easy to get frustrated. But if you look hard enough, you might realize that the newly promoted person just got a lot of heavy responsibilities you secretly didn't want. They're stuck with all of that, and you still have your freedom.

If you led a project that ended badly, perhaps even leading to you losing your job, you learned a lot and hopefully found a better job. Your new supervisor might even value what you learned from getting things wrong previously.

I beg you, please think about silver linings. It calms your limbic system, helps you view every experience as a learning opportunity, and fosters adaptability. It gets you into the mode of thinking about multiple backup plans, making it possible to have more pathways to success. It makes you an indispensable problem-solver at work, in your community, and at home.

When you deliberately review this list each morning—The Favorite Person Practice, the Three-Foot Radius, and Silver Linings—you train your brain to think about those things throughout your day. Remembering your favorite person lifts you and makes you kinder to others, thus bringing more joy (or at least less crankiness) to them and you. Focusing on your three-foot radius means you have greater clarity of your priorities; thus, you can accomplish more and fret less. Reflecting on the silver linings reminds you that there is always more to be grateful for.

These practices are deeply kind. When you do them, your ego takes a backseat, and blame and anger become noticeably quieter. You can think about actions you want to take next because feelings of hurt and surprise are replaced by compassion and a yearning to help. You successfully shift your mindset into problem-solving and values-driven actions, and move beyond instinct-driven decisions.

That's why we talk about kindness as a practice. What you practice the most makes you grow, and it makes those actions more familiar and comfortable. With a strong kindness practice, you show up as a better version of yourself more often. Before long, you find that you've trained yourself to do it as a reflex. Kindness becomes your new instinct!

By using the sparks listed above, I hope you begin to glow from within—radiating joy, even on your hardest days. And as you lead with kindness, you become a beacon, not just of how to live but of how to *create* joy every single day.

With all that light—your own and the light reflected by those who followed your example—your joy won't just return. It will expand.

May that joy be fully yours. And if you ever need a spark to relight the flame, reach out. I'm right here beside you.

As President of Our Future is Kind, **Michael G. Neece** teaches people how to use the power of kindness to create innovative, productive, and efficient teams.

His wide-ranging experience includes leadership and educational roles in traditional corporate settings as well as planetariums. He has delivered more than 750 sessions about team building, kindness, the wonders of the universe, and the curiosity invoked by space exploration. Michael has developed a unique approach to helping teams thrive by talking about kindness through a cosmic lens.

As host of the podcast, "Our Future is Kind," he interviews executives, futurists, politicians, artists, writers, and community leaders to help his audience ponder, "What should the future be like? Who will be there? How can we craft it carefully into what we want and deserve?"

His book, *In Kind: Consciously Craft a Meaningful Life and Career*, is a comprehensive roadmap for leaders who want to build a corporate culture that's rich in psychological safety. Its practical tools and exercises are meant for anyone seeking career success, whether they are starting out, starting over, or in dire need of a kinder workplace and life.

His role as a father to members of the LGBT community, combined with his fervent belief in the worth and worthiness of all people to have a seat at the table, adds to his interest in building a kinder future. Aligned with this, Michael is a co-founder of The Human Summit, an event that brings together those who want to drive more connection among disparate communities.

Michael resides in North Carolina, where he enjoys playing guitar, juggling, climbing stairs for charity, and hiking. He is also an avid reader and writer.

Connect with Michael:

Website: https://OurFutureIsKind.com

Instagram: https://www.instagram.com/michaelgneece

LinkedIn: https://www.linkedin.com/in/yournextkeynotespeaker

YouTube: https://www.youtube.com/@YourNextKeynoteSpeaker

CHAPTER 15

IT'S (FINALLY) ALL ABOUT ME!

TAKING CENTER STAGE IN YOUR LIFE

Lulu Pearl Trevena, Artist, Coach, Retreat Leader

MY STORY

If you think reinvention requires Botox and beige, buckle up, it's about to get intimate, and possibly a little juicy. Liberation at this age comes with stretch marks and a lust for more—welcome to the second coming.

Small mountains of discarded tissues scatter the floor of the enormous dome structure, soggy with the remnants of weighted storylines closing. Runny noses glistened beneath trembling lips, eyes swollen and rimmed red, droopy, but clear. Bodies post-convulsing, sobs cracked the air wide open. Screams tore loose, primal and unfiltered, shuddering through every soft curve of the healing cocoon. Until only fragmented echoes clung to the air, drenched with relief. Hearts softened.

At the end of each day, shadows met—the heavy emotional lifting complete. For now, we folded into each other, a tangle of limbs and re-regulating breaths. We found our way, exhausted, crawling and bottom-shuffling, to the healing pile of the cuddle puddle.

Heads nestled into shoulders, backs curved to hold the weight of sorrow gently slipping out, unrestricted. Smooth fingers entwined, and hairy legs tickled, just a little, infusing warmth, comfort, and no attachment to who or what body part met.

Safety. Softening.

Maskless. Blissfully and utterly spent.

Time floated in suspended peace.

A year earlier, after the first day of the shadow work retreat, I lingered at the edge of the cuddle puddle; curled small in embryo pose, not yet ready to fold into the touch of strangers newly met. Personal space, right?

Gently, my eyes took in slivers of light; eyelids flickered, opening luxuriously, catching a sudden sparkle of warm eyes, wide with post-storm joy, close by. Then grins unfurled, and elastic, uncontained, broad, contagious smiles spread wide as hammocks in summer shade. Laughter, warm and free, rose from bellies as peace settled like a weighted blanket: soft, sure, and earned.

What happens at a Shadow Work Intensive stays at the Shadow Work Intensive!

And yet, I strutted home full of vitality, a new woman—as ME.

The glow-up was undeniable—an embodied freeness. I felt more liberated in my 60s than I ever did in my vivacious, youthful, take-on-the-world 20s, now, undeniable embodied wholeness, sassy and wise.

I rebirthed myself in the lush countryside of the Netherlands. And I birthed myself, center stage, as *The Boudoir Poet*.

The deeply transformative two weeks drew to a close when the facilitators announced a social night. Performances (skits, music, and poetry) were on their wish list. At first, it seemed no one was up for it. We had been peeling back layers multiple times a day, and the thought of spending time rehearsing or practicing felt somewhat of a burden.

That soon turned around, and the common room began to hum with energy. Some arrived carrying instruments; others searched for the best lounging spot to absorb what would unfold. Mattresses and oversized cushions of varying colours and shapes were arranged in a loose half-circle, forming an amphitheater haphazardly, yet organic and inviting. An off-white sectional couch, casually integrated, added to the eclectic seating.

Delightfully, the line-up for the night became a radiant celebration of community. Joy, lightness, tenderness, human merry-making, and laughter—the richness of heart and soul connection.

At the retreat center, there was no alcohol, drugs, or substances to distort or escape whilst on our healing journey. Only vegan food was served—all the vices weaned out of each of us, everyone clean and open.

What remained were softer humans, reveling in their raw, luminous aliveness.

My black miracle bodysuit, its shoestring straps clinging delicately to my shoulders, cinched me in at the waist and lifted my breasts into a full, voluptuous curve. It matched my flowing black palazzo pants, wide-legged and grounding me, my feet bare, toes brushing the coolness of the floor. Over it, a soft blue lace cardigan floated, barely there, sheer and whispering softness in every thread.

I prepared two poems to share, each one carefully crafted with the antics, flavour, rawness, delicious heartfulness, and a little spice of the last two weeks. They pulsed with raw moments I hoped would land in the hearts of the thirty-two souls present, our group of men and women, spanning from their early twenties to the life experience of their seventies.

We became a rare, bonded family that unfastened its secrets, aired its grievances, and discovered a binding, amplified love for the sweet truth in each human being.

Arjen finished his performance. The room pulsed with high-vibe energy. "Next up is Lulu!" the MC announced.

With my emerald leather phone case in hand and poems queued and ready, my fingers reached instinctively for a ruby-red silk gerbera that I spied resting nearby. *A pop of colour,* I muse. My eyes catch the shape of a Chicago-style (think Chicago on Broadway) open-back wooden chair—simple, low-backed, sturdy. I take it with me, walking with purpose to the center of the performance space.

There, I rotated my fingers and twisted the chair around so its back faced the audience, every section open, the design skeletal yet sensual. I placed the mysterious found gerbera and my phone gently on the seat.

Then, with a slow, deliberate forward bend at the side of the chair, I slide my hands down my thighs along with my soft palazzo pants, sensuously, unapologetically, stepping out of them, like shedding skin.

The audience erupts—revelry.

I straddle the chair, facing the audience, bold and bare-legged, in my one-piece, snug body suit. I place the red gerbera at my feminine mound, as a sacred symbol, with playful rebellion, and theatrics. I was poised.

My hands steady, I slid to the notes tab on my phone. I leaned forward into the wooden frame, my breasts pressing gently, and paused, rising in my seat. I elongated my spine, stretching just enough for my feminine assets to rest on the top rung, held tenderly in the black fabric of my miracle bodysuit. "Hmmm," I audibly punctuate the moment slowly.

The audience—they are with me. Sass meets reverence. It was a communal moment of embodied audacity.

Who says sensuality has an expiration date? Who decided the energy of fun, freedom, and flirtatiousness was reserved only for taut, young adult bodies, as if ripeness doesn't deepen with time, as if desire doesn't mature like fine wine into something far more intoxicating?

My poems were skillfully witty, clever, and wise. They held a mirror to our shared journey, part confessional, part celebration, and part burlesque tease.

It wasn't something I ever imagined doing. But I did.

And when I took that center stage, I claimed it. I *commanded* the space.

This was not performance. It was reclamation, embodied, fierce with joy. Viva. . .the cracking open of roles worn thin, the shedding of invisibility from an unseen, unappreciated marriage. Post-divorce, I stood visible.

I didn't play a part.

I finally showed up for myself, as myself, and being fully seen.

I was the only performer who made money that night! Tucked cheekily into the strap of my bodysuit by Court, a muscular, magnificent Viking of a man, his gesture was half-appreciation, half-dare, and fully delicious.

None of it was planned. My intention was to *read* poems, wanting them to take center stage, but the props whispered, the stage beckoned, my introversion subsided, and I said yes!

To the risk.

To the *me-ness* of the moment.

This. . .

. . .was finally *all about me.*

A week after returning from the Netherlands, a digital photo arrived. It was a delightful surprise; I didn't know I was captured in time.

But there it was: proof of a night where I let my entire embodied free-spirited woman speak, be seen, mature in body, playful with an audience, and allowed my sensual self to unabashedly shine.

Some days, when I need a little joy-laced reminder, I open my phone photo album. And like a very Jamie Lee Curtis in *True Lies* moment, I whisper to myself, "I did that!"

Shadow work in a safe community is the most powerful way to do shadow work. It's like standing under every spotlight at once, while the headlights of an oncoming car race toward you at 100 miles an hour. The heat in your body rises in unrelenting waves. Sweat drips. There's no escape. You are center stage in your life; you are utterly and completely exposed.

Not physically naked. Existentially naked.

This nakedness goes deeper than skin, beyond tone, texture, or surface dermal layer. It exposes the raw truth beneath. No mask, no persona, no shield. There is nothing to hide behind. And literally, all the utterly exhausting running, dodging, and sidestepping comes to a halt.

This is vulnerability with a capital V, and it is non-negotiable. Courage accompanies it, full-bodied and alert.

It's as if your psyche splits open, your patterns spill out and lay bare at your feet, and the illusions you've unknowingly built your life upon are exposed.

The gnarly lies that have taken root and lived in your mind rent-free for years, once sneakily shaping your choices and stealing your power, are brought into the light. They don't survive the exposure. They're seen and lovingly evicted.

You face yourself. Entirely.

Safety is the paramount invitation to deep healing work, no matter the type. So is community; being witnessed by loving others as we unravel and restore, as imperfectly perfect humans. This is the brave warrior's journey: a calling to release, to love, to live a little more Heaven on Earth.

For years, I believed that if everyone just "did their work," the world (my world) would feel easier. Simpler. Less exhausting. Kinder. But here's the kicker: their life is theirs.

I've spent a lifetime doing mine; healing, exploring what it means to be a soul in a human body. *Who am I?* has been my constant companion.

In the early days, I thought I was broken. I carried that belief like a quiet weight, convinced I needed fixing. Maybe the Universe had stuffed up. Or maybe it was all the verbal belittling flung at me over the years that stung and stuck, especially for a sensitive, empathic soul.

Now? This exploration feels less like punishment, more like freedom. It's layered, rich, and alive, with infinite curiosity about the wild, precious human experience.

And still, I let others' opinions keep me small. Their judgments left me tiptoeing, walking on eggshells, silenced. I spent decades putting others first, barely noticing how diminished I became.

Wildest of all was the energy I wasted overthinking interactions, obsessing over words they probably never gave a second thought. Anyone else? Here's the raw truth: in some strange way, over-caring made me feel a little superior. If I cared more, I could declare myself "better." But even that came at a cost, as I judged myself for judging. Exhausting, right?

Eventually, I let go of the fantasy that others would invest like I do. Their capacity is theirs. It's not mine to manage or control, and definitely not to carry.

When I finally let that land, I exhaled deeply, an archaic breath I didn't know I held.

That's when I began to put myself first.

Maybe that sounds selfish. I thought so too, initially. But truly, it *is* about me, not in a self-absorbed way, but in a life-giving, boundary-honoring, soul-reviving, hallelujah kind of way.

This is *my* life. I'm the one living it. And you are the one living yours.

I've spent too long accepting less. My natural compassion and humility through over-giving once drained me. Somewhere along the way, I believed my worth was measured by how much I gave, did, endured, and sacrificed. You, too?

No more.

Now, my compassion doesn't cost me myself.

I've learned stronger boundaries.

I've stopped wishing others would meet me.

Instead, I meet myself.

And those who truly want to meet me with reciprocity and depth, they will.

This shift hasn't made me harder. It's given me more room for love, clarity, creativity, and focus. I want that for you, too.

Because putting ourselves last isn't noble—it's a quiet tragedy.

And every woman needs to hear that.

I'm finally okay with putting myself first.

Now it's your turn.

In the spark section that follows, I offer a gentle yet powerful invitation that beckons you toward a joyful opening into your own preciousness and freedom at any age. You're encouraged to stretch gently beyond the familiar, arriving at the edge of your comfort zone with grace, not force or pressure, but a soulful nudge into possibility. Start practicing The Art of Life Sweetness.

THE SPARK

"Be brave, be fierce, be visionary.
Mend the parts of the world that are 'within your reach.'
To strive to live this way is the most dramatic gift
you can ever give to the world."

~ Clarissa Pinkola Estés, Ph.D.

Aging is on our terms. Grey-haired rinses are of a past era. It excites me that, even in my 60s, I'm still growing, learning, and evolving.

Our self-care and self-love are not luxuries; they're the very expression of our life force. So often, we search outside ourselves for the nourishment we crave, believing it'll come from elsewhere. No, you don't have to read evocative poetry in a bodysuit, but challenging yourselves, your mindset, and your fixed ways merits unabashed loving attention—by you.

The truth is: What we seek is already within us.

Life is made of meaningful moments—precious and potent—and when we tend to them with care, they deepen. Routines offer grounding, yes, but it's in stepping beyond the familiar edges that vitality amplifies. I believe we live much of life in practice mode; refining, reshaping, and remembering ourselves, one choice, and one moment at a time.

ART OF LIFE SWEETNESS PRACTICES

Maybe it's time to slow down, deliciously. When I speak of slowing down, I mean with presence, and the subtle awareness of how we use and restore our energy.

In Italy, *la dolce vita* means the sweetness of doing nothing. Yum! And no, I'm not suggesting you sit in a rocking chair just yet.

LIFE SWEETNESS PRACTICE 1: SAVOURING

What if you savoured every single moment, like it truly matters? *Savouring* is a conscious act of choosing presence over pace. We rush through life, barely smelling the roses. When we savour, we become intimate with life's textures, flavours, and sounds, attuning to the whispers of the world and our inner landscape. Our senses, those wild portals of aliveness, invite us to remember that joy isn't a distant goal. It's here, now. And our senses know the way.

Read the following, then try it yourself.

Bring your subtlest awareness to yourself. Make yourself comfortable. You're about to journey through your senses.

Close your eyes. Start with hearing. Listen to nearby sounds. Then stretch to hear what's outside your space. Further still, reach your awareness further outward. Notice tonal qualities, vibrations, and subtleties beneath the sounds.

Now, bring awareness to smell, near and far, and refine it. Feel the air arriving at your nostrils and then leaving.

When you're ready, open your eyes gently. Let your sight softly land on what's around you, not focusing, but inviting in. Allow your gaze to receive. Softly.

Taste can be awakened each day when you sip, eat, or kiss. Stay present to the experience, in all ways.

Now for touch. Feel your clothing against your skin with subtleness and presence. Look down at your hands, and rub the palms slowly across each other. Enjoy this. Your hands are extensions of your heart—precious.

Take this practice with you out into the world on *Wonder Walks*. No phone, no agenda. Let your five senses be your GPS. This walk isn't to get anywhere, but to return to yourself.

LIFE SWEETNESS PRACTICE 2:
SACRED YES, SACRED NO

Each day, choose one sacred yes for your soul (even if small), and one sacred no to something that drains you. Knowing what to add and what to move away from is important. Feel the subtle power in honoring your own rhythm.

LIFE SWEETNESS PRACTICE 3:
PLEASURE PAUSE

Once each day, pause to fully delight in one simple pleasure, intentionally. Pleasure is your birthright. It's not confined to sex, but a 24/7 practice of filling yourself with goodness. True Tantra is presence: *the art of making love to the moment.*

It might be soaking in a warm bath, patting your beloved pet, feeling the breeze brush your cheek, or moving your body to soulful music. The key is to slow down, finely attune, and delight in your senses as guides. Focus on pleasure, delight, and a deepening inner connection to joy.

This is soul medicine.

LIFE SWEETNESS PRACTICE 4:
USE MY FAVOURITE MANTRA

Tender, Tender, Beloved.

Say this mantra often. Let it be a balm; a gentle shift from the long, looping drone of your inner critic. Speak to yourself with the compassion and reverence you've always deserved.

I've created a poem and song inspired by this mantra (link in my bio).

These four practices are an easy starting point, simple and effective. These aren't merely basic practices. The benefits will bear fruit as you use them.

Joy has a different quality than happiness. Happiness comes and goes, often arising from external circumstances. It flutters in on the wings of a good moment, a kind word, a sunny day, an accomplishment, a shared laugh, and just as easily, it drifts away with a change in weather or mood.

But joy—oh, joy is something else entirely.

Joy is a quiet, brilliant ember glowing deep within.

It doesn't rely on applause or timing.

It bubbles up from the soul's depth, freely and unconditionally luminous, like golden sunlight kissing the ocean's surface at just the right angle. Each droplet catches the light, glistening like liquid jewels, riding the wave's crest with effortless elegance and wild delight.

Even in grief or stillness, joy hums beneath the surface, holding a sacred knowing: life, in all its mess and majesty, is worth being fully present for.

In Joy, blessings,

Lulu

Lulu Pearl Trevena is a multi-award-winning author, Soulful Living Coach, retreat leader, and Creatrix of *Live Life with Wonder*. A sacred space holder and truth whisperer, Lulu supports women, especially in midlife and beyond, to reclaim their voice, pleasure, and wise feminine power. Her clients experience emotional release, radiant embodiment, and renewed purpose through quantum healing, shadow work, soulful mentoring, embodied practices, and personalized retreats. Women's Personalized One-to-One Retreats via consultation.

Her published works include the Silver Nautilus award-winning *Soul Blessings*, the *Moments of Transformation* card deck, and the *Epiphany Journal & Playbook*. Lulu is also the visionary behind *Wholehearted Wonder Women 50 Plus*, an international Amazon bestseller and global community.

Wholehearted Wonder Women 50 Plus on Amazon:
https://www.amazon.com/Wholehearted-Wonder-Women-Plus-Confidence/dp/1954047177

All these works are available as soul-nourishing gifts from The Wonder Shop on Etsy, perfect for women ready to remember their feminine magic: https://www.etsy.com/shop/livelifewithwonder/

She invites women to gently shed outdated narratives and awaken to the tender wisdom within. A devoted poet and wonder-seeker, Lulu shares her personal healing anthem: *Tender, Tender, Beloved*, born from the depths of transformation. Listen and receive her song and poem here: https://lulutrevena.live/shop/collage

Explore her writing sanctuary on *Substack, Pearl Lustre with Lulu*, where she shares musings on aging, love, creativity, and devotion to self, open-hearted and deeply reflective with stories and poetry, deepening our shared humanity. Each post is a soft invitation into more soulful living. https://lulutrevena.substack.com/

Lulu lives by the ocean and finds beauty in dawn light, crystal grids, meaningful pauses, creativity, travel, and the medicine of presence. She believes every woman holds the map to her own liberation, and that we are never too "grown-up" for a little wonder.

It's All About Me T-Shirts and Baseball Caps available here: https://livelifewithwonder.com/

Receive your free gift: *Welcome Your Wise Woman*, a sacred download at: https://livelifewithwonder.com/

CHAPTER 16

CREATE YOUR LIFE STORY WITH GRATITUDE ON EVERY PAGE

THE KEY TO MANIFESTING A LIFE YOU LOVE

Jodi DeSantis-Helming, M.S. Ed.

MY STORY

At 2:30 a.m. on February 14, 2015, I experienced a moment that changed the story of my life in an instant. It redefined who I thought I was, shook my entire foundation, and forced me to find a different way to live.

I stood slumped over my kitchen counter, exhausted. I hadn't slept very much over the course of ten days.

The phone rang. It was the cardiologist from Winthrop Hospital. "I am so sorry. . ."

I lay on the kitchen floor, unable to think or move.

This cannot possibly be real. This cannot be happening. He is 47 years old. Eric, my husband, is the greatest dad these two boys could ever ask for. They adore him. We can't lose him. He's the one who is supposed to carry us through our lives- when they go to their prom, when we drop them off for college, when we, maybe someday, walk them down the aisle together as they marry their soulmates. How am I ever going to get through the next year, the next month, the next week, the next day, this next moment? What the hell am I supposed to do now?

After what felt like an eternity, I picked my head up off the floor and wrote—not literally, but in my head. I wrote the story of how my eleven- and twelve-year-old sons and I would proceed from that moment forward.

That story was simple but powerful: *We are okay.*

I said it over and over and over. I said it as I told the horrible news to my sons. I said it out loud to everyone who asked, especially when my children were right next to me, so they knew it too. But I certainly didn't believe it.

How could we be okay? Our lives were turned upside down.

I said it anyway. *We are okay.*

I've said it to myself every day since that dreaded morning. I said it when I took my children to school for the first time since their dad died, as their guidance counselors waited at the school entrance for them. I said it as we sat with the deacon of our church week after week, unsure of exactly what to say to make sense of what had happened, acknowledging that our lives would never be the same again. I said it when the three of us went to Arizona to disperse my husband's ashes on Camelback Mountain, as he asked us to, half joking, one ordinary day back when life felt predictable.

Now, we had to adjust our expectations about how the rest of it was all going to go, what our future would be like, and how we'd relate to one another. We had to come together as a family, no longer the family we thought we'd be, but very much a family nonetheless. We had to learn how to share our feelings, even if that made us uncomfortable. We had to find ways —so many ways —to honor the person who had been the leader of our family. We had to support one another, love each other, and learn how to move forward together in the midst of circumstances that none of us would have or could have ever imagined. Above all, we had to focus on the good in our lives. The story of our lives had changed in an instant, and now we had to rewrite our "script" and create a new story. The only way I knew how to do this was to:

1. Create a new story that would allow us to move forward (and maybe even thrive!).
2. Begin and end each day focused on what was still good in our lives, what we still had, and the blessings in front of us.

A year and a half after my husband passed, my older son, Logan, began attending high school. On the first day of school, I brought him there, to the same school where my husband had taught social studies for 16 years. This is why we decided to move to this community, so that he could look after his two sons as a teacher when they got to "the big house," as the high school was called. Now, suddenly, this became the high school that lost one of their most beloved teachers, the high school where Logan would now have to carry on, the high school where his dad was supposed to be, but wasn't.

"Have a good day, Logan," I said, swallowing the tears trying so desperately to be released. "I love you."

In that moment, in front of the school building, the moment I waved goodbye to Logan, the moment I had to let go and trust, I knew one thing. Our new story was true. We would be okay—somehow. And I think Logan knew it, too. At least that's what I told myself as I drove away and said a prayer of strength and hope for both of us.

Even in the face of unthinkable tragedy, we can make a moment-to-moment decision to choose joy. We're not the ones in control of the circumstances of our lives. What we have in our power is to control where our thoughts take us, how we speak to others, how we speak to ourselves, what we say, how we narrate the story of our lives, and where we place our energy and our focus. This is what I came to realize. This is what I did to make it through the biggest challenge of my life. I rewrote my family's story script, with gratitude at the forefront of every page.

THE SPARK

STEP 1: CREATE THE STORY OF YOUR LIFE, REVISING WHENEVER NECESSARY.

If you begin to pay close attention to the way people speak, you'll notice people tend to tell the same story day after day, even year after year. For example, I have a colleague at work whom I have known for 21 years. Each time something goes wrong for her, she says, "It figures. I always have bad luck." I have a friend who is constantly saying, "I am so overwhelmed!" On the other hand, one of my other colleagues is constantly asking herself: "Who has it better than I do?"

In this way, people tend to use their stories to define themselves. For example, if someone decides, "I have difficulty in romantic relationships," then he'll expect to fail before even giving a relationship a fair chance. Rather than being open to all possibilities, he will label himself as someone who starts to have a negative experience as soon as his relationships get serious. I even saw a vanity license plate once that read: HARD2LUV. This is the story that a person chose to tell herself and others on a daily basis.

The words and phrases we use have a powerful impact on the way we frame our experiences, and consequently, how we experience life in general. If we're interested in creating real change in our lives, the stories we tell ourselves and those we tend to share with other people may be the best place to start. As you become aware of "the story of your life" that you seem to be repeating, you can replace it with the story you'd like to see become part of your new reality.

Guiding Question:

What new story do I want to tell about my life?

When To Use This Strategy:

Use this strategy when the story you tell yourself day after day is no longer helping to move your life forward, but instead is holding you back.

What To Do:

1. Begin to notice the type of language you use when you recount events that happen in your daily life. Do you use positive or negative words and phrases? Do you say things like, "It was awful, horrible, horrendous," or do you more frequently say, "It was awesome, amazing, wonderful?" What is the "story" that you consistently tell people? Do you say that you always have bad luck, or that you just cannot seem to lose weight, or that you are not smart/good/talented enough to get that promotion?

    One of the most effective ways to identify your story is to document in a journal the words, phrases, and expressions you use when you're in conversations with people. Do this for seven days in a row. If you're not sure, ask people who spend a great deal of time with you what your favorite expression seems to be or what words and phrases you tend to repeat most often. You may be surprised at what you discover!

2. If the language you use tends to be negative, it's likely that you're holding yourself back from living your best life possible. Turn your story around. Start saying the opposite. When you change the language you use, your thoughts change accordingly, and so will what shows up in your life on a daily basis. For example, instead of telling yourself, "I don't really have what it takes to be the director of my department," say, "I have so many qualities that would make me an outstanding leader." Instead of saying, "I always have bad luck," say, "Good fortune seems to follow me wherever I go." Observe how your circumstances begin to change as a result of the story you are telling yourself.

3. Remember to post your new story everywhere you tend to look—on your phone, on your refrigerator, and on the bathroom mirror. Tell your new story throughout the day, both to yourself and when you have conversations with other people. It'll help you change the way you think about the circumstances of your life, and as a result, those circumstances will change for the better. Document in your journal how telling your new story makes you feel.

Affirmation:

I have the power to create the story of my life.

Most Important Point:

Our lives are reflections of the stories we tell ourselves every day. Tell yourself a story that makes you feel good.

STEP 2: SAY THANK YOU–FOR ALL OF IT.

"There are two ways to live your life. One is as though nothing is a miracle. The other is as though everything is a miracle."

~ Albert Einstein

The Law of Attraction states that "like attracts like," or in other words, whatever you focus on will expand. When you wish for something you don't have, and focus on the fact that you don't have it (like a great deal of money), you come from a place of lack. The Universe will respond to the lack. On the other hand, when you focus on the abundance you already have in your life (however small it may seem at the time) and express genuine appreciation for it, the Universe continues to deliver more and more blessings to you in that area of your life, whether it be your finances, career, health, or love relationships.

Guiding Question:

How can gratitude enable me to attract more of what I want in my life and less of what I don't want?

When To Use This Strategy:

Use this strategy when you feel sorry for yourself, when you feel the need to get back to counting your blessings, or when you find yourself comparing yourself to others and coming up short.

What To Do:

Start what I call a *Miracles Notebook*. Buy a beautiful notebook and decorate it with pictures of everything you love. Take it wherever you go and begin to document three miracles that occur each day. I explain this idea further in my first book, *Take Three Miracles and Call Me in the Morning*. A miracle, or a fortunate event or interaction, can be small and simple. You found the car keys you were looking for. The gift you needed to give your friend for her birthday arrived at your doorstep just in time, right before you left for her birthday party. The meeting for which you weren't quite as prepared as you would've liked was cancelled by your boss at the last minute.

As you begin to observe and document three miracles each day, the miracles you experience on a daily basis will expand. Soon, the seemingly small miracles will turn into grander ones, like: You got the promotion you wished for. Your beautiful baby niece was born on time and healthy. The loving relationship you imagined finally comes into your life.

When you look for miracles all around you, both big and small, miracles become an increasingly larger part of your everyday life. Remember, what you focus on will expand, in much the same way that when you look for red cars on the road, red cars are seemingly everywhere. Use this strategy to focus on the good in your life each day and bring more of all that is good to you.

Affirmation:

I acknowledge and appreciate all the blessings in my life.

Most Important Point:

Say thank you, not only for the blessings right in front of you, but also for those on their way to you. You can even imagine what it feels like to have those blessings already. Focus on what's good in your life and watch your blessings expand.

Final note:

The loss of my husband was devastating to our family. It changed the story of our lives. It changed how it was all supposed to go. But we found a way. We found a way to rewrite our script, finding gratitude each day for what is still good, for what we have, and for the beauty and the blessings that are very much a part of our lives. We found a way to choose joy each and every day, even if just for a moment. And you can, too.

Jodi DeSantis-Helming is a workshop leader, author, mother of two boys, teacher, and life coach. She has been a nationally board-recognized educator, as well as an educational coach and mentor, in the Mineola School District for 35 years. She has written and published two books, *Take Three Miracles and Call Me in the Morning*, and *The Life You Have Ordered Is Currently Out of Stock*, and numerous magazine columns, such as one titled *The Positive Thinker's Toolkit*. She has been a guest on many podcasts and shows, including the WHPC radio show called Just Relationships and @DoctorNursesRock, a YouTube show with Patty Hodge. She also hosts her own show, *Sunday Night Serenity*, which airs each Sunday night at 7 p.m. (https://us02web.zoom.us/j/81965166790). She conducts workshops and retreats on topics such as:

- Living a grateful life.
- Developing resilience and grit.
- Taking care of yourself, for caretakers and those who tend to place other people's needs ahead of their own.
- Using the Law of Attraction to identify what you want and to bring more of it into your life.

The sign outside her house reads, "Where there is love, there are always miracles."

She offers her workshops nationwide, both in-person and virtually. This is the link to the Gratitude Resources that she has compiled for her workshops. It includes helpful resources for you to use as you continue your gratitude journey.

Connect with Jodi:

Phone: (516) 675-1613

Email: jodidesantis13@gmail.com

Facebook: https://www.facebook.com/jodi.desantis.helming.2025

CHAPTER 17

FROM BURNOUT TO BLISS

THE BODY'S SIMPLE PATH BACK TO JOY

Dr. Heather Robertson, DC

MY STORY

Have you ever finished your day—successfully having crossed every item off your list, answered every email, met every demand—only to collapse on the couch a shell of yourself, running on fumes? You're tired, but not the kind that sleep fixes; you're hungry, but nothing looks appealing. You're thirsty, so you reach for your water bottle, but as you drink, an unsettling thought whispers: *This isn't what I am thirsty for at all.*

I know that feeling intimately. I remember the exact day my own gentle whisper became a deafening roar, the day I didn't just question what I was thirsty for, I found myself completely paralyzed by the answer. My body finally called it. After years of running on caffeine and cortisol, it was done. There I was, 48 years old, sprawled on the floor like a discarded coat.

My phone buzzed with another urgent something. But in this moment, every sound felt distant in comparison to the deafening voices now loudly present in my head, *You're failing*, sneered a familiar voice, *and everybody knows it.* My mouth tasted like stale coffee and the unspoken "nos" I swallowed over the years. My water bottle sat three feet away, full and waiting. I couldn't move to grab it. Not because I was lazy or tired, but because my thirst ran deeper. I was parched for purpose, starved for joy, and dying for a life that wasn't a long, exhausting game of Whack-a-Mole.

And on that floor, for the first time, I finally listened.

What did I hear in this profound moment of forced self-reflection? Here I was, consciously taking the time to be in tune with what was happening in my body. The sound was not enlightenment; it was the frantic screech of a body that had become a smoke detector with a dying battery. You know the sound: it's a wailing cry of something that kept fulfilling its purpose but accepting defeat at 3 a.m., and there you are waving a towel at it, begging for five more minutes of peace. For years, I fanned the smoke of my own burnout while my body screamed the alarm. I felt overwhelmed before—a business owner and busy mom handling life's stuff as it piled up—but this was different. My hormones jumped ship years ago, leaving me a puffy, rage-filled, sleep-deprived ghost of myself. My old coping tools—the deep breaths, morning walks, green smoothies—all rusted under an avalanche of to-do lists.

So, this time, I didn't get up. I didn't meditate, journal, or call a friend. I just stayed down. I let the cold hardwood floor seep into my back. I watched a dust bunny tremble under the floor vent. I listened to my own ragged breath, not trying to change it. In that surrender, a terrifying but liberating thought hit me:

Rock bottom isn't where dreams go to die. It's just the universe finally getting your attention. It's where your body, tired of the nonsense, hands you a map and says, 'Let's go a different way.'

I'll be honest, I didn't love the map at first. It wasn't a ticket to a bright, shiny new world; it was a guidebook to a descent—a quiet, inner excavation of everything that led me to that floor. My journey from burnout to bliss wasn't a triumphant rise; it was an unlearning.

So, I began the excavation. I traded high-intensity workouts for lying in the grass, feeling the sun on my eyelids. I called it "Vitamin D Therapy," but it was really permission to be simple.

I traded my hurried green smoothies for real meals I would actually savour. I allowed myself to nap without apology.

And it felt agonizingly slow and deeply unproductive. And of course, the critic in my head had a field day. *You're being lazy*, it sneered. *You're wasting precious time.*

But a miracle happened. As I stubbornly committed to this stillness, a quieter voice, one I hadn't heard since childhood, began to pipe up over the critic's rant. It was the voice that noticed how the steam from my tea curled in the morning light. It was the sensation of a genuine smile when my dog rested his chin in my lap. These weren't grand moments of joy; they were tiny, biological flickers. My cells sent up a different signal—not an alarm, but a quiet, persistent *Yes! This! More of this, please.*

Those biological embers I ignored began to glow, steadily weaving themselves into the fabric of my days. The bliss I found wasn't a roaring bonfire; it was a quiet, durable warmth. It was the soft hum of contentment as I stirred oatmeal on a quiet morning. It was the unexpected thrill of a cool breeze after years of being too busy to feel it. It was joking with my boys and actually hearing the laughter, not just rushing past to the next task. This new joy didn't need to be deserved or earned. It was simply there, a low-grade current of peace available whenever I tuned in.

And then, the fog began to lift. I didn't forget the secrets to joy; I was simply speaking the wrong language. I used the vocabulary of achievement in an attempt to converse with my soul, a hopeless translation error. You can't think your way into a feeling any more than you can read a recipe and call it a meal. Joy isn't a thought. It's a biological celebration. It's the chemistry of safety humming in your neurotransmitters, the rhythm of balance in your hormones, and the sacred quiet of a nervous system that knows the work is done.

I looked back and saw the truth: my deep breaths and morning walks hadn't rusted. I was just using them wrong. I tried to pour premium fuel into a broken-down car, hoping it would magically fix the engine. But a deep breath isn't fuel for the grind; it's a celebration of the pause. It's a direct memo to your vagus nerve: *The hunt is over. The coast is clear. We are safe.* My walk wasn't a step count; it was a sensory feast. It became about savouring the impossible pink of a sunset, hearing the rhythm of my own footsteps as a drumbeat of aliveness, feeling the air in my lungs as a conversation with life itself.

This was the greatest unlock: my body was never the problem. It was the wisest guide I had, the most loving protector. Its exhaustion wasn't a failure; it was a fierce and final act of love, a divine intervention staged by my own soul to save me from a path it never agreed to. My burnout wasn't a breakdown. It was the breakthrough of a lifetime. The life I built on "should" and "must" had to crumble. I had to detach from the imposter that had slowly taken over my senses. It wasn't a destruction, but a necessary demolition to make space for the life my soul had been whispering about all along—a life that could expand and fully breathe.

The secrets to living my best life aren't locked in a seminar I attended or a book I read. They were etched into my very DNA, waiting for me to get so quiet and so desperate that I finally read the instructions written on my own cells. And I want you to know, the same is true for you. Your map was never hidden.

Your story begins with this single, liberating truth: Your best life isn't out there. It's in here. It's in the dopamine kissing your synapses when you dance in your kitchen for no reason. It's in the way your nervous system sighs when you take a deep breath without a deadline. It's in your gut microbes throwing a party when you eat something that truly delights you.

This is the untold story of transformation. Your fatigue isn't a life sentence; it's the prologue. Your joy is the plot twist, and every cell in your body is a co-author begging you to turn the page.

Science calls this homeostasis. Poets call it belonging. Your body calls it Monday. Because here's the truth that no textbook can teach you: healing is not a destination you reach; it's a posture you practice.

Every time you choose to stand as if your dreams are already true, your spine murmurs, *Finally!*

Every time you rest without apology, your adrenals weep with gratitude. Every time you move toward what sets your soul on fire, you aren't just being positive, you're conducting a neurochemical symphony of bliss.

The world doesn't need a more perfect, polished version of you. The world needs this version, the one whose biology has stopped begging and started celebrating. You've already survived the hardest part: your moment on the floor. The moment you realized the life you were living was too small for the soul inside you.

Now, I want you to try something. Reach out to the part of you that still feels hunched under the weight of "not yet" and tell them this: "Your bones are wiser than you think. Your bowl is deeper than you know. Your body has been waiting your whole life to rise—not for glory, but for joy."

Here is the secret your bones have known all along: You don't have to fix yourself to start living. Your body isn't broken, it's brilliant. That stiffness? It's a nudge toward movement. That exhaustion? It's a love letter begging for rest. Even if your anxiety is just your ancient biology whispering, *Hey, let's rewrite this story together.*

You don't need a guru. You just need to listen inward. The rhythm of healing is already within you, a rhythm of listening, responding, and sometimes dancing like no one is watching.

Every boundary you set rewires your neural pathways for self-respect. Every risk you take in the name of joy floods your system with courage. Every moment you choose curiosity over judgment assures your cells that *we are safe.*

Your cells are alchemists, turning your courage into chemistry. Your spine remembers its strength. Your breath can calm your storm. Your joy is not a reward for being good; it's your natural state, waiting to be uncovered.

Your body has been waiting for you. Not with judgment, but with an invitation. An invitation to rise. Not for anyone else, but for the absolute joy of it.

So, this story isn't about the breakdown. It's about the blueprint I discovered in the rubble.

My burnout forced me to strip away the layers of complexity that I had built my career on: the perfect protocols, the endless research, and every complicated strategy. I had to unlearn my own expertise; what remained were the essentials: breath, water, food, movement.

The shocking truth? The same body that brought me to my knees held the exact instructions for my liberation. I didn't need a complex formula; I needed to learn the native language of my own biology, a language spoken not in words, but in sensation, rhythm, and ease.

I discovered that joy isn't a distant destination to be reached. It's a biological state to be nurtured, moment by moment. And the master keys were the very things I always overlooked as too basic: the breath I took for granted, the water I ignored, the food I inhaled without tasting.

And if I, a doctor of wellness, an expert in health who lost her way, could find the path back to myself through these simple acts, I'm absolutely certain you can, too.

Our cells are not just vessels for life; they're conduits for joy. And we access that joy not by doing more, but by being fearlessly and fully, right here, right now. Ready to turn those sparks into a lasting flame? Let me share the simple, powerful tools that will light your path.

THE SPARK

Now, how do we go from knowing it to living it? We start with the fundamentals. I've distilled my journey into four core practices we will call "Sparks." These aren't just items on another wellness checklist. They're revolutions that reprogram your body from the inside out, shifting your cellular environment from survival to joy. Let's ignite them.

1. The Spark of Breath – The Remote Control for Your Nervous System

We think of breathing as automatic, yet it's the only automatic function we can take charge of at will. This is the direct line to the vagus nerve, the commander of our 'rest and digest' system. When we're stressed, we take shallow, chesty breaths that tell our body we're still in danger. This keeps cortisol high, flooding our system with the chemistry of crisis. It's an exhausting emergency state that we were never meant to sustain long-term. But we can reclaim control in a matter of seconds.

So:

THE RESET BREATH

Inhale deeply through your nose, then take one more sharp sip of air to inflate the lungs fully. Hold for three seconds. Slowly exhale through your mouth. Do this twice. Feel the shift? That is you, sending a direct message of safety to your nervous system.

2. The Spark of Water – The Internal Bath for Your Cells

Hydration isn't just about quenching thirst. Every biochemical reaction, including the production of energy and the feel-good neurotransmitters, happens in water. Dehydrated cells are sluggish, inflamed, and unable to communicate joy. Water is movement. Our bodies are mostly made up of water. It keeps our blood flowing, our joints lubricated, our muscles limber, and our lymph ready for action. It's the juice of life.

Remember my water bottle just out of reach? I was the living embodiment of a dehydrated cell—sluggish, shut down, and utterly unable to connect to the flow of life.

So:

THE FIRST GLASS

Your first act of the day: drink a full glass of water before you touch your phone. This isn't a demand on your system; it's a gift to your cells, replenishing what was lost overnight and setting a tone of nourishment for the day.

- **Pro-Tip:** Keep a bottle with you as you work. Try sipping water before your morning coffee or afternoon slump. You might find it's a more effective boost.

3. The Spark of Mindful Eating – The Ritual of Receiving

Eating under stress activates the sympathetic nervous system (fight or flight), which actually shuts down digestion. You could be eating the most organic salad with the best ingredients, but if you're scarfing it down in a distracted rush, your body interprets that as a stressor, not fuel. Food shouldn't be just calories in for energy out. We overlook its power to truly nourish us. Real healing begins when we stop feeding the patterns that got us into trouble in the first place.

So:

SLOW FOOD IS GOOD FOOD

For one meal a day, just eat—no phone, no screen, no book. Put your fork down between bites. Chew. Taste. This isn't just eating; it's a practice in receiving the goodness the world has to offer. It tells your body, "We are safe. We can enjoy this." Absorb it, digest it, incorporate it into the cellular symphony that is happening inside.

4. The Spark of Joyful Movement – Wiggle Your Way to Joy

One of the most effective tools for shaking off the weight of the day is also the simplest: dance. Why does it work? Because rhythmic, spontaneous movement to music you love is a triple threat against stagnation. First, it disrupts stagnant energy physically, literally shaking you out of a frozen, stressed posture. Second, it forces diaphragmatic breathing as you move and maybe even sing, which immediately signals safety to your vagus nerve. And third, it floods your system with endorphins and dopamine, not because you earned them with a grueling workout, but because you simply gave yourself permission to play. It's a neural cheat code for joy, accessible anytime, no special equipment required.

So:

KITCHEN DANCE PARTY

Ten minutes, three songs: Your only job is to move—tap your toes, click your heels, wiggle those hips, line-dance, tap-dance, tango, twist, or do the hustle. It's a chance to evict the critic in your head and come home to the joyful, rhythmic intelligence of your own body.

Now, we have arrived at the simplest, most radical truth: this isn't optimism; it's biology. The path to your best life isn't paved with punishment; it's built cell by cell, choice by choice, in the quiet moments when you finally choose to listen.

Remember, these tools—the breath, the water, the mindful bite, the kitchen dance—are not tasks on a checklist. This is a practice. This is the daily, sacred work of your cells; it's how you build a life of joy from the inside out. You're not doing these things to get joy. In the mindful doing of them, you're embodying joy. By speaking the primal language of your cells, you're telling them that it's safe to be alive, be vibrant, and be truly, deeply well.

Your assignment is to realize you were never a project to fix, but a living invitation to softness. Your lesson is to drink when you're thirsty, rest when you're weary, and move towards what makes you feel truly alive.

Your body has been waiting, not for perfection, but for partnership. Let joy be the tide you float on, not the shore you struggle toward.

Dr. Heather Robertson is a health professional, guide, and mother on a mission to rewrite the story of modern wellness. She is a chiropractor and wellness coach who specializes in the innate intelligence that guides all healing and provides a roadmap for joyful living.

She has found simple yet powerful ways to empower people to live their best and healthiest lives. Her own journey has taught her that true healing isn't just about aligning spines, but about aligning one's life with purpose, passion, and presence. She now merges her deep clinical understanding of the body with the soul-level coaching to help her clients discover that the fuel for their best life is written into their very biology. Her work is a unique blend of somatic science, cellular wisdom, and practical spirituality, designed to move you from exhaustion to expression.

Beyond her professional credentials, Dr. Heather Robertson's greatest teachers are her two sons. Being their mom has given her a fierce commitment to modeling a life of vibrant well-being, not just teaching it. Watching them embark on their own journeys to make the world a better place is her greatest inspiration and a constant reminder that healing ourselves is the first and most powerful step toward healing our world.

She is the creator of the popular and successful In8 Wellness Program, and her insights have been shared in publications, seminars, and corporate workshops.

You can experience her transformative work through her live workshops, dive deeper in her 1:1 mentoring programs, or begin your journey with her free resources.

Connect with Dr. Heather:

Dr. Heather Robertson–Chiropractor, Thunder Bay, Ontario, Canada

Read my blog, discover my programs, subscribe to my newsletter:

Website: www.innatrisalus.com

Facebook: http://www.facebook.com/in8wellnessIn8

Instagram: http://www.instagram.com/in8wellness

Watch me on YouTube: In8Wellness:
https://www.youtube.com/channel/UCFwDvHFwPAwiTozIU_BmTPg

CHAPTER 18

AGING JOYFULLY

YOUR MOST AUTHENTIC AND FULFILLED LIFE IS YET TO COME

Tina Marie Romero, MBA, MA Diplomacy & Intl Relations

"What if growing older isn't about slowing down—but finally waking up?
Imagine shedding the pressure to prove, please, or pretend, and stepping
into a season where joy isn't earned—it's embraced.
Aging isn't the end of your story; it's the long-awaited beginning
of your truest, most authentic chapter yet. The best version of you isn't
behind you—It's the new adventure you're about to write."

~ Anonymous

MY STORY

October 2020. At the age of 50, at the height of a pandemic, my business partner and I were set to sell our franchise homecare business. Signing the purchase agreement meant that, in only six years, I had made ten times my initial investment. It meant I was financially secure to take a break until I figured out what was next. It meant I was free to reinvent myself and pursue new dreams.

More so, it meant relief from the mounting challenges of a homecare business: severe nationwide labor shortage, numerous state and federal regulations, increased COVID costs and requirements, 30-50% decline in business, shrinking margins, and so on. There were only cons glaring in bright headlights.

And yet, my intuition was yelling something else. I found myself unsettled, anxious, and confused. My heart was whispering something different than what my head was set to do.

"How can I give up the one thing I thought was my life's purpose?" My heart whispered.

I am just getting started. I still have so much more to accomplish with this business.

Although I asked my trusted circle for advice, I realized I needed guidance most from myself. So, I drove six-plus hours to Massachusetts for a weeklong silent retreat.

Situated on the coast of the Atlantic Ocean about an hour's drive northeast of Boston and noted for the spectacular beauty of its rocks, ocean, and woods, Eastern Point Retreat House was the perfect place for me to contemplate and nourish my soul. The natural beauty and silence all around took me to the depths of my heart, where my soul needed me to be.

On my sixth day of silence, I lay flat on top of a large rock, listened to giant waves crashing against its sharp edges, looked up to the clear blue sky, and inhaled a crisp, cool breeze. I closed my eyes, took a long breath, and heard my answer loud and clear:

It's not time to sell. You need to keep the business and buy out your business partner.

"But how? I don't have the money. Can I do this on my own? It was hard enough doing this with a partner, why would I want to do this alone?" I questioned myself.

Because the best version of you is yet to emerge.

I was instantly reminded of my favorite Paulo Coelho quote, "When you want something, all the universe conspires in helping you to achieve it."

You don't need to have answers now. You'll figure it out along the way. I'll be right there with you.

I stood up and started walking barefoot on the sand. As I turned around, my footprints in the sand caught my eye, and this verse spoke out loud to me: "The times when you have seen only one set of footprints, my child, is when I carried you."

A warm breeze wrapped around me. I felt light as a feather, as if I was literally being carried and held by the wind. The confusion I felt six days ago vanished, replaced by an immense peace and clarity that now consumed me.

I can go home now.

The buyout was a million-dollar decision that changed the trajectory of my life. The truth is, my life literally began at fifty. I started living by intention and stopped living by expectations. Life didn't slow down. It sharpened, deepened, and finally became authentically mine.

Five years later, I made more money than ever, bought my dream condo in Manhattan, co-authored two Amazon #1 bestselling books, walked on the New York Fashion Week runway, was on a billboard in Times Square, featured in several publications, interviewed on TV, and had many more once-in-a-lifetime opportunities I never dreamt of.

I'm now living the life of my dreams while successfully running my business as a sole proprietor. Additionally, I am on the advisory board of a homecare industry association and on the board of directors of a nonprofit where I co-curate exhibits at our art gallery.

Despite my added responsibilities, I get immense fulfillment from these volunteer roles. What surprised me most is that these additional roles have not stopped me from consistently going to the gym and playing pickleball five times a week. I discovered that when you nourish and activate your soul, it leads you to your life's purpose, and everything aligns beautifully.

I have a full life, yet I'm never too busy for anything or anyone who brings me joy, because everything I do now is intentional. I'm excited every day knowing the best is yet to come. I'm finally living life on *my* terms, and I want to help you do the same by sharing my SPARK medicine, which got me to where I am today in only five years.

THE SPARK

In my younger years, I was *always busy*, traveling restlessly, attending events due to FOMO, doing things because it was the cool thing to do, and always chasing the next thing on my endless to-do list.

My life was dictated by expectations. I accomplished everything I thought the world expected of me, until that turning point in my life, one October afternoon, lying on top of a rock after six days of silence. That was the first time I made a decision not because of expectations but because I gave my soul the space to breathe, which led me to my next step.

S – SOUL. NURTURE YOUR SOUL.

"Soul, set the worries of this world aside, and allow yourself to soar like a bird on the wind. Listen to the whispers of your Creator calling gently to you, inviting you to remember that just as the body needs food, so too your soul needs to be nourished."

~ Matthew Kelly

Spirituality plays a crucial role in aging joyfully because it provides a sense of meaning, connection, and peace—especially during a time of life often marked by change, reflection, and sometimes loss.

I went to a Catholic school from kindergarten to high school. This foundation solidified my deep faith in God, who created me for a purpose. I consider it a privilege to be alive. My duty every day is to fulfill my life's purpose and reach my highest potential.

Having that faith, however, is vain without the wisdom to discern my life's next steps. It's a universal truth that "We are always one decision away from changing our lives." This is why it's important to take time to nourish our souls so we can hear what it's trying to tell us and help us make wise decisions.

Whatever it is you believe in—God, Nature, Buddha, etc, take some time to be still, and listen. You don't need to go on a weeklong silent retreat. Meditate, pray, go on long walks, write; do something that allows you to slow down, block the noise, and hear your soul speak.

These simple practices are essential when making big decisions, but they can also offer comfort, reduce anxiety, and help us cope with grief, illness, or uncertainty. They foster acceptance and peace with life's transitions.

Studies suggest that spiritual practices are linked to better mental health, lower stress, and even improved physical outcomes. People who feel spiritually fulfilled often experience more joy and gratitude—key ingredients for a happy life.

Spirituality encourages reflection on one's life, values, and contributions. It supports the process of aging as an opportunity for wisdom-sharing, forgiveness, and leaving a meaningful legacy.

Find a spiritual passage or quote that moves your soul and let it carry you through life's ups and downs. Mine has accompanied me all throughout my life's journey: *For I know the plans I have for you, declares the Lord, plans to prosper you and not to harm you, plans to give you hope and a future.* ~ Jeremiah 29:11

P − PHYSICAL. KEEP MOVING.

"The greatest wealth is health."

~ Virgil

Physical activity is like a joy amplifier for aging—it doesn't just extend life; it enhances the quality of that life. Walk, run, swim, dance, bike—do what feels good to you and commit to moving your body every day. Physical activity keeps joints flexible and reduces stiffness. It's not about performance; it's about vitality.

If there's one valuable lesson I learned from serving seniors for more than a decade now, this is it. When clients say, "I'd rather die now," it's usually because they can no longer move around on their own. Sadly, they have all the money to spend but can no longer enjoy it.

It's never too late to start exercising. I wasn't athletic growing up. I never ran, was a bad swimmer, and feared biking on open roads. In my thirties, I got my first road bike and signed up for America's Most Beautiful Bike Ride, a 100-mile century ride around Lake Tahoe. That started my romance with physical activity, training, endurance, nutrition, and goal setting. To date, I've completed several Olympic-distance triathlons, a Spartan Trifecta, the New York Marathon, and numerous races.

Physical activity and exercise are key ingredients for a fulfilling, vibrant life as we age. They release endorphins and other feel-good chemicals. Whenever I start feeling stressed, I go to the gym, play pickleball, or simply go for a walk. By doing this, I automatically change my mood and preserve my inner joy.

"Don't wait for a fall before you call" is a slogan we use in my homecare business. Stronger muscles and better balance reduce the risk of falling. Being physically capable allows us to continue doing the things we love and age joyfully—travelling, volunteering, gardening, playing with grandkids, etc.

You don't need to be athletic to stay active. Join a walking group, take a dance lesson, or a group exercise class. These activities keep you moving and provide social connections that bring so much joy as we age. Movement leads to more energy, better sleep, and a more positive outlook. We shape our physical independence in the future by doing the groundwork now.

A – ATTITUDE. ACCEPT THAT LIFE COMES WITH PROBLEMS.

Attitude is everything.

A good attitude doesn't change the fact that we age—but it changes how we experience it. Instead of merely "getting old," we can live fully and age joyfully.

The most important shift I made in my fifties was to accept that being alive comes with only one certainty—I will always have problems. I learned not to ask "WHY" storms come, but instead to ask "WHEN" and be ready for their unexpected arrival.

Being well-prepared builds resilience and fosters strategic thinking. It gives clarity and mental calm in the face of uncertainty. Having a plan breaks complex tasks into manageable steps, minimizes wasted effort, and enables smarter decisions under pressure.

2024 was my hardest year in business. I fired my scheduler and failed six times with replacements, and another office staff member retired. I worked tirelessly for almost an entire year, led migration to our new scheduling software, and was on call 24/7.

My positive attitude enabled me to handle this difficult phase with calm and grace. Despite all the odds stacked against me, I thrived, somehow achieving year-over-year revenue growth and receiving an Operations All-Star award at our 2024 franchise conference.

Acceptance of the "certainty of problems" brings calm, control, and strength. It encourages flexible thinking, making us better equipped to pivot when things go off course. This adaptability strengthens our ability to bounce back from setbacks.

So, whether you're preparing for life's everyday hurdles or extreme emergencies, aging joyfully is not about expecting the worst—it's about having the right attitude and being ready to face life's twists with a big smile, wisdom, and confidence.

R – RELATIONSHIPS. SURROUND YOURSELF WITH PEOPLE WHO BRING YOU JOY.

"You are the average of the five people you spend the most time with."

~ Jim Roth

Healthy relationships bring joy, connection, and vitality—the key ingredients to not just aging well, but aging joyfully. They're the emotional glue that holds well-being together as life evolves. But the keyword is *healthy*.

Mindfully choosing only healthy relationships and setting boundaries are essential. We can deny it all we want, but the reality is that as we age, we no longer have the same energy we had in our twenties.

You have limited time and energy every day, so you need to guard your energy fiercely. This means being intentional about who you invest it with. This sends a message to yourself (and others) that you matter. Your confidence and sense of worth increase when you stop overextending yourself.

By saying no to anyone or anything that doesn't bring you joy, you get more time and energy for your passions, goals, and people who uplift you. It helps minimize overwhelm and confusion. You think more clearly when you're not mentally drained by unnecessary drama. You bring your best, most energized self to your connections.

Positivity attracts others. Choose to surround yourself with people who share your values and joyful attitude. You don't need hundreds of friends who drain your energy.

K – KNOWLEDGE. KEEP LEARNING.

"Once you stop learning, you start dying."

~ Henry Ford

Running an accredited and state-licensed homecare agency requires continuing education on state and federal regulations, best practices, legal issues, in-services, homecare trends, employment practices, new technology, and many more, to be in compliance and keep my business acumen sharp.

Lifelong learning necessary to age joyfully isn't just about knowledge—it's about keeping your mind, body, and spirit engaged with life. It feeds curiosity and creativity, leading to a richer, more fulfilling life.

Many people like me discover new passions or hobbies later in life. I played pickleball for the first time last year and fell in love with it. I was hooked, but unfortunately, I was bad at it. I lost every match, but instead of giving up, I showed up every day and sought mentors to teach me.

Thank goodness I'm not as bad now as when I started. I'm committed to learning and getting better, so I allocate time for it in my daily schedule. Playing relaxes my mind after a stressful workday and changes my mood since doing something we love releases dopamine, the feel-good hormone.

Learning new skills stimulates our brains and can improve memory and cognitive function. It increases focus and discipline. This is why starting a new hobby is important as we age. Hobbies give structure and meaning to our free time, and ultimately a sense of purpose.

When I was offered a board position in our homecare industry association, I felt inadequate since I didn't have any board experience. Nonetheless, I welcomed the opportunity to learn from my peers. I asked questions and tried my best to understand our advocacies and issues we were tackling. I later became treasurer of the association's PAC (political action committee), which was another role that required me to learn a whole new world of political fundraising.

It was even more daunting when I stepped into a working board of directors role with the task of curating art exhibits. I do not have any gallery experience or an art background, so this was a challenge for me, but I welcomed the opportunity to learn something new and hone my creativity. This role has given me so much joy and newfound art appreciation. Conceptualizing a new art exhibit every quarter keeps my mind creative. My interaction with numerous artists provides immeasurable value and knowledge.

The world around us changes rapidly. To stay current, we need to be open to learning new technologies, cultural shifts, and economic developments. This is essential as we age in order to stay connected and engaged in society.

Joyful aging is the opposite of stagnation. It's never too late to learn something new or start a new hobby. The brain remains capable of change (neuroplasticity) throughout life. The more we challenge it, the more it grows.

I never thought I'll have so much joy being a "pickler" in my fifties and enjoy playing with seniors (some even in their seventies). It makes my heart jump for joy to see them learn something new and age so joyfully. The good news is, so can you using my SPARK!

Tina Marie Romero is an aging expert passionate about helping others age joyfully, grow bolder, and reinvent themselves so they can live their most authentic and fulfilled lives.

As CEO of Synergy Homecare of North Central New Jersey for more than a decade, she has helped families by providing compassionate caregivers for anyone so they can stay and die at home with dignity and independence. Her agency grew from zero to seven figures in less than three years and has consistently received Best of Homecare of Choice and Caring Star Service Excellence Awards.

Uprooting herself from the Philippines in 1995, Tina reinvented herself from a fearful undocumented worker without a voice into a seven-figure businesswoman employing 100+ immigrants, a board member collaborating with business leaders, and a lobbyist advocating for seniors. She is also a cancer survivor whose recovery propelled her to be a triathlete, marathoner, Spartan trifecta finisher, yogi, and dancer.

A two-time international bestselling author, Tina hopes to help people age joyfully by using SPARK as a medicine that made her fifties the most authentic and fulfilled chapter of her life.

When not helping seniors, you will find Tina at the pickleball court, working out at the gym, or drinking champagne by the water at sunset.

Connect with Tina:

Linktree: https://linktr.ee/tinamarieromero

Website: https://synergyhomecare.com/nj-piscataway-08854

LinkedIn: https://www.linkedin.com/in/tinamarieromero/

CHAPTER 19

REPARENT YOURSELF

THE KEY TO INFINITE JOY

Julie Goldberg, Energy Healer, ICF Certified Coach

MY STORY

Everything changed when I realized I needed to love the ugliest parts of myself.

It's early summer 2022, and I'm sitting on the couch, staring into the LED light of my phone screen. I can't stop scrolling. I'm addicted to my phone, afraid to go to bed, and avoiding sleep. It's 2 a.m., and all the lights are on. It's a weeknight.

I need some help.

In the months leading up to this moment, I left an unsafe, toxic relationship, moved back and forth between Airbnbs and friends' houses while keeping my stuff partially in my car and partially in a storage unit (I called it being bougie homeless), and finally, after a whole lot of struggle, I moved into my new apartment.

Even though I was finally in a stable living situation, my external life became disorganized and unmanageable. I stayed up until the early hours

What decisions would I make if I knew little eyes were watching me?

That frame of reference saved me in so many ways. I started to pull myself back up. It didn't happen all at once, but as I integrated this frame into my life, I started cooking better meals for myself, set up a weekly chore chart, prioritized connecting with friends, and got the healing support I needed. In essence, I got my life back. I got my self-respect back. I got order, organization, and sanity back. Over time, I got JOY back.

Once I had my basics covered, I noticed myself smiling more often. I started growing my client base. Eventually, I got my own office locally and started seeing clients online. I noticed I felt grateful every day, at least at some point. I got back to taking dance classes and going out dancing again. I made friends I love. I started facilitating classes and workshops again. I spent time in nature. I laughed more often and rediscovered my inner silliness. I started weaving inner child healing into my coaching. I furthered my education as an energy healer and started doing healings on myself and others. Little by little, I embodied the message, "I did it, and you can too."

If we fast-forward to today, my life is far from perfect, but it's distinguishably better. I talk to myself in a kind, encouraging voice much more often, instead of an endlessly critical one. I do things just for fun, just for the sake of joy, just to make myself laugh. I have safe, healthy relationships with healthy boundaries. I have the capacity to support way more people without feeling burnt out. I feel vibrant and healthy most of the time.

My life is a work in progress, and I'm grateful to say there has been *so much* progress! It's truly a joy and a privilege to be here on this planet and to speak to you through these words.

Now that I've shared my story, I'll offer some practical tips and a meditation I've used for my healing, to grow self-love and acceptance inside myself. I hope that self-love and acceptance start to grow inside of you, too.

Let's get you started on reparenting yourself and reconnecting with your joy!

I did it (and am doing it), and so can you!

THE SPARK

WHAT IS REPARENTING?

Reparenting is a conscious re-patterning of our thoughts, beliefs, and actions towards a healthy, productive, joyful life in alignment with our true Selves.

Reparenting can include adjusting how we speak to ourselves, regard ourselves, and care for ourselves. It can also involve reprogramming and re-patterning around how we relate to others and the world.

To start your reparenting journey, choose something in your current life that you're struggling with or something that's getting in the way of expressing your fullest Self. Next, you'll examine this thought, feeling, belief, and/or behavior and trace it back to the root of where it started. Finally, you'll ask yourself some questions to start to shift the pattern.

Here's an example from my actual life. I procrastinate, and I don't like it. It annoys me to no end. But when I close my eyes, feel deep inside of myself, and ask: *Where did this come from? How old was I when this behavior started?* I see images of myself as a child and teenager being criticized by adults and never feeling like my work or my efforts were good enough. By putting myself in my own old shoes, I can empathize with myself.

It's not a mystery that I avoid certain tasks, because I now have an internalized voice telling me it's already not good enough before I even start. The next questions I ask myself are:

What do I need to heal this?

What does younger me need to feel safe to try, even if it's not perfect?

In this case, younger me needs a whole lot of compassion, love, and understanding, and a kind inner voice that says things like:

It's okay to go for it, even if you mess it up.

If it's not that good, you'll learn something.

You're always loved no matter what.

And so I practice and reinforce that loving voice. Eventually, I start to feel safer taking risks and trying new things, and I procrastinate less.

3 STEPS TO SUPPORT YOU IN REPARENTING YOURSELF

Step 1: Ask yourself: What thought, feeling, belief, or behavior is getting in my way and blocking my fullest expression?

Step 2: Next, ask: Where did it come from, and how old was I when it started? This may take some time to find within yourself and can be done as a meditation. Connect with yourself at that age or ages and start to send yourself empathy and love.

Step 3: Finally, ask: What do I need to do to heal this thought, feeling, belief, or behavior? What do I need to feel safe to start making this change? Provide yourself with the safety you need, and then start making the changes necessary to heal.

A NOTE ON REPARENTING:

Some people have resistance to doing inner child healing because they worry that working on themselves would mean their parents failed. Reparenting yourself doesn't have to be disrespectful to your parents. It's about acknowledging old pain and unmet needs and healing them. Our parents couldn't read our minds or see inside our hearts, as much as we may have liked them to. The needs of a child are nuanced and many, and it would be impossible for someone outside of the self to meet them all.

No matter what kind of childhood you had, you can start to reparent yourself, heal, and reconnect with your JOY.

WHAT IS JOY AND HOW DO I FIND IT?

Joy is our innate state of being; it's a feeling of lightness, excitement, and aliveness, the state we're all born in. After we're born, shit happens. We get hurt. Emotions, beliefs, and negative states can cover our joy. Reparenting helps us feel whole and live in internal harmony. There's joy in simply being ourselves, in having peace in our internal world, and in having gratitude for all of the beauty in our lives.

However, when we (re)discover our gifts, passions, and purpose, a desire to express and share them naturally follows. Joy overflows, and we start to make other people's lives better, too. This joy feels like heart-opening, heart-healing, love, connection, and a feeling of oneness with the Universe.

When we share our joy, it inevitably grows.

SURPRISING TRUTHS I'VE LEARNED WHILE REPARENTING MYSELF:

I was resistant to these truths for years, but I've found them invaluable. I hope that by sharing them with you, you can sit with them and try them on sooner than I did.

1. **Discipline** is essential to achieving your goals. It also builds self-trust, excitement, and a healthy sense of pride (feeling proud of yourself and your accomplishments). Discipline can actually be fun, especially when it supports your dreams.

2. **Consistency** leads to freedom. We need structure, but it has to be the right structure. There is a difference between routines imposed on a child and the routine we create for ourselves as adults. You now have the freedom to create consistency in your life that aligns with your goals and what brings you joy!

3. **Self-worth** is something we all need to work on, even if we think we're "fine." You deserve nurturing love, care, kind words, understanding, fun, joy, silliness, spontaneity, and more. Are you giving these to yourself?

4. **Positivity** is safe. It's okay to focus on what's good in your life. Nothing bad will happen, you won't drop all the balls or forget some critical detail. Constant criticism of yourself and others doesn't create joy. What you focus on will expand and grow. As many people have said, "Where attention goes, energy flows." You might as well focus on the good.

5. **Gratitude** is key. Your life will improve if you continuously ask yourself, "What can I be grateful for in this situation?"

THE EXERCISE: SELF-LOVE MEDITATION FOR INNER CHILD HEALING

This meditation has three parts, which can be done together or individually.

PART 1: INNER CHILD HEALING

Find a quiet space where you can sit up with a tall spine, shoulders relaxed, and your feet planted on the ground.

Bring your hands to your heart (the center of your chest) and close your eyes.

Start to take some deep breaths, in through your nose and out through your mouth, and start experiencing your body from the inside. What does the inside of you feel like? How does it feel to hold your heart?

Bring your attention down to your feet and invite them to relax. Start moving your awareness up through your body, relaxing your ankles, legs, hips, belly, spine, chest, shoulders, arms, hands, neck, head, and face.

Imagine a pillar of white light coming from above your head, flowing down through your central core. Allow this white light to clear your mind. Drop any thoughts, concerns, or discomfort into the white light and allow them to be swept away. Do this part for at least five minutes.

As you continue to connect with your heart, ask yourself, "What age inside of me needs the most healing today?"

Ask that age to come forward and see or feel them in your mind. Connect with this younger version of you. Ask them what they need. Allow them to speak to you about what they're experiencing.

Start to flow love to this younger version of you, surrounding their feelings and needs in your love. Start making a plan with them on how to get their needs met as you continue to wrap them in your love.

Continue flowing love, listening, and talking to them until they feel fully safe, heard, and met.

208 | JOY UNLEASHED

PART 2: SELF-LOVE

Once this younger version of you feels full of love and like they've gotten everything they need, bring the attention back to the current you.

Feel your heart and start to generate love. See this love as a white light growing inside of your heart. When this loving light has filled your whole heart, allow it to grow into your chest, shoulders, arms, and hands, back into your heart, creating a circuit of love flowing from you back to you. Allow yourself to run this circuit of self-love for at least five minutes. If it feels right, you can also run the energy all over your body, like it has its own circulatory system, filling your whole being with love.

PART 3: EXPANSIVE LOVE

Allow the abundant love inside of you to move out beyond your body, until it fills the entire room. Take your time and expand your love into the entire building. Then into the surrounding area, then into the whole neighborhood. Fill your whole city or town with your love. Then expand your love into your whole region (state, county, area), into the whole country you live in, and eventually send your love out into the whole world. Imagine all of the people, animals, and plants receiving your love as it overflows out of you. You can stay here or continue expanding your love beyond the Earth into our solar system and the entire universe. Get as big as you want with your love!

Slowly start bringing your energy back into your body from however far out you expanded. When you're ready, open your eyes.

*See the links in my bio to get an audio recording of this meditation

A FINAL NOTE:

No amount of harsh criticism will evoke your brilliance. We all need encouragement, nurturing, and LOVE to continue growing towards our limitless potential.

You are LOVED and you are LOVE. Always.

Julie Goldberg is an energy healer and ICF-certified coach specializing in inner child healing, embodiment, and soul-level transformation. Julie is passionate about serving those who are ready to know themselves, step into their divine nature, and live life with joy.

For over a decade, Julie has worked with clients on physical, emotional, and energetic healing. After earning a B.A. in Dance from the University of Oregon and writing a thesis on somatics, Julie danced professionally in New York City. She became a Pilates instructor, personal trainer, and myofascial release practitioner before transitioning to energy healing and coaching.

As a healer with the Modern Mystery School, Julie offers ancient healing modalities from the lineage of King Solomon. These healings are a part of a path of progression that starts with a Life Activation. Life Activation supports clients in igniting the light within them and reconnecting to their highest purpose.

As an inner child healing and trauma-informed coach, Julie supports clients with emotional integration—helping them reconnect with the parts of themselves that were neglected, silenced, or wounded and uplift them with love. She also leads workshops on consent, communication, and embodied movement.

Julie lives in Durham, North Carolina. She loves dancing, hiking, swimming, and making fruit preserves in mason jars. On Saturday mornings, you can find her at the farmer's market and in Zumba class, a routine she created for her inner seven-year-old. :)

Connect with Julie:

Free Self-Love Meditation: https://julie-goldberg.kit.com/selflove

Facebook: https://www.facebook.com/julie.goldberg.739/

Instagram: https://www.instagram.com/julie_goldberg_/

Book a Consultation to Explore Working with Julie:

Website: https://trianglelightcenter.com/

More Resources:

The Modern Mystery School Certified Professionals List: https://modernmysteryschoolint.com/certified-professionals/

Adult Children of Alcoholics and Dysfunctional Families: https://adultchildren.org/

CHAPTER 20

UNCONDITIONAL LOVE

QUESTIONS THAT SPARK PEACE, HARMONY, AND JOY

Jeanie Davidson, Transformational Coach

MY STORY

"Stay back, don't come near me!" she shrieked through barren eyes.

My daughter's words cut through my heart. I wasn't touching her. I wasn't even close. But the phone in her hand told me she wasn't talking to me; she was performing for someone else. That was the moment I realized something was terribly wrong.

Earlier that day, her cherry-red Jeep Cherokee appeared in the driveway, just like any other school day. It was a Friday. My neck strained from sitting at the computer all day, but excitement built as I anticipated having a lovely family night at the Fort Worth carnival. Her sister's friend laughed in the other room, happy about their sleepover. The night felt utterly delightful, like a nice escape from a busy, distracted, monotonous week.

I walked up the wooden steps and cracked open her door to tell her good night.

"Stay back, don't come near me!" she shrieked through barren eyes.

Puzzled, I stepped inside, asking in concern, "Honey, are you okay?"

"Get away from me! Don't you dare touch me! Get your hands off me!"

"Honey, what are you talking about?" Palms open, near the door, about nine feet away, and confused, "Huh? I'm way over here. Are you okay?"

Then, I realized something felt off. Her words didn't match her tone or expression. It felt insincere, like a performance.

My eyes shifted to the clutched cell phone in her hand, covertly by her side.

I said, "Wait a minute, are you on the phone? Who are you talking to?" She shifted as I approached. Shocked and distracted by my observation, she barely noticed as I quickly grabbed the phone and saw that she was talking to her boyfriend, and oddly, his dad. I picked up the phone and said, "Emma needs to go." Then I hung up. I stared at her in utter disbelief.

Then anger set in, and I asked suspiciously, "What the hell are you doing?"

"I want to move in with Dad. I can't stand it anymore. I'm leaving." She started down the stairs, dragging a suitcase. She was a senior in high school, recently disconnected from friends after a dispute over a boy. I knew she was going through something, but she was so secretive! I read the parenting books and tried to have the conversations. Still, somehow, I couldn't reach her to understand what was going on behind those often gleeful, sometimes sporadically angry eyes.

But this? I have no idea what this is.

And by this point, I was scared by her abnormal behavior and urgency to leave–not to mention, raging inside over being falsely accused of apparently attacking her.

A few years before, she tried to run off with an older boy in high school. She romanticized things in a way I secretly wished I could, but clearly she wasn't thinking straight. So, I grounded her from her car, and began driving her to school. To my surprise, despite the "inconvenience," we bonded again. She returned to a more relaxed, cheerful version of herself once she accepted the punishment.

After this strange episode, clearly, she needed to be grounded again. I tried to take her car keys away, but she threw herself to the ground over them. My husband and I tried peeling them from her clenched hand, and it became more of a scene than I'd like to admit. She clenched harder through tears, and we peeled her fingers away, finally getting the keys. At the time, it was an act of fear and anger; now, in retrospect, I wonder if it was about control. But either way, I didn't want her driving in that state with such odd behavior. I was scared and hurt.

She took off on foot along Camp Bowie Boulevard to McDonald's, made a frantic call to her dad to pick her up, and in the coming days, refused all other contact. Her dad went along with it, probably wanting to feel needed and valuable (understandable, yet infuriating).

She somehow implied to her school that she was abused, and I felt completely betrayed, like my intentions and sacrifices for her were spat in my face. I was a single mom for so long, and I made hard decisions for her well-being. She was my whole world. *How on Earth could she lie to people and disparage me in such a thoughtless way?*

A friend who worked in the school district called. "Is everything okay?" His concern seemed tinged with judgment, signaling that the accusations were taken seriously and intervention was needed. Humiliation rushed to my cheeks; my heart pounded like a time bomb.

I tried to be a conscious parent. And while the frantic episode of retrieving keys on the kitchen floor wasn't my best moment, I knew what her life consisted of, and I couldn't understand why she was saying such things.

What if something has happened that I don't know about?

I was ready to throw my husband under the bus if he'd done something to her. But I couldn't imagine it being possible. This wasn't in his nature, which is part of why I chose him as a young, single mom.

"Please have her talk to this therapist," I convinced her dad before they left the state for his new job.

He conceded. She just turned 18, but authorized me to speak with the therapist, who confirmed that there was no abuse. However, like any angsty teenager, she was irritated when we commented on the provocative clothing she had tried to wear, and when asked to babysit her sister.

Yet, she still kept her distance, and I remained confused. She only attended one session before she took off and had to finish her last month of senior year at a completely new high school out of state.

Every day, I stared at her room, felt her absence, and bawled grief-filled tears. I felt like she died.

I needed support, but, angry and offended, my husband couldn't give it, claiming he was glad she left. I started to hate him. My other daughter, so young, only knew her sister had disappeared unexpectedly, and she was mad too. So, nobody was on my side. And admittedly, I was hurt and angry myself, but my grief was stronger.

I didn't know it at the time, but this was the beginning of the end of my marriage.

The day her graduation arrived, she didn't want me there—another slap in the face. I pictured all of her dad's family there, thinking I was a bad mom. Yet, I couldn't let her graduate without her own mother being there. My ego wanted to hide under the bedcovers until this passed, but I felt called to go for her sake.

That was when I became acquainted with unconditional love, not as a lofty ideal, but as a brutal choice.

When I arrived, Emma's eyes were stone cold. I felt her bottled-up emotions, hiding beneath the surface like a concrete barrier. I wanted closeness with her and maybe even a little appreciation, but none was to be had. I persisted, despite constant tears pressing in the back of my eyes, ready to fall, but I held them in.

I cried on the day of her graduation, though she didn't know it. I cried for her and mourned that she didn't get to graduate with her childhood friends, but among strangers.

Thankfully, we bonded in the days that followed. But then a series of more unconventional behaviors surfaced, and her dad called me, not knowing what to do.

Ultimately, it was determined that she suffered from bipolar disorder. She was an A+ student, a lovely daughter and fun sister, and now I didn't recognize her. It took time to get her on track, where she didn't feel ashamed of taking medication. I repeated conversations with her when she didn't remember them. My one golden nugget of advice was, "Honey, everybody has something. Some people take medication for their heart or blood pressure. This one is yours, and there's nothing to be ashamed of. Just do it and see what happens. We can make decisions later, when things settle down. I love you."

After a lot of love, effort, and my broken-down ego, she started thriving. She continues to grow, create a good life, and move toward goals, while reconnecting with old friends. I'm so very proud of her. I see what she's gone through and how far she's come, and I love her so very much.

I'm not sharing every bit of the story, but it's sprinkled with more despair-filled moments where I thought I lost her forever. If I'd let my ego and hurt run the show, I would have.

I later volunteered for a non-profit organization helping runaways and others in tragic circumstances. I found myself wondering how many teens and young adults exposed to homelessness, drugs, and human trafficking might be suffering from a mental illness their family didn't know about or just couldn't bear. I can understand their position. I felt myself on the brink of giving up so many times. Because when your heart is broken and your pride is crushed, over and over again, it's so hard to love your way through it.

But this is my daughter. I cannot let her fall beyond reach, and certainly not to self-destruction.

No, I don't enable her. Yes, I hold her accountable to a high standard for herself, but most of all, loving her unconditionally has been the path to the wonderful place we now find ourselves.

I can't imagine what regret I'd feel if she had been lost to the world by what was given to her. It's her cross to bear, and she bears it beautifully.

THE SPARK

Why tell such a heavy story in a book about joy? It's reality—tough, hard reality. And it will always be here. My relationship story is one of many I've experienced firsthand and through clients who've come to me in despair over broken relationships—conflicts about gender identity, addiction, narcissism, boundaries, suicide, and other trials, tearing their lives apart. Many of them have carried hurt, shame, and worry for years—years darkened with dread, robbed of peace and joy. They thought it couldn't change, and hope was lost. But I'm here to tell you that hope is never lost. When you face it head-on, through the lens of unconditional love, anything is possible, including newfound joy from what seemed lost. I've seen that spark of light in their eyes as new, happy stories unfolded before them—so beautiful, so meaningful. This is what life is for.

What relationship issue is stealing your joy? The spark I offer here is to check yourself. Question your motives and decisions, especially when they could create substantial distance between you and your loved ones. We know that when people are dying, reflecting on past experiences, what matters most is their relationships with those they love. To honor that, here's a way to shift your perspective.

Grab a piece of paper and a pen. First, activate your body's relaxation response and ability to focus by taking three to four slow, deep breaths (each time, inhaling to the count of four, holding for two, exhaling for the count of six). Feel good? Great. Now, bring to mind the difficult person or situation, and quickly answer the following questions, stating the first thing that comes to mind for each. Short, fast, and honest.

1. What do you currently feel from this person or situation?

2. What would you rather feel?

3. Why would you rather feel this way?

Now, flip the perspective. Imagine that person looking you directly in the eyes. Let them answer these same questions through you. Short, fast, and honest.

1. What do they currently feel from you or this situation?
2. What would they rather feel?
3. Why would they rather feel this way?

I'm impressed with your willingness to answer these questions. It's not always easy to see from multiple perspectives, but this is a beautiful start. You may have felt an immediate shift in the momentum of what's been happening. Even that matters. If you didn't feel it, that's okay, too. By simply asking the questions, you've just opened up a new space in your brain (and heart) that wasn't there before. Return to these questions each day to shift your view, and watch it change before your eyes. You'll find an expanded version of this tool, along with vital resources to accelerate healing, progress, and love, at www.JeanieDavidson.com/Joy. Let them refresh you daily to transform this situation. By the way, the LUMiN™ Assessment + Breakthrough Session has been known to change lives in an instant.

If you've given up, you're about to give up, or you think it's too late, I want to offer you a bit of hope. You're more powerful than you can imagine. When you tap into unconditional love, answers unfold, and healing shows up. My daughter later rewarded me with beautiful gratitude for sticking by her side beyond the difficulties. It brings tears to my eyes and fills my heart and soul when I remember this moment. She said, "Mom, you always gave me good advice, and I will always listen to you in the future. Thank you for being here for me. I love you so much."

Unconditional love isn't just an idea; it's the path forward.

I have a special map for you at www.JeanieDavidson.com/Joy

Jeanie Davidson is the creator of The LUMiN™ Method, a breakthrough process that helps people break free from destructive patterns, build certainty in their decisions, and create measurable progress toward the life they want. An award-winning author, certified hypnotherapist trained through an internationally accredited program, and featured coach in the award-winning film *Zero Limits*, Jeanie has guided hundreds of people through life's toughest challenges, transforming loss, shame, and conflict into renewed peace, purpose, and joy. She leads the Flow to Freedom community, is the founder of Rise Studios, and is a proud single mom of three.

Connect with Jeanie:

Website: https://www.JeanieDavidson.com/Joy

CHAPTER 21

A SENSORY SYMPHONY OF JOY

THE FIVE SENSES ARE YOUR MAP; JOY IS THE DESTINATION

Maggie O'Hara

"Let yourself be silently drawn by the strange pull of what you love. It will not lead you astray."

~ Rumi

MY STORY

I was a ghost long before I knew what one was. I grew up learning how to disappear without ever leaving the room.

For much of my life, I felt invisible—like I was quietly moving in the background, unseen and unheard. The world asked me to fit into boxes that never felt right, and I wondered if my voice even made a difference. But when I started creating through color, scent, sound, texture, and taste, I found a language beyond words. Creativity woke up my five senses, and in doing so, it woke me up. Today, I no longer hide. I shine my light boldly, using art and story to help others rediscover their own brilliance.

* * *

The grown-ups talked over me again. I sat quietly at the corner of the table, knees pulled up to my chest, tracing patterns in the condensation on my glass. I wrinkled my nose at the smell of Mum's cheap cigarettes. Their words moved fast, loud, and confident, like I didn't need to be part of the conversation, like I wasn't even there. My dad's motto was "Children should be seen and not heard."

"Let it go," I whispered to myself, as the cat meowed and I allowed the flicker of frustration into the secret place in my heart where all the unsaid things went.

I learned early how to disappear—how to make myself invisible to avoid drawing attention, how to bury my feelings so deep no one would ever find them again.

But joy, was clever. It slipped through the cracks, like sunshine through the floorboards.

It showed up in the rusted old VW Kombi van at the bottom of our yard, where my best friend Dawn and I spent whole afternoons pretending we were crossing deserts or driving through fantasy lands.

"You be the navigator," she said, handing me an old map from her dad's shed, all creased and torn.

"We're going to Morocco today," I announced, finger pointing to a sun-bleached corner, "and we'll stop for magic carpets and pink lemonade!" We could almost taste the Turkish delight and mint tea, which we made with mint leaves and water.

We laughed so hard the whole van shook, the smell of dust and rust mixing with the scent of salty Athel Pine trees on the breeze.

The van became our ship, our plane, our portal. There, I wasn't small. I was an explorer, a storyteller, and a creator of worlds.

We lost hours building fairy gardens behind the shed, making delicious mud cookies with mud icing running through our fingers, or whispering stories to each other. I scribbled in notebooks, doodled in the corners of school pages, and hummed made-up songs as I sewed tiny outfits from fabric scraps my mum saved for me.

No one told me it mattered, but I felt it deep inside my heart—being creative was how I stayed alive.

My teacher told Mum, "She's very quiet; she's always last to be picked for sports, she just blends in. But she is a sensitive soul, and off with the fairies most of the day."

Why didn't they say, "She's creative and has such a vivid imagination, she could be anything she chooses to be"?

One day, I said to Mum, "I've written and illustrated a story." She smiled and said, "That's nice, love," before going back to the laundry. I smiled too, and folded the pages quietly and slid them under my bed.

It wasn't for anyone else, anyway. Creating made me feel like I existed. It was enough.

Back then, my joy didn't announce itself. It didn't sparkle on command. It whispered, softly, persistently, like a secret only I was meant to hear.

You're only eight, but with your imagination, you could easily write a children's chapter book if you write a few pages every night. Use it as your creative writing homework.

It was always there, even as I moved through the demands of adulthood. It whispered when I scribbled poems on pieces of scrap paper in cafes or late at night when my ideas came. It flickered in the glow of vanilla-scented candles arranged on the dinner table, nestled between vases of bright flowers and handmade place cards with uneven lettering, which made me smile. It was in the tiny garments I designed and sewed for my young children, wild colours, mismatched patterns, and clothes which couldn't be found in shops.

Each act of creation felt like I reclaimed something that was once lost.

"Why do you always go to so much effort?" someone asked once, watching me rearrange the decorations and decor on the Christmas table for the third time.

"What does it matter if something isn't right? No one will even know."

I shrugged. "Because it matters to me."

They didn't need to understand. It wasn't for them. It never really was.

It took years before I realised my curiosity and constant urge to explore the next idea wasn't a flaw to fix. It was how I was wired. I was creative and slowly unleashing my inner joy.

One morning, notebook in hand, I looked out at the sun sparkling across the ocean and laughed softly to myself.

This may be what it means to be multi-passionate, to carry mirrors inside which catch the light differently depending on how you turn.

Writing, illustrating, painting, teaching, weaving stories, or setting ornate tables, none of it was separate. Every piece and passion reflected the same source:

My joy, my light.

These days, I don't chase joy. I collaborate with it. I bring it into my day on purpose, through rituals that anchor me in the here and now.

Before I sit to write or paint, I open a tiny amber bottle of essential oil and let the scent of lavender or wild orange rise to meet me, and take three slow breaths.

You're safe here, and I believe it. I light a candle on my desk and watch the flame flicker to life, a small reminder that the spark inside me still burns.

Music follows. Not loud or jarring, just Koshi chimes, with soft frequency tones, and meditative high frequency music, depending on the outcome I'm after for the day. I enjoy the music that moves through your chest before you notice it in your ears.

Then, there's colour, always colour, on my canvases, in my journals, in the cushions and clothes around my home. Joy is a shade, a feeling, and a palette. The brushstrokes are not just visual, they're emotional, intuitive, and healing.

My fingers crave texture. I'm tactile and love to touch everything.

When my children were young, so that they wouldn't feel and touch everything, I would say, "Hands in our pockets in this shop."

In truth, it was for me, too. Even to this day, if it looks tactile, my fingers will move slowly to touch the furry fabric or silky soft cushion.

Creating isn't just thinking—it's feeling, grounding, and remembering I'm alive.

And taste? It surprises me every time. A square of dark chocolate is often tucked into the corner of my mouth as I edit a page. I have a piece right here with me now, sitting next to my warm spiced chai.

When someone comes to visit, I ask, "Would you like a spiced chai or tea?"

I don't wait for a special occasion to start unpacking my grandmother's teacups from their little cardboard boxes. Having a cuppa with a friend or on my own is a celebration of being in the present moment.

Outside is where I come home to myself.

I don't walk for exercise. I walk to see and feel.

I trail my fingers across ferns, breathe in the musk of damp leaves, and listen to the chatter of kookaburras overhead. Sometimes I pause, close my eyes, and let the earth speak in her quiet language. I sit under a tree, legs crossed, breathe slowly, and let it all move through me.

That's where I remember: joy isn't something I need to earn or achieve. It's not pleasing someone else. It lives inside me. In the flame. In the fragrance. In the first sip of tea. In the breeze on my cheek. It lives in the act of noticing.

And now, I don't just notice it. I live by it.

THE EXHIBITION THAT CHANGED MY LIFE

The gallery lights dimmed just enough to let the colours take centre stage. I took a deep breath, the soft scent of lavender and varnish mingling in the air. My heels echoed on the polished floor as I walked past the final piece—each canvas brimming with emotion, alive with colour.

A woman stood frozen in front of a large piece, her phone raised. The moment she lifted it, digital butterflies, yet astonishingly real, burst from the artwork and floated into the air. She gasped.

"Did you see that?" she laughed, spinning around to catch her friend's arm. "It flew right past my face!"

Nearby, a child squealed and reached toward the sky, chasing another illusion. Laughter rippled through the room as everyone reached for their phones to see these magical illusions.

That was the moment—the exact one. I watched their eyes widen, their bodies relax, and their minds open. It was as though time bent and let us all return—for just a breath—to childhood, back to a place where magic was real and joy was simple.

This wasn't just an exhibition; it was a portal, a celebration of healing:

You get to feel this. You get to come alive again.

Every piece was inspired by one face.

I asked myself, "How many emotions live inside this one face? How many feelings can I evoke using the same face and different colours?"

Then, with the help of a developer, we brought those artworks to life, literally. Through augmented reality and an app, each canvas didn't just hang; it came alive with different coloured butterflies. This is being seen a lot more now, but in 2022, it was new technology and captivating.

Butterflies danced and darted through the space. It was art, but also alchemy.

One guest, misty-eyed, touched my arm. "I haven't felt this kind of wonder since I was a little girl," she whispered.

I swallowed hard. "That's exactly why I made it."

The night changed something in me. I didn't just want to create art. I tried to guide others back to that place, their inner child, their untamed joy. We spend so much of our lives being serious, responsible, and striving for perfection. In doing so, we forget how to be free.

But joy never leaves us. It waits patiently, like a childhood friend on the front porch, hoping we'll come out to play again.

Not everything I make is meant to be seen. Some of it is just for me. I write poems that never leave my journal. I paint messily, not for galleries, but for my soul. My notebook is full of ideas and thoughts. There's freedom in privacy, knowing that not all art needs to be pretty or posted. That, too, is a form of joy.

Joy doesn't have to perform. It just has to be felt.

And here's the truth: you don't need to be an artist or a writer or even particularly "creative" to feel this. You need to be present. Engaging the senses is one of the quickest, kindest ways to come back to yourself.

When your thoughts spin, when the noise gets too loud, the senses become anchors. They say, "Come back. Come home."

Start small.

- Smell your morning tea before you sip it.
- Stand barefoot on the grass and watch the sunrise with your hands tucked in your sleeves.
- Run your fingers across something soft, or rough, or beloved.
- Listen to the song playing in the background. Let it move you.

Joy isn't always evident. Sometimes it's the flicker of candlelight against a wall. The sound of a cat meowing. The weight of a stone or crystal in your palm.

These are the quiet doors back to wonder. And they're already partly open; you need to push them wide open. Wonder isn't lost, it's just waiting quietly, ready to be found again.

Curious how to step through those doors? Here's one of my favourite ways to invite joy in. A small ritual you can try yourself.

THE SPARK

Here is a simple, beautiful activity that you can try at home.

CREATE A SENSORY JOY ALTAR

Purpose: Reconnect with your inner child and awaken joy by engaging all five senses in one simple, beautiful practice.

What You'll Need:

- A small space, like a shelf, a windowsill, or a corner of a table
- Items to represent each of the five senses

Instructions:

Sight – Colour That Delights You: Choose a small object or artwork in a colour that makes you feel alive. It could be a photo, a flower, a crystal, or a postcard. Let it be something that feels like joy when you look at it.

Smell – An Uplifting Scent: Add a candle, incense, or a few drops of essential oil on a cotton ball. Citrus (like orange or lemon) lifts the mood, while lavender soothes.

Sound – A Chime or Melody: Place a small bell, koshi chime, or a playlist of your favourite high-frequency music nearby. Please take a moment each day to listen with presence.

Touch – A Textured Treasure: Choose something with texture: a smooth stone, a piece of fabric, a feather, or a tactile object that brings comfort. Touch it when you feel disconnected or stressed.

Taste – A Treat Just for You: Keep a small jar with treats, such as herbal tea bags, dark chocolate, cacao, or a favourite spice. When you visit your joy altar, let yourself indulge mindfully, tasting with your eyes closed.

How to Use It: Visit your Joy Altar each morning or evening. Light the candle, listen to the chime, hold your textured object, and take three deep breaths in, hold, and release. This will ground you in the present, reconnect you with yourself, and help you find joy in the stillness.

Living joyfully isn't about perfection or having a life free of challenges. It's about choosing to show up—fully and kindly—for yourself, with curiosity, creativity, and compassion. Whether you're painting a canvas, scribbling your thoughts, walking barefoot in the garden, or simply savoring a quiet cup of tea, you are honoring the precious inner child who still dreams, explores, and delights.

This simple ritual of your Joy Altar invites you to pause, breathe, and reconnect. It's a gentle reminder that joy lives within you, waiting quietly to be noticed, embraced, and nurtured.

So today, and every day, say yes to joy. Say yes to yourself, because you deserve to live a life where your soul can shine freely, brightly, and unapologetically.

If you would like to learn more about bringing joy and creativity into your life or to awaken your inner child, reach out below and connect. We can let our inner children find joy together.

Maggie O'Hara is a multi-passionate author, artist, and creative visionary whose work invites people to reconnect with themselves through story, art, and the senses. A pioneer in the wellness and creative industries, Maggie created Australia's first fully interactive affirmation card deck, combining her love of art, fascination with technology, and soulful self-discovery to inspire thousands to embrace their inner wisdom.

Her creativity flows across many forms. As the author of enchanting children's books, Maggie takes young readers on global adventures that celebrate culture, kindness, and curiosity. Her stories weave in playful details, like a hidden mouse on every page, encouraging children to explore both the world around them and the magic within.

As a digital artist, Maggie's vibrant, nature-inspired works have captivated audiences, with her debut exhibition selling out and affirming her place as an innovative voice in contemporary art. She is also a proud co-author of two #1 Amazon bestsellers, expanding her reach into the world of personal growth and inspiration.

At the heart of all her creations is Maggie's belief in the healing power of creativity. She finds joy in embracing the five senses—through colour, scent, texture, sound, and taste—as a pathway to connection and self-love. Whether through words, images, or ritual, Maggie's work reminds us that creativity is not only an art form but a way of living more fully, joyfully, and authentically.

Connect with Maggie:

Website: https://www.maggieoharas.com

Facebook: https://www.facebook.com/maggieodigitalart/

Instagram: https://www.instagram.com/maggieodigitalart/

LinkedIn: https://www.linkedin.com/in/maggie-o-hara-25622713b/

YouTube video of the exhibition:
https://www.youtube.com/watch?v=OCv9MBQEmqU

Linktree: https://linktr.ee/maggieohara

CHAPTER 22

TEARS, TRUTH, AND TRIUMPH

HOW JOY IS A JOURNEY BACK TO SELF

Rebekah J. Zayit

MY STORY

To tell the truth, I secretly used to feel guilty about not having joy. From the time I was a small child, I knew that Christians were supposed to be joyful, and I thought joy equaled happy. At the age of four, I watched my father, a Presbyterian pastor, greet his congregation with a sincere smile. When their faces responded with cheerful attention, I was convinced it was I alone who didn't feel happy. The trouble was, I should've had more joy than any of them. . .because "joy" is my middle name.

I did not yet know myself.

As my childhood progressed, I experienced sexual abuse, depression, and several traumatic incidents. By the time I reached fourteen, I was so disconnected from myself that I loathed my own body. I didn't trust my body, and I didn't trust myself. I tried to trust God, but that just left me feeling lost.

When I was sixteen, my struggle with bulimia led my parents to enroll me in a Christian inpatient treatment center for females with eating disorders. It was weird having a nurse come into the bathroom with me each time I had to go, but back then, I shrugged my shoulders and went with it.

One bright Sunday afternoon in the center's commons room, I slumped over the green chenille arm of a sofa and sighed. The other girls were walking, shifting, and making their way toward me. I longed for quiet time to read and journal, but that would have to wait.

It was time for our weekly residents-only meeting. Attendance was required, and we'd been told to discuss any concerns or issues regarding community living. This was the only time we gathered when the staff wasn't present.

Suellen, our elected resident leader, plopped down on the brown leather couch opposite me and tucked a blond curl behind her ear. "Ladies, let's get started," she said in a shrill tone. A flurry of tennis shoes and strappy sandals came pounding through the hallway. As two residents passed me, I heard the new girl, Mary, whispering to Bethany.

"How many calories are in toothpaste?" Mary asked, flashing a nervous glance toward Suellen as she bent near Bethany's ear.

"Mary," Bethany chided softly, "you don't swallow toothpaste."

Mary was new, so she was allowed to ask things like that. I had been there for four weeks; the unspoken rules were different.

A few minutes later, after Suellen formally announced our agenda, I noticed the fog of my daydream dissipate. Carol, a fellow resident, was saying my name.

"Rebekah," she stated, "I see you not participating. In fact, we can all tell you're not really trying."

"Wait, what do you mean?" I sat up a bit straighter. "Sorry. I'm tired today, and I just got distracted for a moment."

"No." Carol looked at me hard.

"We mean overall, not just in this meeting."

Wait, what?!

Why is this the first time I'm hearing of this?

Staff told us we should first address any conflicts with each other individually. If we couldn't resolve it that way, we were supposed to then take the issue to the staff or the resident meeting. I'm confused. We're supposed to be practicing Matthew 18, right?

I found my voice, albeit shaky.

"Okay. . ."

Then Suellen jumped in. "Yeah, Rebekah, we still see you trying to escape and avoid your issues. You can't get better that way."

"Right. . ." I replied, "But in what way are you talking about?"

My stomach fluttered as all meeting eyes bored into my brain. More voices chimed in:

"Yeah, Rebekah."

"Rebekah, you haven't been working the program."

Suellen continued, "You didn't do what we were told to in Art Therapy. The counselor said you had to choose your own design and not ask other girls' opinions."

"I stopped when she told us that," I reminded her.

"Yes," Suellen countered, "but you looked uncomfortable from then on."

Huh?

"How about when you play the piano?" Now Julie was chiming in. "We've seen your face through the two-way window when you're playing, and we see how you're using it as an escape."

Wait. . .isn't playing music to express emotion a good thing?

Suddenly, even more voices talked all at once, and my stomach jumped from fluttering to heaving.

I'm working so hard. . .but clearly, not hard enough.

I jumped from my seat, the cacophony of their words sinking to the floor as I hopped over some girls seated on the rug and headed for the porch door. My old friend Nausea sat up attentively and waited.

Lila, one of the older residents, tall and muscular, suddenly stood. She was completely blocking my path.

"No, Rebekah," she said sternly. "Don't run away."

At that moment, I knew if I opened my mouth to speak, my old friend Nausea would unload on her.

Through stinging tears, I reached up, put my hands on her shoulder, and pushed.

I rushed from the room before my old friend started yelling.

Outside, my stomach grew quiet. I needed to cry in private, but our bedrooms were locked. There was nowhere to go that wasn't common.

I turned and fled down the stone path, past the counselors' offices, past the stables, and headed up the hill nearby. I climbed up high enough that the human sounds from below were muffled.

I cried.

I prayed.

I went back down.

Apparently, I was gone for thirty minutes.

During those minutes, they couldn't find me.

During those minutes, the girls told the staff that I assaulted Lila.

A staff member was assigned to physically be with me at every moment until I was discharged from treatment. I was discharged that same afternoon.

I had failed treatment.

And I did not yet know joy.

Eight years later, I left my eating disorder behind, married a man in the Catholic Church, started having babies, and began the life of which I had always dreamed. And that was the life God called me to. . .until it wasn't.

He filed for divorce on a Friday morning. I didn't see that one coming. Twenty years and six children after our wedding, he began repeatedly insisting I find a marriage intensive therapy retreat we could attend as a couple. I researched thoroughly and kept him abreast of my findings. Just as we selected one and I was about to schedule it, he went and filed. He came home mid-morning that Friday with the news to surprise me.

I didn't know then that much of him had been hidden. I didn't know the assaults that were still to come, nor how those assaults would strip our children away. I lost them, an identity, and a whole way of life.

I didn't know how close I was to joy.

Our parish priest recommended a series of homilies to me, entitled *In the Beginning*, given by Cardinal Joseph Ratzinger. I located the series online and printed a hard copy for myself. As I did, I suddenly felt a sharp heaving, as though someone had punched me in the stomach. Yet I felt no pain.

Ratzinger's writing was scholarly, fascinating, and funny. He shared an account of Creation I had never heard before. He said knowing where we come from is of vital importance if we wish to know who we are. I silently agreed. I may have felt uncertain of who I'd become, but one thing was for sure: my identity was bigger than me.

My eyes glued themselves to the pages. Then I read:

"In Israel herself, the creation theme went through several different stages. It was never completely absent, but it was not always equally important. Creation became a dominant theme during the Babylonian Exile, for Israel had lost her land and her temple. According to the mentality of the time, this was something incomprehensible. . .it meant that the God of Israel was vanquished. . .and a God who could not defend His worshipers and His worship was seen to be. . .a weak God. Indeed, He was no God at all; He had abandoned His divinity. And so, being driven out of their own land and being erased from the map was, for Israel, a terrible trial: Has our God been vanquished, and is our faith void?"

Void indeed. I heard the dearth of self in those cries. If Israel did not know who God was, she no longer knew who she was. What if I no longer knew who I was? Did that mean I no longer knew God? Yes, the foundation of my former life was smashed into bits, chewed up, and spit out all over the place. I asked myself again and again: *Who am I?*

I thought I was who God called me to be. . .

So is God dead?

Is He deaf?

Or is He just infuriatingly silent?

I continued to read.

It turns out that the land Israel inhabited, the place where she knew and worshiped God, was not a restriction for Him after all. It turns out that God is not restricted by any one piece of land, person, vocation, or way of life. Nor is He restricted by our expectations of the future. He never has been. It was Israel, not God, whose view was limited by her own perceptions.

But why would a good God allow His own children to be carried off into exile, even slavery? Because Israel's beliefs about herself were intricately connected with her beliefs about God. One could not be torn down without destroying the other. As the ancient prophets responded to their people's needs in exile, they found that the Creation story now bore critical importance. It was during the crisis of exile that the prophets "opened a new page" of Creation. It was then that Israel's shattered view of herself was completely unmade.

Only when that view was unmade could it then be remade.

And when she was remade. . .only then could she see His face.

It was only when the life and identity for which I worked so long came crashing down that I looked anew at myself and at Him. I found that He wasn't punishing me for my deficiencies; He was clearing the rubble so I could be close to Him. And He *so* wanted to be close to me.

When I was ready, when I was able to see, He gave me the gift He'd been waiting to give me all along: a deep, profound experience of joy.

Joy is the finding and retaining of the truth of who we are, regardless of the circumstances around us.

Last summer, I had the opportunity to take some of the kids to Kentucky, to a cabin high on a mountain. We planned our favorites: hiking, climbing, wading, and swimming.

The cabin itself was quite high. On its expansive outdoor deck lined with blue-cushioned chairs, my fourteen-year-old daughter sprawled through the night air, beckoning.

"Mom!" she called, "come outside when you're done!"

"I will," I answered, tucking the last of the younger kids under his covers.

I gathered the mugs of peppermint tea she left steeping in the kitchen and carried them to the porch. This was our shared space: stargazing. Years before, we'd found a phone app that we could point at the night sky to learn the names of any heavenly body. This girl had always had a voracious appetite for learning, and we relished finding new stars, quizzing each other on constellations, and discovering new favorites.

"Hi," I greeted her as I slipped out the screen door.

"Look at this!" she said, pointing upwards at a constellation. "I already found Canis Minor."

I was stunned, though not by her finding the constellation. The night sky—far from town lights and neighborhood homes—was brighter, darker, and clearer than I'd ever seen it.

"Whoa, this is amazing," I whispered, sliding onto a cushion next to her. "I didn't even think about this place being a great one for stargazing."

"This is even better than the field we went to fall last," she murmured in reply. "We can see everything up here because of our height, and because there's no light pollution."

"Wait! Did you see that?" I shouted suddenly, my arm pointing to the left, my legs rising out of the chair. "It went down so fast; it almost looked like a shooting star!"

"Where?" my daughter asked, and I showed her the intersection of two nearby pines above. "Maybe it was an airplane," I began.

She pointed excitedly, "No, look–there's a plane over there. See how it's moving?"

"Yeah," I agreed. "The streak I saw went a lot faster than that."

Suddenly, we both sat up straight.

"Look!" she shrieked. "That's another one!"

"Wow," I breathed. "That's incredible."

We watched as two, then three, four, five more stars shot across the sky. It was the only time either of us had ever seen that many, that close, in one night.

I looked at my daughter's face, bright with the moon, then turned back toward the high, dark valley above, studded with twinkling gemstones. In that moment, she was her, I was me, and we were who we are together. I inhaled the scent of pine as she rested her head on my shoulder.

Did you bring us here for this? This is for us, isn't it? I asked Him.

Right then, I saw that no matter what was to come, this realness, this connection, could never be stripped from either of us. She and I would share this experience forever. My chest swelled suddenly with elated, exhilarating joy.

"I love you," I whispered.

"I love you more," she answered.

THE SPARK

CURSIVE WRITING

Sometimes the tool that's the biggest help is one you can actually do.

I once had five children as a single, homeschooling parent, and my youngest was two years old. My reality did not include more than a few minutes per day to sit down to do anything.

I've used this spark while standing at my stove, breaking up ground beef in a pan, as well as in doctors' offices and school pickup lines.

Cursive writing – not print or manuscript – is an activity that crosses the midline of the brain. Activities that cross the brain's midline provide key support in our brains' building new neuropathways. Any therapies, healing work, inner child work, new boundary setting, friendships, or prayer in which we participate, all must, in order to sustain healing, form new, actual paths in our brains. While many activities that cross the brain's midline are full-body actions, cursive writing is one you can do regardless of physical fitness, mobility, or location.

Further, it's eminently flexible and adaptable. I can write anything and never run out of things to write; I begin and end just as quickly. The best part is that it's not necessary to form new thoughts each time you use cursive writing. This spark works just as well if you're copying someone else's words. For about a year, I copied the Psalms.

Set Up:

1. New to cursive writing?
   https://mailchi.mp/rebekahzayit/freedownloadableworkbookgiftoftimeseries2

2. Collect sheets of paper, your preferred writing utensil, and, if you like, a clipboard. I use a pencil because it provides a bit more resistance between me and the paper as I write, which helps me to focus. If you find a pen or colored pencil works better for you, use that. If you'd rather download my free templates, click here:
   https://mailchi.mp/rebekahzayit/freedownloadableworkbookgiftoftimeseries2

   a. Choose a passage that is roughly one or two paragraphs from a source you love. A portion of a narrative (story), a poem, song lyrics, a prayer— any words that speak to your heart. The key here is that stories connect us to ourselves and to one another as human beings. Both stories and relationships are formed in the right side of the brain. In using this spark, we seek re-connection with ourselves. This is why I recommend using a poem, prayer, or portion of a story as your pre-selected passage.

   b. If you are a person for whom any words are sometimes too much, or you don't have something that currently speaks to you, try writing a list. List the names of people to whom you are close, places you've visited, or animals you find fascinating. What matters is not the content of your writing, but the movement of your hand.

   c. When you have a sense about which option sounds best to you, simply begin and try it. It's okay to try one, then switch it up. Better to choose and change than to stay still.

3. Remember: no one will see this. It's not being graded. If it's messy or misspelled, who cares? The value is the actual physical movement of your hand as it connects to your brain. Don't censor yourself. If you make a mistake, keep going. Sometimes, making a mistake can itself turn out to be very healing. You're not writing a novel; you're retraining your brain. Keep going.

4. Next time you're overwhelmed, pull out your clipboard and begin writing. Set a timer for ten minutes, or simply write until you notice your body beginning to relax. The general target time is three to twenty minutes—again, notice your own body and honor it.

5. When you have written in cursive during a period of stress or hyperarousal for more than a minute, and you find your breathing and heartbeat to be more regular than when you began: you are seeing success!

The takeaway: When we're growing new neuropathways, activities like cursive writing can blaze trails for us. They don't walk the trails instead of us, but they make those trails possible.

Want more ideas for digging deeper? Visit: https://rebekahzayit.com/

Rebekah Zayit is a coach who specializes in helping people grow spiritually, especially during difficult life transitions. She is also a writer, speaker, copyeditor, and the proud mother of six. With a professional background in psychology and language, she helps people find clarity and the confidence to move forward. Rebekah loves to help her clients uncover obstacles, move through their stuck places, and reconnect to themselves with joy.

Rebekah earned her B.A. in English Rhetoric and her M.A. in Clinical Psychology. Rebekah's career has been as multifaceted as her passions: she's counseled clients facing substance abuse and dependence, homeschooled her children, and taught students of every age in classrooms, small groups, and one-on-one. Now working remotely, Rebekah partners with individuals and organizations as a coach, writer, and copyeditor. She is known for asking excellent questions, creating space for breakthroughs, and helping others express themselves with impact.

Rebekah loves to pray; she is a devout Catholic who deeply values learning with people from all perspectives. She continues to be a self-proclaimed "grammar nerd," and she watches way too many videos on Meyers-Briggs.

Throughout her journey, Rebekah has maintained these strengths: the ability to form genuine connections, to hear the unspoken, and to guide others through creative problem-solving toward true transformation.

Rebekah is happiest when drinking black coffee, writing, reading, and hiking through the woods with her children. Rebekah's passion for language, nature, and human beings continues to bring her ongoing adventure and inspiration.

Connect with Rebekah:

https://rebekahzayit.com/

CHAPTER 23

THE POWER IN BELIEVING

HOW TO ATTRACT 4000X FASTER

Debra Guerrero

MY STORY

I know what you're thinking.

What power?

Is it magical?

Where can I buy it?

Well, it's not magic, and you can't buy it. You're born with it. It's a gift from the I AM—The Divine, the Creator, and this little one was created to share this hidden secret at this time with you.

THE LITTLE ONE'S STORY

This little one was born into a fight-or-flight response. She knew and felt things deeply and did her best to stay still and quiet. So even at seventeen months of age, her parents took her to the doctor to see why she wouldn't take a step. Once she did start walking, she ran. It still took her quite a while to come out of her shell.

The little one knew, in the depths of her being, that she was called to minister and love God's children—the world. She was chosen, and she was an empath.

This was a 'holy crap' moment when she realized just what she was here to do!

At age four, the little one and her family moved to Iowa, from Louisiana. Her mother didn't want to move at all.

It took longer for the little one to get dressed to go outside than she spent playing. After the third day of snow, this little one wanted to know when it would go away. She was missing back home.

The nights were long—her mother was afraid to be there at night without her father. The little one's mother sewed during the night to avoid going to bed. Her mother laid the little one and her sister at each end of the couch to sleep. The little one put a knife under her cushion. She was already learning to hide and cover things up. But as long as she took care of her mother, it was okay to take on the responsibility. To her, anyway.

Months after the little one started her protection patrol, she felt she was doing well, until her mother got the phone call. That phone call dropped her mother to the floor, screaming, "It's all your dad's fault my mom died!"

As they drove back to her grandmother's celebration of life in Louisiana, she made plans for how to take care of her mother. She leaned against the back of her mother's car seat and told her, "I'll take care of you from now on, Momma."

In the summer, her mother started taking the little one and her sister to the pool. By this point, her mother had groomed the little one to be her caretaker. Her mother also taught others how to abuse and control the little one.

Her mother said, "How about we skip the pool today and go pick out that special toy you've been wanting?"

Aware of her voice and body language, the little one knew she needed to go with her mother, even though she wanted to stay and play.

They barely walked down one aisle at the store when a tall man approached and placed his hand on the little one's left cheek.

Tears flowed down his face as he said, "She should be mine."

The little one was so confused. She looked up at her mother for help and froze, waiting for an explanation. It wouldn't come.

"I don't trust anyone but you, little one," her mother said.

At age six, they moved to Texas. By this time, the little one's mother had separated her from others and had her believing her father didn't love her because she was supposed to be a boy. Since her father never said anything, she believed her mother.

A year later, they moved into a home that was built for them. The little one's parents took her to see the house while it was being completed. Her father said, "Guess which house it is." And she did. She saw the look on her father's face as he asked her mother, "Did you tell her?"

The little one possessed an uncanny knack for sensing what lay ahead, speaking truths before they unfolded. But when she noticed the unease her words stirred in others, she quietly taught herself the art of silence.

It was a great time and place for the little one. She loved the outside. It was her happy place! She discovered that down the block, across the ditch, and through the woods was a lake, and an old farmer man in blue jean overalls who she adored. A mile in the opposite direction, crossing through a cattle field, was the church the family attended. Inside the church was a special feeling that grabbed the little one in a deep, moving way. Her parents noticed and laughed it off. They didn't understand.

At age eight, during the summer, the little one decided to talk with the priest at the church every Wednesday at 2 p.m. The little one had burning questions deep inside, like, "Why do we only sing three songs? Don't they feel Him? Don't they know God is speaking?"

The nun and priest attempted to get the little one to go to nun school for years. "I'm never wearing what the nuns wear," was all the little one said. She wore tennis shoes and cowboy boots.

There was a calling, and it showed. The little one's connection with God was certainly unusual.

The summer before the little one turned nine, she was mowing their lawn, and it was hot. She went inside the house for some water. A voice on the TV caught her ear as it vibrated throughout her body. She stopped in mid-step to hear this woman. This woman's voice burned into every fiber of the little one. The woman was wearing a long white ruffled dress, and she said, "Don't grieve the Holy Spirit." The little one didn't know who she was, nor who the Holy Spirit was; she just knew this was her friend, and she wanted everything the Spirit had to offer.

The little one had already seen the movie of Jesus's life and fully believed. His words were, "You are to do all I did and more." Well, this was all she needed. She knew the Spirit would help, so she planned to go back to the church. The little one was eager to speak with the priest. When he came out, she told him with great excitement about the lady she saw on TV in detail. She confided to the priest that she had been practicing walking on water, but always failed. "Nothing I try works," she admitted. "Will you teach me how to do it?"

His look and his half-laugh took aback the little one. She told him, "Well, Kathryn Kuhlman said I was to do all Jesus did and more. If you can't teach me, can you take me to someone who can?" He said he couldn't, nor did he know who could. The little one was surprised. She asked him how he got his job as a priest!

By this time, the little one had mastered covering up whatever needed to be covered, and that certainly included emotions, which are energy in motion. Her little nervous system couldn't hold them down anymore, though she tried. They put her on spasmodic medication to help stop her vomiting.

As the little one grew, she grew closer to her mother. She learned to read all of her signs. She learned to read the room, where everything was, and who was where. Her mother even complimented her on her knowledge. It was essential to know when, what, and how she may need her. Often her mother gave her the look or said something, and that meant she needed to stay wherever her mother was. She couldn't go with others, and that left the little one often lonely.

The summer before the little one turned nine, she had her own business. She wanted to ride go-karts with her friends. When she asked permission from her father, he said, "You can go if you have the money." It took her less than three minutes to think about it and ask, "If I have the money, will you take us?"

He said yes, and that's all she needed to know. She headed to the garage and got her bucket, dish rag, and soap. Now the little one moved with confidence. Her father asked, "What in the world are you doing?"

"I'm going to wash cars for a living," she told her father as she headed out the door.

She had no time to talk because cars and people with her money were waiting. Her father laughed as she walked out. His head turned, and his eyes widened when the little one came home with a little over twenty-seven dollars. Plus, a list of cars to wash the following Saturday!

Before the age of eleven, the little one cleaned houses and did odd jobs around the neighborhood, always looking for ways to make money.

The little one had a nonstop business mind, always looking for ways to make her mother's life better. She knew that would take money—and she was confident she could earn it. Even though she loved swimming, the lake, and playing, she hired a few boys to handle some of the jobs she took on. They earned their pay, and she earned hers by giving them the opportunity to work.

When the little one was eleven, her mother was having several affairs. She used the little one as an excuse and dropped the little one off somewhere for hours. Or the little one drove her mother and dropped her off, then hid the car from her father and others. This cut so deeply into the little one. She didn't just hurt and lie to her father; she lied to friends and family, too.

Her sister was given a Fiat X19 for her sixteenth birthday. She had a photo shoot all around that little blue convertible car by none other than the man her mother was having an affair with. The little one smiled, joked, and laughed, all the while busting open inside, thinking: *Dad has to know!*

Her sister was cute as could be, acting like a car model in her navy blue and white outfit, clueless about the affair and the fact that the little one was the one helping her. The little one now had to protect her sister from this man. Without saying why, the weight was on her shoulders.

The little one always felt alone, and the harder she tried to be good, the harder it got, though she had the Holy Spirit and I AM.

Her mother found other men. At age seventeen, the little one had her own boyfriend, and she got caught. She was a junior in high school and pregnant—a complicated pregnancy, too. She was in and out of the hospital, alone, and scared.

She was now totally under the control of her mother. Even attending church and seminary was difficult, and the physical abuse was preferred over the mental abuse.

Her life wasn't heading where she desired. She kept going and attempting to be what she knew God and her agreed on—her scroll. Class after class, the more she grew, the more her family laughed.

By this time, the little one was all grown up on the outside.

That knowing in her gut of why she's here and what she was to do never left. It fueled her. The more her family laughed, the more classes she took.

At a business meeting, a tall, older woman caught the little one's eye in a way no one had. It was clear she must meet this woman walking with purpose. The little one was getting ready to present and start her training, so there was zero time to waste. She excused herself and immediately went over and introduced herself.

This friend was different. There was a quick, deep connection.

She believed in her, and that's all it took.

They became the best of friends. Twenty-five years her senior, they were like Lucy and Ethel. And let me tell you, they got in it just like Lucy and Ethel.

That belief in herself allowed the little one to connect with her own heart; the blocks released as she became herself. She knew her passion was a gift from the I AM, and it was to get her to her purpose. She couldn't get enough knowledge and hands on training in frequencies, releasing blocks, and finances.

She became certified in Ho'oponopono, EFT, and ordained as a Reverend, as well as trained in multiple energy modalities, including stones, touch, Reiki, crystals, energy portals, colors, frequency-specific microcurrent, and finances, where many of our blocks originate.

There was laughter where tears would generally be, and the tears became tears of joy as she saw miracle after miracle before her.

Every time someone threw dirt on her she shook it off, grinned inside, and took a step up out of the hole she was in. It all stemmed from her friend, Joanna Devine, believing in her.

Her motto is: Everyone is welcome at the table. That's what Jesus did—loved all. Even when He knew their heart and intentions, He didn't change. He stood on love and allowed it to change the heart—the foundation.

The little one, none other than Debra Guerrero, served wherever she went, including Dr. Joe Vitale, and she attended the first Ho'oponopono event with Dr. Hew Lin in Texas.

As Dr. Lin spoke, a fire burned in her. She knew this was the missing piece in churches, schools, and the world. She wept with the knowing—this was I AM's heart.

THE SPARK

It's not in the judging, telling others what, when, or how, or keeping them in counseling for years.

There's a faster way, as I'll teach you how to shift your energy in seventeen seconds.

We have seventeen seconds for the first thought to come in. In these seventeen seconds, we must release the negative thoughts or words before the second seventeen-second thought or word comes in. At this point, the physical body is beginning to respond. Suppose the thought remains, and another seventeen seconds of thought builds on it. The third seventeen-second chemicals are being released into your body.

You, the owner of your life, have complete control of what chemicals are released inside you. Positive or negative—it's your choice.

I know, you were taught it was outside of you and that stuff happens. No!

Everyone and everything outside of you is not responsible for your emotions and life. Your emotions are a magnet for attracting exactly what you're putting out. They're like a seed for your garden. What you plant, is what you harvest.

The opportunity to live your life in *Joy Unleashed* comes from your decision. Seventeen seconds is all it takes. Connect this with Ho'oponopono practice and you will shift your life quickly, on solid ground.

Once you have control back over your thoughts that holds space in your head rent-free, I'll teach you to use Ho'oponopono for the fastest way to reach ZERO—total freedom. I believe in You!

Ho'oponopono is a Hawaiian practice of reconciliation and forgiveness.

There are four phrases used: I love you; I'm sorry; Please forgive me; and Thank You.

I created a *How to Reach ZERO* workbook to help you reach zero quicker.

Release the negative thoughts and be the person you're created to be, and you'll attract 4000 times faster by being authentic.

It's looking in the mirror and laughing at what you're attracting and learning that the faster you love it—the faster it's released or brought in and the quicker you create the life you desire.

My life's mission is to believe in you, to see you play full out, and to embrace your scroll. Live your life!

So if you have the opportunity to take care of the person who you think hurt you, you may step up in love and be honored to do so.

I was able to be the caretaker of my mother. Less than a week before my mother graduated to the next realm, she looked up at her grown daughter and softly said, "I'm so sorry, Debra."

I smiled and said, "Mom, I forgave you long ago. Thank you, Mom, for being what I needed. To get me where I needed to be, for such a time as this."

A tear dropped, as she believed.

To believe in others is to heal the world.

I hope you connect with me. I've held intentions for all your blocks to be released, including financial, and that you're living the life of your dreams!

Debra Guerrero is a seasoned speaker, trainer, and entrepreneur with over 30 years of experience in energy, frequencies, and finance. She launched her first business at age eight and embraced spiritual healing early in life. Today, she's CEO of Bold Rulers, a brand of frequency-infused products, and Awaken the Banker Within. This system teaches how to profit while paying bills and unlock the secrets of true financial empowerment. Additionally, Debra Guerrero offers speaking services, as well as individual and corporate training. She is guaranteed to shift the atmosphere and make you laugh.

Driven by her life's purpose—her "scroll"—Debra inspires others to awaken the love of God within and become the creator-owners of their lives. Her transformational teachings break barriers and spark miracles.

Certified in multiple modalities, she embodies the Elijah spirit, shifting atmospheres and elevating vibrations wherever she goes—focusing on the present and the future.

She reminds us we are spirits navigating a physical experience, and some of us have truly lived boldly within it! Embrace laughter as you awaken, and shift into your personal flow—the flow of your divine scroll.

Debra believes in you and looks forward to seeing your visions become your reality.

Connect with Debra:

Email: Debra@BoldRulers.com

https://www.debraguerrero.com

https://www.boldrulers.com/

https://www.AwakentheBankerWithin.com

CHAPTER 24

BETRAYAL

SACRED MEDICINE FOR BOUNDARY SETTING

Angel Gold

MY STORY

"He isn't going to tell her his ex-sex buddy is on this trip."

What do you mean he isn't going to tell her? My body became rock-still as I sat there, staring into his eyes, searching for some sort of compassion, empathy, or authenticity—something that would make that sentence sound less grotesque.

Here was this human, a captain in the fire service, mentoring his officer to lie to his girlfriend while conspiring with the front-line workers in the group to cover it up before their two-week rafting trip.

That red-flag moment is now etched into my bone marrow as the first stage of failure of my trust and respect, not only for the man I chose to couple with, but also for firefighters and front-line heroes altogether.

This wasn't my first encounter with "front-line" violating boundaries without remorse. Years earlier, the father and fire captain of one of my gymnasts cheated on his wife. Through his chaos addiction, I helped raise his daughter, a talented athlete with a luminous spirit.

One night, after years of knowing me, he crawled on top of me during a movie at his family's home.

"I've always wanted you," he whispered, pressing his mouth against mine.

"What the fuck are you doing? You are married!" My body revolted. I shoved him off, walked out the door, and filed him in the mental folder with the other four front-line workers with whom I had similar experiences.

My mind races back to the pyramid grounds where I met my last partner—his action to connect and his physical proximity bordering on betrayal of his wife, who waited for him at home.

My nervous system fired in the red zone as my carefully crafted words dripped with sweet venom, "You know, my first shamanic teacher shared, when you come into my world, you're going to eventually love me, hate me, and want to fuck me." Our eyes locked, stillness permeated the space between us, "Well, I'm definitely at number three." His striking blue eyes flashed as the dimples in his cheeks deepened.

With COVID reshaping our lives, half a year later, I found myself in the States with this man who had pursued me on ancient grounds.

Newly single and hungry for the supply of my medicine.

Shortly after my arrival in the States, I had a full hysterectomy and the most epic shamanic death I've experienced to date.

My Dream

Raging white water, crashing against the cradling of Mother Earth,
shifting directions, rolling balls of fury,
spraying rainbow-filled droplets of water
as the river thrashes down the ancient carved-out liquid trail.
The sun beats down, reflecting off the cool misty spray,
drying the logs and branches hanging into and over the river.
He's face down, jammed in the logs,
the water rushing over his lifeless body
as Pacha Mama calls him home.

Gasping for air, my eyes shot open as my hand reached for my heart.

My eyes fell upon the big lump of a husband, all tucked in, breathing peacefully beside me. *He's alive. . .you can breathe*, I repeat silently to myself until my heart comes back into a resting space.

I chose not to tell him; *it was just a dream, right?*

Two days later, he looked at his phone with his eyebrows furrowed. "The white-water rafting group says the river may be too dangerous to be on; a man has been missing for a couple of days now."

My mind goes into overdrive: *You must tell him! His life may be in danger!*

*Someone **just** died on that river, and now you're going to let your husband go.*

My truth is, I cannot control anyone's actions.

And, I could provide him with the information I received, and he could then make a better-informed decision. So, I chose to share my dream and request that he stay acutely aware of his surroundings. "If you get a red light when you're out there, just call it and don't go!" He agreed.

The surgeon's office calls: there has been a cancellation. *Do I want to have my hysterectomy next week? He will leave three days after my surgery if I move it up.*

Am I okay with healing by myself?

Ooh, this is a big test, but should I even have to test myself at this point?

Or is this a test for him?

Is it fair to ask him to stay home when this group has been planning it for months? Nah, I got this, I'll be fine!

Surgery day arrives, I'm tucked into my room, my husband has gone for the night, and I'm ready for dreamland. Screeching pierces my ears as desperate words form in a female voice: *Get away from me! Get him out of here!*

Wailing, scurrying carts, the shuffle of feet, squeaks off the floor as humans shift in the hallway. More deep voices arrive with more shuffling, as she continues to wail. *I can't stand it. What's going on out there?*

My heart pounds in rhythm with the throbbing in my womb space.

Adrenaline pumping through my veins shoots me out of bed to peer out from behind my flimsy curtain door. My swollen eyes are bombarded with a handful of black security vests as I'm hit by an energetic wall of searing trauma.

Shell shock hurls me back into my bed as the panic attack sets in.

I can't breathe, I can't breathe, I can't breathe—nurse!

The next three days and nights are filled with dream after dream of the violence I've already processed in this lifetime. Experiencing it on a whole new level, drug-induced, the excruciating womb pain aligns with the new experiences and creates complex trauma.

While my husband packs for his trip to perhaps face his own death.

I don't remember coming home. The phone call, however, is branded into my cells. "Oh ya, no problem, that sounds great!" His eyes sparkle as he shares, "She's going to ride in my boat with me." My heart sinks into my already traumatized body.

The one you have already polarized. The one you already broke my trust with.

"You're going to leave me here, torn apart and traumatized, to go play on the river with another woman?" The posturing, minimizing, and gas-lighting commence, as our voices heighten, the phone rings, "Ya? Sounds good." The energy shifts in the room. "They figured out another scenario, you'll be happy to know, she isn't riding with me."

For sure, my heart sinks to depths I'm not sure it will return from. *Right now, I am so happy with the decisions you are making.*

The morning arrives. He stands in the doorway of our bedroom and looks down at me. In my hazy mind, I attempt to memorize every particle of his being. My heart shatters as I hear the last "goodbye" seep from my moist lips, and tears fall down my cheeks.

I must let him go. This is the Shaman's way.
Attach on the inhale and detach on the exhale.
How am I going to do this alone? I can't do this! Don't leave me!
Can't you see, I need you right now?
He must choose. It's not your choice. You must let him go.

As I heard the truck pull away, deafening stillness entered the room, and something died inside me.

The next 24 hours became a trauma and drug-induced space of out-of-body experiences.

I willed myself to go into intentional deep meditation.

As usual, I ended up on the top of the Pyramid of the Sun in Teotihuacan, Mexico. And was reminded: *We're all one. You have access to him and his energy, whether it's on this physical plane or not. You've already experienced this with others. You did choose to marry a firefighter!*

Every day, he puts his life on the line. Every day, he may not come home tomorrow.

This is the life I chose. This is the story I created.

The wonderfully crafted experiment the Universe and I danced through shed light on mental triggers around domestic violence, betrayal, and abandonment. My physical body writhed in excruciating pain and was inundated with drugs my brain couldn't process.

This led to a lethal combination and perfect storm when I was left with only one day of help and then left isolated at home to heal alone.

The contents of the pill bottle accidentally spilled into the palm of my hand.

Stillness permeates the room as I have a chat with the Universe.

I'm done playing this way.
If you want to use me as your vessel to serve humanity, I need a softer way.
I have succeeded in my pursuits in this lifetime; I have nothing to prove to anyone, and I just watched my soulmate, my warrior, walk out the door.
I'm putting down my sword.

I absolutely could leave this Earth right now and be so proud of what I have already accomplished in healing my ancestral lines in this lifetime.
I'm not scared of you, Angel of Death.
If you want me to stay and be in service,
I want a new storyline filled with joy and service.
So mote it be.

Clearly, I chose life at that moment, and my mission with the Universe was sealed.

He was gone for a week with no contact.

My phone rings and I pick it up expectantly, "Hey! A guy on the river had a satellite phone, just checking in to let you know you were not wrong. As soon as we got to our drop-in place on the river, we found the dead man and got him to the ranger's station and back to his family."

I was fucking right.

Adrenaline rips through my traumatized body and takes a seat in my chest. *Am I just right about the dead body, or am I right about his behavior with the woman on the trip? This group has already proven they will protect their own.*

We are human, and the greatest and most powerful teaching that got me through this whole ordeal was the fact that we, as humans, can hold duality.

I love you with everything that I am. And you dropped me.

It reminded me that I am whole, all by myself.

I got through that ordeal without the help of my significant other.

I don't need him. I chose to have him in my life in this role we agreed on.

It led to further communication around what unconditional love, relationships, and boundaries look like, and what I wanted and needed from a business partner versus an intimate partner.

The clarity from our experience and communication led to a deeper yes from both sides to continue with an intimate relationship.

THE SPARK

What I didn't understand at that time was that I entered the darker and dangerous cycle of trauma bonding.

Trauma bonding is a consistent loop of affection and abuse that creates a process addiction in the brain, which, when it goes unchecked, can wreak havoc in a person's life, just like any other addiction, such as drugs and alcohol.

But at that moment, what mattered most wasn't psychology.

It was my choice:

Stay broken or alchemize betrayal into joy.

Minimizing the severity of what a hysterectomy does to a woman on all levels is traumatic. Adding domestic violence, betrayal, and abandonment triggers during the same time makes me question how I got out of that situation alive, with no therapy or hormone treatment.

Yet, on the other side of that coin, my psychic abilities were through the roof and on laser point. Books and podcasts came flowing through me. Yet, the more I started to flourish, the more my partner sabotaged, distracted, and diminished me.

In April 2024, the ultimate betrayal played out on the very same grounds, where he pursued me as we led our first group retreat with another teacher.

Boundaries once again were crossed in the most brutal public display on the lunar eclipse in front of thousands of people, as I lay at their feet and watched him rub himself against her backside in ceremony as she howled in full kundalini orgasm.

You would think that would've been the severance, but no.

I forgave him.

But his treatment after that night revealed the truth:

I was not his divine partner. I was his supply.

In the beginning, knowledge doesn't always bring action. Especially when you love them and thought you were creating the same storyline.

When it becomes clear that you're being used, the real transformation happens, yet it takes time—time to build the energy to act.

It takes time to discern if what you're experiencing is real or a trauma reaction.

I realized, through all the relational and medical trauma I experienced, I had no idea who this new person emerging was. I needed help. I needed mirrors and safe spaces to connect with other humans who could hold this level of initiation and see me through to the other side, bringing me back into the light.

Laura Di Franco drafted into my storyline shortly after my hysterectomy, and I chose to step into her brave healer container and not look back. I wrote in three of her books, was a lead author of my own book, and when this experience happened in Teotihuacan, I chose Laura as my mentor and healer, once again.

This cosmic breadcrumb led me to Shari Alyse, as Laura and I, with another Brave Healer lead author, headed to California to be on Shari's show, Good Morning Joy, fully supported by my husband, so I thought.

Shortly after it aired, another bullet arrived.

What I have learned

is that some humans love setting up the fall,

with a smile on their face and a sniper rifle at their back.

"Now you know what it's like to live this lifestyle; you can go find it again with somebody else. I want a divorce," he said matter-of-factly, like he suggested where to go and eat dinner. "I don't believe in divine union, and I don't want to change my behavior; my behavior keeps hurting you, and I'm comfortable the way I am, so I'm going to release you."

Weeks later, papers were filed, and I was shipped back to Canada.

"You get the gold medal for the smoothest divorce."

Two months later, his predatory pattern repeated with another woman.

I sought more joy. I sought safe connections. I surrendered to the brutal detox as I dissolved the thought patterns he seeded in my brain.

You can't live without me.
Nobody can hold a container like I can.
I am more powerful than Don Miguel Ruiz.
Nobody can ground you like I can.

For a short while, I believed I couldn't live without him. Trauma bonding is real.

The suicidal ideation was real. My psychic gifts were seductive.

I can access the other side; I have loved ones on the other side; I can be of more service from the other side. My trusted advisors are on the other side; I can advise from there.

I kept reminding myself: *You chose life on Earth. You made a commitment to the Universe to share your medicine on the other side of this humiliating initiation.*

Survival had me heading back into the gymnastics world for work, a space I hadn't entered in 15 years after a decorated career of coaching world-class athletes. *I can be of service here. I just want some time to play with the kids and give my inner child some fun.*

After a few short months, the Universe rudely reminded me: *That's not where you belong, and* re-routed me in full surrender to the path laid before me to share this medicine.

Trust became my goal: trust in myself and faith in the Universe, which I believed had me.

The downloads started coming again, and my psychic abilities came back online.

The more I allowed myself to become still,

the more magic showed up in my world.

As Shari and I danced in our own grief portals, our connection grew, this book came to fruition, leadership opportunities showed up in our Brave Healer community, collaborations started forming and I felt my soul coming back online in the most humble and beautiful way as I turned my pain into alchemy through the written word and the most healed version of myself to date.

I wrote *The Boundary Queen* ritual guide by allowing my psychic channel to expand and tap into dimensions and ancestry I hadn't previously accessed.

This throne initiates names, seals, and enforces sacred boundaries when language blurs your "No." Not in rage, but in sovereignty.

Use it when:

- You feel hooked after you've said no (dream-loops, "check-ins," ritual nostalgia).

Example: Imagine an ex texting "just to check in" months after you've already closed the door. Even though you've said no, the pull of old rituals (like late-night conversations or shared memories) makes you question yourself. That's when this boundary practice is needed most.

- Your "Yes" only counts when you're the one shrinking.

Example: A colleague praises your work but insists you take a smaller role so they can "shine." Or a partner only welcomes your yes if it means you dim your light to keep them comfortable. In those moments, your agreement comes at the price of your own radiance—and that is not a true yes.

- Anyone who tries to outrank your body's truth with titles, ceremony, or cosmic poetry.

Example: You're in a spiritual circle, and the leader insists, "Spirit told me you should. . ." even though your whole body contracts. The titles or sacred language don't change the fact that your no is clear. That's when you anchor in your Royal Edict and claim your sovereignty.

How to wield it (fast):

1. Crown check-in: Hand on heart + womb. Write three Bone-Truth lines your body agrees with.

2. Royal Edict (fill + speak):

I am the Boundary Queen of my field.

I do not consent to _____.

Effective now, _____ (clear limit).

If crossed, I will _____ (action I can enact).

My 'yes' is sovereign and reserved for right relationships.

3. Seal and enforce: One candle, pinch of salt, speak:

> By breath and bone, I guard my throne;
> My iron no is set in stone.
> Within my chest, I bless
> The tender bloom of velvet, yes.

Then block/mute, revoke access, and end shared loops—no debate.

Go deeper and claim your crown with the eBook now:

The Boundary Queen

Divine Feminine Protection · Reign Without Apology

Inside: Seven done-for-you edicts, clean exit scripts, glamor-busting checklist, daily throne practices, altar pages, and printable decrees.

Get the guide on the Skool Platform →

https://www.skool.com/fire-heart-mystery-school/classroom

> Closing oath
> I am the keeper of my gate.
> My word is law in my body and field.
> Only what is in right relationship may enter.

Angel Gold is a shaman, author, and creator of *The Boundary Queen*.

Angel assists women who've bled for broken dreams reclaim a clean yes, and an iron no, so they can build lives in right relationship with their bodies, their gifts, and their connection to Source.

If your intuition has been glamoured by titles, telepathy, or "divine purpose," she's here to cut the spell, gently, clearly, and for good.

Her work weaves Toltec and Celtic-rooted wisdom, ritual, and practical throne architecture (aka: what to do with your phone, your calendar, your money, your access points) so your **velvet yes** is protected and your power stops leaking through loopholes.

What Angel teaches:

- **Divine Feminine Protection:** boundaries that bless your nervous system and your calling.
- **Throne Architecture & Law:** daily practices that make sovereignty a habit, not a fight.
- **Glamor-Busting Discernment:** spot false light, ritualized loopholes, and spiritual trespass
- **Clean Exits:** scripts and rituals that end entanglements without explaining your no

She's written international bestselling work, led circles and courses across North America, and midwifed thousands of humans through endings that became beginnings.

Her medicine is sassy, sacred, and surgical: say less, mean more, move on.

If you're done shrinking for "almost" and hungry to guard the gates of your life, come in.

Start with The Boundary Queen (my signature guide), then step into training, rituals, and community designed to keep your field clean and your crown on.

Enter here → www.angelgold.ca

Iron no. Velvet yes. Sacred life.

Connect with Angel:

Website: https://angelgold.ca

Instagram: https://instagram.com/iam.angelgold

YouTube: https://www.youtube.com/@angel0gold

CHAPTER 25

MANIFESTING MIRACLES

BECOMING A CONSCIOUS CREATOR OF YOUR DREAM LIFE

Renata Angelo

MY STORY

Imagine transforming your deepest desires into reality, living a life free from pain and filled with purpose.

When someone tells you, "You can't," you have two options: believe them or prove them wrong! This is true when it comes to health and wealth. In both instances, you are the creator of your reality. I learned it the hard way.

Who are those people? Where am I? My mind raced a hundred miles an hour. I smelled the asphalt and heard the ambulance coming from a distance. *Why can't I move my legs?* I was lying on the ground, paralysed from the waist down, unable to move my legs, my motorbike totally smashed.

A handsome French guy knelt by my side and held my hand. With a teary eye, he said, "I am so sorry. The sun was shining into my eyes, and I didn't see the red light."

"It doesn't matter," came out of my mouth. He looked so handsome. For a moment, I didn't care that I couldn't move my legs. Being 23, I was thinking about how cute he was.

This is how I met my first spiritual teacher. His name was Philippe. He introduced me to inspiring books and helped me explore personal and spiritual development. This changed my life forever.

I spent some time in a wheelchair and on crutches. I learned to walk again, but chronic back pain persisted 24/7 for a year. I did everything doctors told me to do, but there was no relief from the pain.

One year later, at a check-up, the doctor looked at my eyes and said, "There's nothing more we can do. You must learn to live with the pain."

It was as if the bomb dropped. Hope was crushed.

Learn to live with the pain? No way. I either want to find the cure for chronic pain, or I don't want to be here.

Even though I loved life, spending 24/7 in pain, I wouldn't want to live.

Little did I know at that time that our thoughts create our reality.

The very next day, I went to pick up a Thai takeaway for dinner with my friend. I was so hungry. It was getting dark and raining heavily. We parked the car, and I ran across the street to the shop. Suddenly, I heard my friend screaming: "Renata! Renata!"

I stopped instantly. A car I didn't see raced around the corner and passed me by a few millimeters. My knees shook as I realized I could've died. I collapsed in my friend's arms.

After a few moments, I started to question: *Could my thoughts really create my reality? If yes, I must be more careful about what I think about and what I wish for.*

I realized I didn't want to die. And at the same time, I didn't want to live in pain. *What should I do?* I started to look for a reason to live through the pain.

If I am able to find the cure for chronic pain, I'll be able to help the people who are suffering now, but not only them, but also future generations.

That was the moment I chose to live. I chose to keep going—for you. I did it for every single one of you holding this book in your hands right now. Whether you are living with physical pain or emotional pain, you're the reason I chose to live and never give up till I find a cure for chronic pain.

But suddenly a little voice crept in whispering: *Who are you, Renata, to find the cure for chronic pain when doctors could not find it? You don't even have a medical background.*

Hmm, yes, it's true I don't have a medical background, but those who have it haven't found a cure yet, I thought.

My biggest advantage is that I have the pain, and I don't have to do expensive clinical studies that take time; I can test everything right away, and I will know what works. This is my advantage! I got excited!

Because I don't know where to look, I might start looking in different places where doctors or scientists don't look.

I was ready to start my quest to find the cure for chronic pain! I had a mission.

How did it go? Well, I tried everything from a Western medicine perspective, and after a year, I gave up, recognizing that I can't walk west expecting to see a sunrise.

So, I turned around 180 degrees, and I tested everything from Eastern medicine. Still no success.

Another year later, I realized I might need to stop looking for the answers outside, because they might not be there. *Perhaps I should look inward.*

This realization came to me slowly, during a meditation session where I focused on my breath and allowed each inhale and exhale to guide me to a place of stillness. As I sat in silence, I started to feel a deep connection with my inner self.

Thoughts began to quiet down, and for the first time, I felt a sense of peace that I hadn't experienced. This practice of meditative contemplation became my daily refuge, where I explored the vastness within. And that was when magic started happening.

During meditation, I was inspired to learn to swim properly. Doctors always said swimming was good for my back. However, I never felt that it would be of any help.

Maybe I'm swimming wrong?

I decided to learn to swim properly. I went to the pool, and as I did my laps, someone started criticizing my swimming style.

"Elevate your elbow more," said the guy in the lane next to me.

"Who are you?" I asked him, feeling confused and criticized.

"I'm training for a swimming championship."

"Cool," I responded, thinking, *I'd better listen!*

We talked, and he introduced me to his coach. I decided to get some professional lessons.

Suddenly, it hit me: *Perhaps my thoughts truly shape my reality?*

I wanted to learn how to swim properly, and that day someone introduced me to a swimming coach. Coincidence? Maybe. Maybe not.

I started training three times a week, and my freestyle improved.

One month passed, and I attended another training session. The coach decided to change the routine.

"Hey, Renata, jump in the pool and do two laps, then three, and then one." He said.

"I can't swim three laps without stopping and taking a break to catch my breath. I have never done it before in my life," I immediately responded. I knew where my limits were. I knew I could swim 50 meters freestyle without stopping and catching my breath.

"It's about the time that you do it!" The coach said in a firm voice.

I didn't protest. I jumped into the pool, swam 25 meters, and then turned around to swim 50. As I came close to the wall, I said to myself, "I can do it." I touched the wall, turned around, and swam 75 meters without stopping!

I broke my limit! I screamed with excitement. "I did it! I did it!" My eyes shone with happiness. I got out of the water and jumped like a little kid with excitement, not caring what others thought.

I know swimming 75 meters freestyle without stopping is a breeze for many people. But it was my personal limit that I broke! I was overjoyed. My joy was finally unleashed!

"I told you you could do it!" Coach smiled, high-fiving me.

"I can't believe it!" I said, leaving with the biggest smile on my face. I broke through my limits. I felt like I could do anything! My belief shifted.

Two days later, I attended another training. This time, I jumped into the pool just to warm up. As I swam, I passed the 50-meter mark. This time, I knew I could do more than 50. I passed 75 meters, 100 meters, and 200 meters, but to my surprise, I wasn't out of breath. So, I continued to 500 meters and could still keep going. I passed the 900-meter mark.

How is this possible?

I had plenty of energy and breathed easily. I passed 1 kilometer with joy and ease and felt like I could swim forever.

I finally stopped and felt stunned. *How is this possible? What changed? Nothing physically. The only thing that is different this time is my belief and knowing that I can swim more than 50 meters.*

That shift in belief unlocked my potential.

Where else do I have limiting beliefs that sabotage my success?

And now I'm asking you. Where do *you* have limiting beliefs? How would your life be different if you were able to identify and replace them?

THE SPARK

Grab a pen and paper, and write down the limiting beliefs that sabotage you.

If you could replace them, what new beliefs would you like to have? Let's have a look at what else can happen when we change beliefs.

There was one belief that when I shifted it, it created the biggest miracle in my life.

Being brought up in a communist country where everything was about science, I was a very pragmatic person. I didn't believe in intuition or God. When I acknowledged Him and did what He told me, I experienced a quantum healing. I was healed, and my chronic back pain was gone forever. I share the full story and how it happened in a movie, ZERO LIMITS.

That fascinating story of quantum healing and the manifestation of a miracle gives hope that anyone, including you, can overcome pain, whether physical, emotional, or financial.

Inside of you, there's a potential far beyond your wildest dreams and expectations. You can manifest miracles.

As Henry Ford said, "Whether you think you can or think you can't, you're right."

Let's examine some key principles for doing this.

I recommend consciously choosing beliefs that run your life. There are no right or wrong beliefs, only supportive or unsupportive ones. Take a moment now to pause. Breathe in deeply, and as you exhale, bring your awareness to your body. Notice any sensations or tensions you may feel. By anchoring yourself in the present moment, you empower your ability to choose beliefs that truly serve you. This simple act of awareness can begin to transform your life.

As Wayne Dyer said, "When you change the way you see things, the things you see will change."

Most of our beliefs were acquired during childhood, and we rarely question them. They were influenced by our family, media, educational system, and the country's political system.

Your beliefs can either support or sabotage your success. Be very careful about what you say. Let's take a challenge. For the next 30 days, speak only what you want to become true. Be especially careful what you say after the words "I am." Only speak what you want to manifest.

The biggest shift happened in my life when I changed my belief about whether God exists. When I first consciously spoke to Him and He answered with clear guidance, I decided to follow it, and a miracle happened.

Here's another principle of manifesting miracles. Act on your inspiration. Nothing happens without action. The biggest difference is that most people act based on their goals or habits. Sooner or later, they usually burn out or give up because you can only go so far with willpower.

When you act on your inspiration (meaning you're in contact with spirit and follow the guidance), you find yourself in the right place at the right time. You will say the right things to the right people, and coincidences start to happen. You're in a state of flow as you manifest miracles.

To make this actionable, take a ten-minute break today. Sit down into a meditation and then write down one inspired idea or action that comes to your mind. Next, think of the smallest possible step you can take toward it—a simple action you can complete within five minutes. This could be sending an email, making a quick phone call, or jotting down a few notes. Taking this micro-action will help build momentum and decrease any feelings of overwhelm, paving the way for more inspired acts.

An important key to success and manifesting miracles is also overcoming your fears. Fears are like darkness, and you don't need to fight them. You just need to turn on the light. In this case, it's a matter of having faith that things will work out and that you can do it, faith in God (or whichever power you believe), and faith that the universe has your back.

To move forward, I had to learn to set aside my ego. If we want things we never had, we must do things we never did. We must let go of all things that no longer serve us, not only old limiting beliefs and attitudes, but also the ego. As Wayne Dyer says, "Ego stands for Edging God Out." If we let Him in, we increase our probability of success.

Everything in the universe is energy. We need to tune into the right frequency—a frequency of joy. Joy is a frequency of healing. When you combine faith and joy and act on your inspiration, miracles will begin to happen. Expect miracles, and you might start seeing them.

We can increase our frequency by adopting an attitude of gratitude. That will elevate our altitude. Reach for the stars. You're one of them. Shine bright like the star you are. Don't play small. We live only once, so let's make the most of it.

Life is about giving. Once we turn our focus from what we can get to what we can give, there are no limits. You can always give more smiles, kindness, and more words of encouragement. And since our outer world reflects our inner world, the more you give, the more you'll get.

Life will become an incredible adventure worth living. Be in your heart more than your head. I've seen many people turn their lives around when they landed in their hearts, got rid of their fears, believed in themselves, and spoke only of what they wanted to manifest; a quantum leap occurred. I've seen everything from countless spontaneous remissions to people doubling their income, even adding zero to their income. Anything is possible.

If you want to increase your chances of success, be very selective of the people you spend time with. I personally can handle negative people in my life only in homeopathic dosages, meaning very little. The five people you spend the most time with will have a direct impact on your happiness and the level of income you receive.

Let me share a story of Helen, who transformed her life by upgrading her circle. After joining a Quantum Coaching mastermind group, her circle expanded to include successful, supportive, driven entrepreneurs. In just a month, her outlook on life shifted dramatically, and she added zero to her income. Surrounding herself with positive, ambitious individuals elevated her mindset and opened opportunities she never thought possible.

Surround yourself with positive people who think big and who believe in you. The best thing you can do is to hire a coach. Someone who believes in you more than you believe in yourself. Your future self will thank you for it. You don't need to do it alone. All successful people have their coaches; be one of them, too.

Create a vision board and place it in your home or office. Our environment shapes us. Declutter everything you don't need and repair or discard anything that's broken. Pay attention to feng shui at your home and workplace. Your environment influences your success. I love creating vision boards and having them around me as they remind me of my goals and dreams. I see them, and it helps me feel as though I'm already experiencing them.

They help me to cultivate a feeling of gratitude for all the wonderful things that are coming my way, as if I already have them. That feeling of gratitude brings them closer. Feeling and living life as if your dreams have already come true will increase the probability that they will.

Give what you want to get. Want more money? Help more people become successful. Would you like more love? Be more loving and more kind. Would you like to experience more fun? Be funnier. Would you like to experience more magic? Create more magical moments for others. Give first what you want to get.

As Tony Robbins says, "The secret to living is giving." And there's no limit to how much we can give.

You are a miracle itself. There's nobody like you. No one has the same skills and abilities. You're truly unique. You have the potential to manifest miracles. It's time to unlock your potential and become the best version of yourself! You have potential far beyond your wildest dreams.

Renata Angelo is an internationally acclaimed transformational speaker, business mentor, and visionary coach, recognized as one of today's leading voices in personal and professional development. She's a featured teacher in the award-winning film *ZERO LIMITS*, nominated for 36 international film festivals and winner of 20 prestigious awards worldwide.

Her journey is one of resilience and inspiration. After a devastating motorbike accident left her facing years of chronic pain and a diagnosis of lifelong disability, Renata refused to accept those limits. Instead, she discovered the power of the subconscious mind, quantum healing, and manifestation. Through her own transformation, she found her mission: to help others overcome challenges, unlock their potential, and create success with joy and ease.

Renata is an international bestselling author who has co-authored two powerful books with world-renowned leaders: *Pushing to the Front* with Brian Tracy and *Performance 360: Success Edition* with Sir Richard Branson. She is also a sought-after keynote speaker, regularly invited by major corporations to motivate their teams, elevate performance, and increase sales.

As the creator of the *Quantum Coaching Program*, Renata helps entrepreneurs accelerate growth and achieve extraordinary results at quantum speed. With her unique gift of identifying subconscious blockages that sabotage success, she guides people to release limitations, reprogram their mindset, and step into the best version of themselves.

Her mission is to remind the world that there are truly no limits—only possibilities. To support you on your journey, Renata invites you to book a **free 30-minute strategy session** at www.renataangelo.com/calendar, where she will prepare your personal *Quantum Manifestation Blueprint* to help you unlock your greatest potential.

Connect with Renata:

Websites: www.RenataAngelo.com
www.QuantumJourney.com

LinkedIn: www.linkedin.com/in/renataangelo

Youtube: www.youtube.com/@renataangelo.official

Instagram: www.instagram.com/renataangelo.official

Facebook: www.facebook.com/renataangelo.official

CLOSING CHAPTER

CONGRATULATIONS, YOU MADE IT!

You've just journeyed through *Joy Unleashed*—25 incredible Sparks, 25 stories, practices, and moments of light shared by real humans who know how to access joy even when life gets messy, complicated, or downright unfair.

And if you're like most people finishing a book, you might be thinking: *Okay, now what? Do I have to glow and skip down the street?* No. That's optional.

Joy isn't about pressure. It's about access. And the good news? It's yours. Right here. Right now.

The Sparks you've discovered aren't just pretty ideas to nod along to and forget. They're invitations. Tools. Tiny doorways back to yourself.

Back to the part of you that knows how to laugh even when things suck.

Back to the part of you that can feel fully alive even if your inbox is on fire, your kid is screaming, or your heart is a little bruised from life.

These authors show us that joy is doable. It's not a fantasy or a privilege. It's available to anyone, anywhere, at any moment.

And yes, that includes you.

Some authors shared stories that made me nod so hard I almost spilled my coffee. Others offered practices that made me stop and think: *Huh, I could do that.*

All of them shared openly and vulnerably, showing that accessing joy isn't about perfection or Instagram-worthy moments. It's about connection, curiosity, courage, and a little willingness to try even when life feels messy.

Joy isn't a destination. It isn't something you achieve and put on a shelf like a trophy.

Joy is alive.

It breathes.

It wiggles.

It sneaks up on you while doing dishes or folding laundry.

It sits in your chest when a song makes your eyes well up.

It whispers in the quiet moments when you let yourself just be. And sometimes, it'll smack you in the face when you least expect it, and you'll thank it for that, even if you look ridiculous.

So what now?

Take your Sparks. Play with them. Experiment. Mix them together. Break them, bend them, try them in ways that make sense to you.

Every author in this book poured themselves and their truths onto these pages.

They're living, breathing examples of what's possible when you choose joy.

Connect with them. Ask questions. Share your story. Let this community of heart-led humans remind you that joy grows when it's shared, not hoarded.

Life is too short to do it alone. Too short to wait for perfect conditions. Too short to hide your light.

Every moment you spend leaning into joy, connecting to your truth, and sprinkling it into the world matters.

You have a front-row ticket to your own life.

It's time to show up fully. Boldly. Laughing. Crying. Dancing (even if your dog thinks you've completely lost it. Maybe you have, just a little).

Your joy is here. It was always here.

Joy Unleashed is your guide to reclaiming, living, and amplifying joy in every corner of your life.

Step boldly into your life. Spark it up. Play with it. Laugh until it hurts. Cry if you need to. Dance like nobody's watching (even if your neighbor is judging from across the street. They are secretly wishing they could be you).

Never apologize for shining.

And don't forget: these 24 extraordinary humans you've met in these pages are still out there, doing the work, living the truth, and offering their guidance. Let them help you stretch, grow, and live even more joyfully.

Joy isn't just something you find in a book. It's something you share.

Something you live. Something you let ripple outward into the world.

Joy Unleashed is your invitation to do exactly that.

KEEP THE JOY GOING

You've finished *Joy Unleashed*, but this is just the beginning. Joy isn't a luxury or a "nice to have." It's your birthright. It's who you are. Don't hoard it. Never feel guilty for it. Nobody has ever benefited from someone withholding their joy.

Watch *Good Morning Joy + Joy Drive.*

Inspiring stories, tools, and laughs from incredible guests.

Available on Amazon Prime, Roku, Tubi, Apple TV, BINGE Networks, and YouTube https://www.goodmorningjoyshow.com

Follow Me on Social Media

Daily inspiration, tips, and encouragement to live joyfully.

Instagram: https://www.instagram.com/sharialyse

Facebook: https://www.facebook.com/sharingwithshari

TikTok: https://www.tiktok.com/@thejoymagnet

LinkedIn: https://www.linkedin.com/in/sharialyse

YouTube: https://www.youtube.com/sharialyse

Hire Me to Speak

Bring an authentic, relatable, and transformational experience to your team, community, or audience. Spark connection, purpose, and joy!

Connect With Me Directly

Share your story, ask questions, or just say hi.

Visit https://www.ShariAlyse.com

Joy isn't a reward. It's a practice, a choice, and a life fully lived. *Joy Unleashed* is your guide, and I'm here to help you keep sparking it–every day, unapologetically, fully alive!

In Joy,

Shari Alyse

RAMPAGE OF APPRECIATION

My heart is bursting with gratitude, joy, and awe as I write this. To the 24 incredible souls who trusted me and this process: thank you. You said yes to going deep, to excavating your own stories, and to sharing your light with the world. We all know that going within isn't always comfortable, but you did it with courage, heart, and vulnerability. While this book is about joy, we all know the path to finding it sometimes means digging through the hard stuff first. I am forever humbled and honored to hold your stories in these pages.

To the incredible, badass, inspiring, epic soul, friend, and publisher, Laura Di Franco, you lit up my heart from the moment I met you. The road to here was not always easy, but I am so glad we made it. Thank you for supporting me on every level and helping make multiple dreams a reality. You truly are the wind beneath so many wings, and because of you, so many people get to experience joy.

To my mom and dad, who will always be my everything. There will never be words big enough to capture my gratitude or my love. You gave me my roots and my wings. Dad, I know you've earned your wings back, and I feel you with me. Mom, I'm beyond grateful you are still here, holding me, cheering me on, and reminding me who I am when I forget. You are my forever best friend.

To John, my other half, my greatest love, and sometimes my greatest challenge—thank you for loving me as I am. You accept the whirlwind that is me, even when you don't fully understand it, and that is the kind of love that steadies me while I fly. I love you deeply and endlessly.

To Tami, Ariel, and UG: this year has tested us all with the loss of Dad, Grandpa, and your big brother. Through heartbreak, we held each other up and gave one another space to heal and laugh. Without you, this book wouldn't exist.

To my family: this year has shown me in the most powerful way how blessed I am to have our blood running through my veins. Your love is my anchor.

To Charlotte and Iris: thank you for loving Dad and me through his toughest season. You carried me in ways you may not even realize and gave me the gift of finding unexpected joy with him. I will treasure that forever.

To Declan and Denise (DeDe): thank you for constantly reminding me of this amazing life I have created and for seeing me so fully. You've been my space holders, my reality checkers, and my comic relief when I needed it most. Bonus points indeed!

To Felicia: Thank you for your consistent belief in me and support of my dreams since we first met. More Chai Chats to come!

To Anna: thank you for believing in me and giving me the foundation and structure to help build my dreams. I love you, Hugo, and your family.

To my friends: you are the ones who cheer for me even when I'm doubting myself, who listen to my endless dreams and worries, and remind me of my wings when I forget I have them. Thank you for reflecting back the best of me.

And to God: thank you for every single blessing, every lesson, every person who has crossed my path. Those who've chipped away at my heart, those who've healed it, and those who've filled it to overflowing. I am the luckiest woman alive to feel what I feel right now. Alive. Full. Loved. Love. And pure, unapologetic JOY.

www.ingramcontent.com/pod-product-compliance
Lightning Source LLC
Chambersburg PA
CBHW061603120626
46550CB00004B/1594